MANHATTAN G

Foundations of GMAT Verbal

GMAT Strategy Guide

This supplemental guide provides in-depth and easy-to-follow explanations of the fundamental verbal skills necessary for a strong performance on the GMAT.

Foundations of GMAT Verbal, Fifth Edition

10-digit International Standard Book Number: 1-937707-01-6
13-digit International Standard Book Number: 978-1-937707-01-9
eISBN: 978-1-937707-14-9

Note: *GMAT, Graduate Management Admission Test, Graduate Management Admission Council,* and *GMAC* are all registered trademarks of the Graduate Management Admission Council, which neither sponsors nor is affiliated in any way with this product.

Layout Design: Dan McNaney and Cathy Huang
Cover Design: Evyn Williams and Dan McNaney
Cover Photography: Alli Ugosoli

INSTRUCTIONAL GUIDE SERIES

SUPPLEMENTAL GUIDE SERIES

MANHATTAN
GMAT

May 29th, 2012

Dear Student,

Thank you for picking up a copy of *Foundations of GMAT Verbal*. I hope this book provides just the guidance you need to get the most out of your GMAT studies.

As with most accomplishments, there were many people involved in the creation of the book you are holding. First and foremost is Zeke Vanderhoek, the founder of Manhattan GMAT. Zeke was a lone tutor in New York when he started the company in 2000. Now, 12 years later, the company has instructors and offices nationwide and contributes to the studies and successes of thousands of students each year.

Our Manhattan GMAT Strategy Guides are based on the continuing experiences of our instructors and students. For this volume, we are particularly indebted to Jennifer Dziura. Jen has logged literally thousands of hours helping students improve their verbal skills—this book is derived from that wealth of experience. Stacey Koprince and Tommy Wallach made significant content contributions as well. Dan McNaney and Cathy Huang provided their design expertise to make the books as user-friendly as possible, and Noah Teitelbaum and Liz Krisher made sure all the moving pieces came together at just the right time. And there's Chris Ryan. Beyond providing additions and edits for this book, Chris continues to be the driving force behind all of our curriculum efforts. His leadership is invaluable.

At Manhattan GMAT, we continually aspire to provide the best instructors and resources possible. We hope that you will find our commitment manifest in this book. If you have any questions or comments, please email me at dgonzalez@manhattanprep.com. I'll look forward to reading your comments, and I'll be sure to pass them along to our curriculum team.

Thanks again, and best of luck preparing for the GMAT!

Sincerely,

Dan Gonzalez
President
Manhattan GMAT

HOW TO ACCESS YOUR ONLINE RESOURCES

If you...

> **are a registered Manhattan GMAT student**

and have received this book as part of your course materials, you have AUTOMATIC access to ALL of our online resources. This includes all practice exams, question banks, and online updates to this book. To access these resources, follow the instructions in the Welcome Guide provided to you at the start of your program. Do NOT follow the instructions below.

> **purchased this book from the Manhattan GMAT online store or at one of our centers**

1. Go to: www.manhattanprep.com/gmat/studentcenter.

2. Log in using the username and password used when your account was set up.

> **purchased this book at a retail location**

1. Create an account with Manhattan GMAT at the website: www.manhattanprep.com/gmat/register.

2. Go to: www.manhattanprep.com/gmat/access.

3. Follow the instructions on the screen.

Your one year of online access begins on the day that you register your book at the above URL.

You only need to register your product ONCE at the above URL. To use your online resources any time AFTER you have completed the registration process, log in to the following URL: www.manhattanprep.com/gmat/studentcenter.

Please note that online access is nontransferable. This means that only NEW and UNREGISTERED copies of the book will grant you online access. Previously used books will NOT provide any online resources.

> **purchased an eBook version of this book**

1. Create an account with Manhattan GMAT at the website: www.manhattanprep.com/gmat/register.

2. Email a copy of your purchase receipt to gmat@manhattanprep.com to activate your resources. Please be sure to use the same email address to create an account that you used to purchase the eBook.

For any technical issues, email techsupport@manhattanprep.com or call 800-576-4628.

Please refer to the following page for a description of the online resources that come with this book.

YOUR ONLINE RESOURCES

Your purchase includes ONLINE ACCESS to the following:

⊳ *Foundations of GMAT Verbal* Online Question Bank

The Bonus Online Drill Sets for *Foundations of GMAT Verbal* consist of extra practice questions (with detailed explanations) that test the variety of Foundational Verbal concepts and skills covered in this book. These questions provide you with extra practice beyond the problem sets contained in this book. You may use our online timer to practice your pacing by setting time limits for each question in the banks.

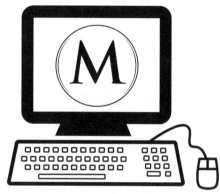

⊳ Online Updates to the Contents in This Book

The content presented in this book is updated periodically to ensure that it reflects the GMAT's most current trends. You may view all updates, including any known errors or changes, upon registering for online access.

TABLE *of* CONTENTS

Introduction

Welcome to *Foundations of GMAT Verbal!*

This book will improve your English for the rest of your life.

Yes, this is a book about the GMAT. But it is not a book of tricks or quick fixes. It is a book about how sentences work, how arguments are constructed, and how written English is used and understood in the United States.

If English is your first language, 90% of this book will still apply to you. The section on vocabulary in Reading Comprehension is primarily oriented towards English language learners, but the rest is applicable to absolutely anyone struggling with GMAT Verbal.

If you are not a native speaker of English, this book will not only help you with the GMAT, but it will also help you understand written English in various contexts throughout the rest of your life.

Either way, this book will open your eyes:

- You may discover that words you thought you knew can be used in ways you weren't aware of. (Did you know that *qualified* can mean *limited*?)
- You may also discover that passages you thought you understood actually have additional meaning that you missed on a first reading.
- And you may discover that the way even educated native speakers communicate in spoken English is not actually considered correct in written English. (Did you know that *I have done more studying than has he* is correct, and *I enjoy the videos of major dance divas like Beyonce and Shakira* is incorrect? The word *like* should be *such as*.)

If you have been studying for the GMAT and struggling, or if you haven't really begun yet (but decided to start here because you know you will need extra help on Verbal), then this book is for you.

This is certainly not the only book you will need in order to succeed on the GMAT. You will also need *The Official Guide for GMAT Review, 13th Edition*. No one should take the GMAT, ever, without knowing the *Official Guide* inside and out — and at various points in this book, we'll ask you to refer to a particular page in the *Official Guide* and do work out of it. So you might as well acquire a copy as soon as possible.

We also recommend that you "graduate" from this book to the *Manhattan GMAT Strategy Guide Series*, which includes individual guides to *Sentence Correction*, *Critical Reasoning*, and *Reading Comprehension*, as well as five additional books on quantitative topics.

In our experience, most successful GMAT test takers spend between 100 and 200 hours studying. Surely, some people spend less time — and some spend more.

Does that sound a bit depressing? If it does, I'd like to set the record straight — *if you really spent that much time just studying for a standardized test, that would be a big waste of the limited time we have here on Earth.* However, that's not what we're about to do! What we're about to do is, well… pretty awesome.

There are certain aspects of the GMAT, such as Data Sufficiency questions, that are quite specific, and pertain only to the GMAT. But there are many other aspects of the GMAT—such as manipulating percents or decoding difficult word problems—that are excellent skills for your career and for life. You know what other parts of the GMAT fall into that category? *Everything on the entire verbal section.*

Since you are beginning with a foundational book on GMAT Verbal and will require even more study after this book, you are going to be spending a lot of time on this. The time you spend now is an investment in your future. It will provide you with a competitive advantage throughout the rest of your career. As a result of the studying you are about to begin:

- You will do better on the GMAT.
- You will be able to communicate better.
- You will be perceived by others as smarter (studies show that people with larger vocabularies are perceived as more intelligent and are paid more).
- You will be better able to understand the idioms and sentence patterns used in speech, business writing, academic writing, and the media.
- You will become a more rigorous thinker. Instead of saying, "I just don't believe that argument," you will be able to point out, "That argument depends on an unjustified assumption" or "That argument's second premise doesn't support its conclusion."
- You will be able to impress your friends with your fun and fearless use of semicolons; this will make you popular at punctuation parties.

Are you convinced yet?

Let's get started!

About the Author

Jennifer Dziura is a Manhattan GMAT instructor who has taught and tutored more than 2,000 students in over a decade of standardized test teaching. She has achieved a perfect raw score of 51 on the GMAT Verbal (and actually, she's also achieved a perfect 51 on Quant).

Jennifer is an expert in working with non-native speakers. She has taught in a Korean-American study academy in Queens, is the author of a set of 1,000 vocabulary flashcards, and even took a research trip to India while writing this book.

She majored in philosophy at Dartmouth and has since been a guest speaker at many universities on topics including time management, career advice for young people, and making punctuation fun.

She has contributed to over a dozen educational books, including a logic textbook for which she wrote various exercises involving ninjas.

She believes that everything is learnable.

Comments from Jennifer's students at Manhattan GMAT:

"Jen was VERY engaging and knowledgeable. She was enthusiastic about the material, and I felt that she really wanted us to succeed. She was funny too!"

"As a venture capital investor I am often confronted with concepts that are very complex, yet need to be communicated in a way that people from a variety of backgrounds can understand. I have to say that in this area Jen is well above the majority of the people I have encountered."

"Jen is very engaging and enthusiastic about the material. She relates the explanations to real-life examples, making them easier to decode and understand."

"Jen is arguably the best teacher I've ever had, at any level, in any subject."

Chapter 1
of
Foundations of GMAT Verbal
Part 1: **Sentence Correction**

Words & Sentences

In This Chapter...

Chapter 1:
Words & Sentences

A GMAT Sentence Correction problem looks something like this:

> The hospital adopted a number of cost-saving measures, <u>to eliminate some administrative personnel and raising</u> fees for certain elective services.
>
> (A) to eliminate some administrative personnel and raising
> (B) to eliminate some administrative personnel and rising
> (C) eliminating some administrative personnel and raising
> (D) by eliminating some administrative personnel and the rise of
> (E) eliminated some administrative personnel and raising

The answer choices represent possible replacements for the underlined portion of the original sentence. Choice (A) is simply a repeat of the original.

What Is Tested

First and foremost, Sentence Correction tests **grammar**. It does not test every little rule—for instance, you are not evaluated directly on comma placement, and no one cares whether you end a sentence with a preposition.

However, you need to know the main rules of English grammar. You don't need the technical names. Rather, you have to know how to apply these rules in context and under exam pressure.

Here's the good news:

> If you can read this simple sentence, you already know a ton of grammar.

Words play specific roles in sensible sentences. Grammar is what governs those roles, which are as important to comprehension as dictionary definitions.

Here is the same sentence again, with the words in alphabetical order:

a already can grammar. If know of read sentence, simple this ton you you

What incomprehensible gibberish, even though you know the meaning of every word!

Whether English is your first or your fifth language, you are making wonderful sense of the words that you are reading right now. As you read normal grammatical sentences, your brain is doing much more than looking up concepts in your mental dictionary. On the fly, your brain is assembling those concepts into complete thoughts, ones that someone else already had.

That's what grammar does for you—it lets you think someone else's thoughts. Each grammatical sentence that you read or hear represents a thought that jumped from another person's brain into yours.

What is a sentence? **A grammatical sentence is a complete thought.** Grammar is what makes sure that the thought is complete.

Without grammar, there would be no communication—or very little. Society would crumble. At least, we would be pointing a lot and getting very frustrated with each other.

Of course, if everyone's internal grammar genie worked perfectly all the time, Sentence Correction would not exist. The genie can be tricked. In particular, humans are awesome at understanding *spoken* language, but reading ability has been grafted into our heads late in the course of evolution.

So you can be more easily fooled by written text, especially when the text uses constructions that are totally legal but rarely heard.

In addition, you should recognize that you're *too* smart. (Good excuse, right?) You are far better than any computer at figuring out garbled messages. At times you instantly grasp what the writer means—and that makes it even harder to spot subtle grammatical flaws in the actual message.

This is why you should refine your intuitive knowledge of grammar. Work to **articulate the rules explicitly.** They will set you free. Consider this example again:

If you can read this simple sentence, you already know a ton of grammar.

Look at the words one after another. How would you classify each one grammatically?

If you started to think of terms such as "nouns" and "verbs," you're on the right track. Here are the words, classified by their **part of speech** in this sentence:

Noun:	sentence, ton, grammar	**Verb:**	can, read, know
Pronoun:	you	**Adverb:**	already
Adjective:	this, simple, a	**Conjunction:**	if
Preposition:	of		

The next few chapters will focus on these seven parts of speech. You will learn their characteristics, as well as commonly associated errors. You will practice spotting these parts of speech and associated errors in simple sentences.

By the way, some languages clearly indicate the part of speech right on the word itself. For instance, the ending -*skii* on a Russian word screams, "I'm an adjective!"

English does very little of this sort of thing. What part of speech is *believe*? It's a verb, but you just have to know that. Don't worry, you do. In a pinch, you can make up a simple test sentence, as we'll see later.

It gets trickier to pin down words such as *light* and *sound*, which can easily take on more than one part of speech. The choice depends on context. In other words, it depends on the *other words* in the sentence:

Noun:	There's no **light** in here, and I can't hear a **sound**.
Verb:	Can you **light** a match? Wait, what does that **sound** like to you?
Adjective:	My head feels **light**. I hope we get out of here safe and **sound**.

Even when you know the part of speech of every word in a sentence, there's still more to do. Read the following two sentences, and think about how they paint completely different pictures of reality, even though the parts of speech are the same in both examples:

1. Mary tickled Joe, who sat still and frowned quietly.

2. Joe tickled Mary, who sat still and frowned quietly.

Word order matters immensely in English. It tells you who did what to whom.

In the first sentence, the noun *Mary* is in front of the verb *tickled*, so *Mary* is the **subject** of *tickled*. Who did the tickling? Mary. Meanwhile, *Joe* is the **object** of *tickled*. Who was tickled? Joe. In addition, *Joe* is the effective subject of *sat* and *frowned*. Who sat still and frowned quietly? Joe.

The second sentence reverses the grammatical roles of the nouns *Mary* and *Joe* by swapping their positions. As a result, the real-life roles of Mary and Joe are also reversed. The sentences describe different situations.

Word order is one aspect of **sentence structure**, which is as important to grammar as parts of speech are. In later chapters, you will practice spotting errors related to sentence structure.

In addition to testing grammar, GMAT Sentence Correction also tests your ability to pick an answer choice that makes the most sense. You must ensure that the intended **meaning** comes through clearly. Even grammatically perfect sentences can have unclear or unlikely meanings. Take a step back, and make no assumptions. For example:

> The spill has greatly affected the Gulf of Mexico, where thousands of office workers toil despite the pollution.

This perfectly grammatical sentence implies that thousands of office workers work *in* the Gulf of Mexico, which is a body of water! When the original sentence doesn't make sense, pick an answer that fixes the problem. For instance, it is very likely that the office workers work in the *area surrounding the Gulf of Mexico.*

Finally, the GMAT tests **concision**. Can you say the same thing in fewer words? Fewer is better, of course, but beware: many students overfocus on this issue. After all, concision is easy to assess: which answer choice is shorter? That's much simpler to figure out than a tricky pronoun issue.

As a result, students often pick the shortest answer while ignoring far more important grammatical issues. Those "extra words" may not be extra at all—they may well be needed to make the sentence clear and grammatically correct.

In fact, it's probably safest for you to **minimize or even ignore concision** at this stage of the game, so that you won't be tempted to apply the principle inappropriately.

As you solve a Sentence Correction problem, you should prioritize the issues this way:

1. **Focus first and foremost on grammatical issues.**

2. **If more than one choice is grammatically correct, choose the one that most clearly reveals the author's intended meaning** (whatever you think that is).

3. **If you *still* can't decide, bring in concision—carefully!**

Listening to Your Ear versus Learning Grammar

Students who just play it by ear on Sentence Correction don't tend to do very well.

The GMAT is very interested in testing things that people say all the time in casual speech, but that are actually incorrect. For instance, according to GMAT rules, the following sentence contains *five* mistakes:

> I credited the counselor for the astute observation that each of the students are different than their friends in ways that affect their development.

Your ear might tell you that the above sentence sounds funny, but your ear will probably tell you that the correct version sounds funny, too:

> I credited the counselor WITH the astute observation that each of the students IS different FROM HIS OR HER friends in ways that affect HIS OR HER development.

Don't worry about the particular grammatical issues we've hinted at above. Right now, we just want to make the point that playing it by ear is a backup plan or a last resort.

You will need to learn the rules of grammar. In order to understand and apply the rules, you will need to start with the contents of this book.

The Answer to the Question

Did you solve the question at the beginning of the chapter? If not, turn back to it, then return with your answer.

Here is the original sentence again:

> The hospital adopted a number of cost-saving measures, <u>to eliminate some administrative personnel and raising</u> fees for certain elective services.

And here is the corrected version:

> The hospital adopted a number of cost-saving measures, <u>eliminating some administrative personnel and raising</u> fees for certain elective services.

The word *and* is a conjunction—the most important one. When you see *and*, ask yourself, "What's in the list?" In the incorrect sentence, we have *to eliminate... and raising....* When you have *X... and Y...*, make *X* and *Y* **parallel**. That is, *X* and *Y* should be comparable in meaning, and they should have the same form.

In the correct version, *eliminating* and *raising* are logically comparable. They tell you more about how the *hospital adopted a number of cost-saving measures.* Specifically, they are two actions that the hospital took to cut costs.

Second, *eliminating* and *raising* have the same form. They are both *-ing* forms of verbs.

The correct answer is (C). None of the other choices are properly parallel. Choice (B) (*to eliminate some administrative personnel and rising fees...*) is only parallel if you claim that the hospital was eliminating rising fees—and that doesn't make sense. The hospital was *raising* fees. Separately, it was *eliminating* some personnel. Those are the parallel actions.

Fear not! In later chapters, we'll go into these issues in more depth. Let's go ahead and get started with nouns, pronouns, and adjectives.

Chapter 2 *of*

Foundations of GMAT Verbal

Nouns, Pronouns, Adjectives

In This Chapter...

Chapter 2:
Nouns, Pronouns, Adjectives

Nouns

A noun is a word for a thing, place, person, animal, or idea. These words are nouns or can be nouns:

kitchen	case study	love	Tuesday	product	stop
children	cleanliness	Afghanistan	fluidity	the rich	cry
removal	division	water	finding	production	administration

A few of these words are commonly found as other parts of speech. For instance, *love, stop,* and *cry* can all be verbs:

Used as nouns: Can you feel the **love**?   This is my **stop**.   I want to let out a **cry** of joy.

Used as verbs: Wait, you don't **love** me?   **Stop**!   I want to **cry**.

Ways to Spot Nouns

How can you tell when a word is being used as a noun?

First, ask yourself whether **the word is being used to describe a thing**. It could be an abstract thing, such as an emotion (*love*), an event (*discussion*), a quality (*cleanliness*), an action (*removal*), or a result of an action (*production*).

This test of meaning will generally work fine. If you get mixed up, though, investigate **where the word is in the sentence**. How does the word relate to other nearby words? What is its role?

As you saw earlier with *Mary tickled Joe*, a noun can play the role of subject (*Mary*) or object (*Joe*) of verbs (*tickled*).

If you're not sure of the exact grammatical role, **look right in front of the word**. If you find markers such as *the*, *a*, *an*, or *my*, you've got a noun. These little words tell you that a noun is coming… eventually. For example:

the **love**   *my* **stop**   *a* **cry**   *the* crazy, mixed-up, passionate, wonderful **love** that we have

As a last resort, **insert a silly noun** in place of the word in question. You might get a silly sentence, but it will be grammatical if the original word is a noun. Try the word *cheese* in the *love*, *stop*, and *cry* examples:

Original words used as nouns: Can you feel the **cheese**?   This is my **cheese**.
                                 I want to let out a **cheese** of joy.

These sentences are weird, but they're grammatical. You're not sure what a *cheese of joy* is, but it sounds kind of good. Now, try the other examples:

Original words used as verbs: Wait, you don't **cheese** me?   **Cheese**.   I want to **cheese**.

These examples make absolutely no sense. Therefore, you know that in the original versions, *love*, *stop*, and *cry* were not being used as nouns.

Categories of Nouns

You may have noticed some unusual nouns on the list above. There are several different kinds of nouns, which are discussed here.

It's not necessary for you to memorize the grammatical terms below. Your goal is simply to be able to recognize that all of these strange nouns really are nouns.

Notice that some nouns seem to be made from simpler words. *Cleanliness* and *fluidity* are made from the adjectives *clean* and *fluid*. Most nouns made from adjectives are **qualities**. Sometimes, an adjective with a *the* in front (*the rich*) can function as a noun: *The rich love these nice cars.* Here, *the rich* is really just a short version of *rich people*.

Nouns can also be made from verbs. *Removal* comes from *remove*. *Discussion* comes from *discuss*. Both *product* and *production* come from *produce*. You might also put into this category words such as *love*, *stop*, and *cry*, which have the same forms as nouns and as verbs. They might have been verbs first; it doesn't really matter.

Many of these nouns made from verbs represent **actions** or the results of actions. Be careful! Verbs represent actions too. The difference is that in the noun form, the action is a *thing*, even if abstract. So the action can play the role of a noun in a sentence.

Try putting *the* or *this* in front of an action noun. Write short sentences to see how action nouns work as subjects or objects. For example:

> The **removal** was great.   This **discussion** inspired me.   I like this **product**.
> I like this **production**.

Some nouns (*Tuesday, Afghanistan*) are spelled with capital letters. These nouns are **proper nouns**, nouns that name specific items. All other nouns are **common nouns**. Some words can be used as proper or common nouns, as in *Harvard University* and *all universities*. When *university* is used as part of a proper noun, it is capitalized. When it is used as a common noun, it is lowercase. You don't need to memorize capitalization rules for Sentence Correction; simply recognize that both proper and common nouns are perfectly good nouns.

Some nouns (*case study, post office, dog collar*) contain more than one word. These are **compound nouns**. Some compound nouns are hyphenated (*gun-carriage, attorney-at-law*), and others have been welded into one word (*landlord, bookkeeper*). When you see two nouns in a row, the first noun is usually modifying the second noun, and together they form a compound noun. In essence, the first noun becomes an adjective. The second noun stays a noun. For example:

> kitchen sink   = a kind of *sink*
> love poem   = a kind of *poem*
> dog collar   = a kind of *collar*

Collective nouns refer to groups composed of members (*administration*). In American English (and GMAT English), these nouns are singular. That is, an administration (or *jury, company, family, majority, society, army*) may have many people in it, but it is considered **only one thing**. In American English, we say *The army IS advancing* (not *ARE advancing*). In British English and in some non-American dialects, many of these nouns would be plural, as in *The family ARE on holiday* or *Manchester United HAVE scored again*. For better or for worse, the GMAT tests American English, so get used to *The family IS on vacation* and *Manchester United IS a soccer team*.

If you find this switch hard to get used to, ask yourself, "How many families are there?" Just one. *Family* is singular.

MEMORIZE IT!

Jury, navy, company, administration, tour group, agency, family, couple, duo—all singular!

Again, you don't need to memorize terms such as proper noun and collective noun. Just recognize that not all nouns look like *dog, week,* or *table*. Some nouns look like *Presidency, mother-in-law, swimming pool, denial, celebration, August,* or *empiricism*.

Drill 2.1 — Find the Nouns

Circle all of the nouns in the following sentences. Most sentences contain more than one noun.

1. Companies in the United States receive certain protections from imports.

2. Jane Austen wrote *Pride and Prejudice*, a novel that in 2005 was adapted into a film starring Keira Knightley.

3. The primary purpose of the passage is to present an alternative explanation for a well-known fact.

4. A recent study has provided additional support for a particular theory about the origin of the fruit bat.

5. I am only happy if you are happy; my happiness depends on yours.

Answers are on page 135.

Singular and Plural

Dog by itself refers to one dog. You often put *a* or *the* in front of *dog*, as in these examples: *I saw a dog walking down the street. The dog was a cocker spaniel.* Either way, the noun *dog* is **singular**.

To talk about more than one dog, make the noun *dog* **plural** by adding an *-s*. For instance: *I have three dogs.*

Some languages do not emphasize the difference between singular and plural. English does, for better or for worse. If your native language does not distinguish singular and plural, pay close attention. Even native English speakers can get tripped up on this issue, and the GMAT loves to exploit tricky cases.

First of all, in English you can count some things but not others. **Count nouns** can be counted normally. They have a singular form when you have just one of them, and a plural form when you have two or more of them. Most plural forms add an *-s*. *One pencil, two pencils, seven pencils.* You talk about how much you have of a count noun by using numbers or other words (*many, few, more, fewer*).

Mass nouns represent "stuff" (*bread, water*) that can't be counted directly without adding a word such as *piece* or *cup*. *One piece of bread, two pieces of bread; one cup of water, two cups of water.* Most of these mass nouns do not have

> **MEMORIZE IT!**
>
> Use *amount* for something you can't count, and *number* for something you can count. For example, "A great *number* of friends have shown me a great *amount* of kindness."
>
> *Less* and *fewer* work the same way. Use *less* for something you can't count (*I have less stress this term than last*) and *fewer* for something you can count (*This express lane is only for people with ten items or fewer*).
>
> This means that most grocery stores are incorrect. Virtually all of their signs say "10 items *or less.*" Since items are countable, *less* should be *fewer*.

plural forms in standard English (*breads? waters?*). You talk about how much you have of a mass noun by counting units (*pieces* or *cups*) or by using *much, little, more,* or *less.*

Some abstractions are mass nouns (*fluidity*), while others are countable (*concept*). You can usually use common sense to tell whether you have a mass noun or a count noun. Simply ask, "Would it make sense to say I have seven of these, for example?" You can have seven *pencils, degrees, heart attacks,* etc. You cannot have seven *breads* or *brilliances.*

Nouns Wrap-Up

Good work! You're building a solid foundation for GMAT Sentence Correction.

Recognizing nouns will be the first step in identifying the subject of a sentence (which is either a noun or something functioning like a noun) and in determining whether a pronoun is correct.

Pop Quiz!

True or False: The sentence "I have a great amount of homework and a great amount of deadlines" is correct.

Answer is on page 131.

Grade Yourself

Throughout this book, we'll ask you to grade yourself on how well you understood a section. Why? Well, one of the most important factors in learning is *metacognition*, or thinking about thinking. We don't just want you to read the material—we want you to check in with yourself regarding your level of understanding. Second, these boxes are a practical way for you to mark certain subjects for later review. And third, it's fun to get an A sometimes!

How did you do in this section?

- ☐ **A** - I totally get this!
- ☐ **B** - I'm okay with this. Maybe review later if there's time.
- ☐ **C** - I'll make a note to review this later.

Pronouns

A pronoun is a word used in place of a noun or noun phrase. All of these are pronouns:

he	his	it	they	myself	their
who	those	everyone	somebody	each	its

Unlike nouns, there simply aren't that many pronouns in existence. You already know them all. On the GMAT, the issue will never be that you come across a pronoun you've never heard of. The real issue is that pronouns are so common and so unassuming that you blow right past them. By their very nature, pronouns do not call attention to themselves! They're stand-ins, substitute teachers, the totally quiet people at the party. For this reason, on a GMAT problem, they're often the most important folks around.

Categories of Pronouns

As with nouns, it is not necessary to memorize the grammatical terms for these types of pronouns. However, you should be able to recognize all the different kinds of pronouns *as pronouns*.

Personal pronouns are what most people think of when they think of pronouns. You use personal pronouns such as *she* or *them* because it sounds silly to say "Cory did Cory's homework in Cory's room" rather than "Cory did his homework in his room." Personal pronouns can be divided into subcategories:

Subject pronouns: I   you   he   she   it   we   they

Subject pronouns are used as the subjects of sentences or clauses (whole sentences that can serve as parts of larger sentences). Subject pronouns perform verbs. Examples: *He ate. The rain fell as **they** continued practicing.*

Object pronouns: me   you   him   her   it   us   you   them

Object pronouns serve as the object of a verb. That is, verbs get done to them. *I like only **you**.* Object pronouns can also be the objects of prepositions: *What do you think of **it**? Give this to **her**. I see through **them**.*

Possessive pronouns: mine   yours   his   hers   its   ours   your   theirs

These pronouns indicate ownership. Don't confuse the possessive pronoun *its* with the contraction *it's*. "Its" indicates that there is something that belongs to whatever "it" is. "It's" means "it is."

You might be wondering, where are *my, your, her, our,* and *their*? These **possessive adjectives** are a kind of cross between pronouns and adjectives. They're technically

2

adjectives because they modify nouns (*my sheep, your water*). They don't stand in place of nouns, as real pronouns do.

However, like the true possessive pronouns (*mine, yours*), possessive adjectives have to refer back to a noun—the person or thing doing the possessing. Pay particular attention to *its* and *theirs*.

The noun that a personal pronoun stands in for should be clear. This is also true of possessive adjectives. For instance, *Representative Nancy Pelosi and the lobbyist had a heated disagreement about **her** agenda.* Whose agenda? The Senator's or the lobbyist's? Even if you feel like you could figure it out from context or common sense, the sentence is wrong (unless the lobbyist is clearly indicated to be male).

Reflexive pronouns (*myself, ourselves, itself,* etc.) are formed by adding *-self* to the end of possessive pronouns or adjectives. Example: *The executives rewarded **themselves** with bonuses.*

Some people say *myself* when they should say *me,* as in *Bill Clinton will be sitting at this table with my husband and myself.* People who talk like this think they sound fancy, but they are just wrong. You can use a reflexive pronoun correctly when the person doing the action and the person receiving the action are the same, as in *He hit himself in the head* or *The dog groomed itself.* The other correct use is to provide emphasis, as in *I made this gift myself.*

Interrogative pronouns (*who, whom, whose, which*) are used to ask questions.

Demonstrative pronouns (*this, that, these, those*) are used to point out a specific thing. *Are **those** my shoes? **That** is my car right over there.* These same words can be used as adjectives: ***that** car, **those** shoes.*

Indefinite pronouns are very important on the GMAT. They take the place of nouns, but do not refer to specific people, places, or things. For instance, instead of saying "All people have an inherent sense of justice," you could say "*Everyone* has an inherent sense of justice." *Everyone* is an indefinite pronoun.

Notice in the example above that when you switched from using *All people* as the subject of the sentence to using *Everyone,* the verb changed as well—from *All people **have*** to *Everyone **has.***

This is because **most indefinite pronouns are singular**, including *everyone.* This fact is tested on the GMAT very often, because in a way it's counterintuitive. If you tell *everyone* in a classroom to stand up and *everyone* obeys, how many people stand up? As long as there was more than one person to begin with, you'll have a plural number of people standing. In some languages, the typical way you refer to *everyone* is with a plural pronoun. Not in English!

Here is a list of indefinite pronouns:

> everyone, someone, no one, anyone
> everybody, somebody, nobody, anybody
> everything, something, anything, nothing
> all, many, more, most, much, several, some, few, both, one, none

2

each, either, neither

another

any

other

ADVANCED TIP:

Technically, there is another type of pronoun. **Relative pronouns** are pronouns, such as *which* and *that*, that are used to relate a subordinate clause to the rest of the sentence: *The book **that** fell on the floor is great.* Other relative pronouns include *who, whom, whose, when, where,* and *why.* It doesn't really matter for purposes of the GMAT that these words are technically pronouns. You can just think of them as words that introduce modifiers. Modifiers will be discussed later.

Some of the indefinite pronouns above can also be used as other parts of speech. For instance, in the sentence *One should learn about grammar in order to succeed on the GMAT,* the word *one* is an indefinite pronoun—it is standing in for a noun, such as *a student.* However, in the sentence *One is the loneliest number,* the word *one* is a noun. In the sentence *I have one pencil,* it is an adjective.

Other words about number *(many, several)* are used much more often as adjectives than as pronouns. For instance, in the sentence *The lake has several swans,* the word *several* is describing *swans,* so it is an adjective. *Several* is a pronoun only when it is standing in for a noun, as in this exchange: "Do you have any swans?" "Why yes, I have *several*!" In this case, *several* is standing in for *swans* (while also providing helpful information about the approximate number of swans).

MEMORIZE IT!

If the pronoun ends with *-one, -thing,* or *-body (anybody, everyone, something,* etc.), it's singular. Even more importantly, the word *each* is singular.

You will see the word *each* on the GMAT repeatedly. So it is necessary to repeat this important piece of information:

***Each* is always singular.** It may at times *seem* plural. But it never will be.

Drill 2.2 — Find the Pronouns

Circle all of the pronouns in the following sentences. Include possessive adjectives.

1. It is clear to everyone that Chairman Frankel will have to resign his position.

2. If one wants to drive over rugged terrain, one will need a vehicle far more powerful than mine.

3. Everybody at the comics convention is hoping for a chance to get an autograph from each of the celebrities.

4. While Dave isn't tall enough to play in the NBA, he is certainly taller than most.

5. Who just saw me spill soup all over myself?

Answers are on page 135.

Antecedents

An *Antecedent* is the word or group of words that a pronoun refers to. In the sentence *The company was forced to cut staff so that it could avoid going out of business entirely*, the pronoun is *it*, and the antecedent is *the company*.

2

Not all pronouns have antecedents:

*   An indefinite pronoun such as *anyone* will not have an antecedent.

*   The pronoun *you* is often used without an antecedent, both in reference to a specific person (*Will you please take out the trash?*) and in reference to "the reader" or people in general (*You should learn about pronouns if you want to do well on the GMAT*).

*   In a few circumstances, the pronoun *it* doesn't need an antecedent, as in *It's raining* or *It is hoped that taxpayers will use these refund checks to stimulate the economy*. Notice that *it* here comes at the beginning of the sentence.

However, take a look at this sentence:

> They always say the grass is greener on the other side of the fence.

Who are *they*? This sentence is considered incorrect. The pronoun *they* always needs an clear antecedent. The same is true of *them, their, it* (except for the exceptions mentioned earlier), and *its*. When you see one of these pronouns, **find its antecedent.** If the antecedent is missing or unclear, you've got problems.

The sentence above could be rephrased correctly—and more informatively—in this way:

> CORRECT: An old proverb says that the grass is greener on the other side of the fence.

In real-life speech and writing, an antecedent is often in a different sentence than the pronoun: *I'd like you to meet my brother.* ***He's an anesthesiologist.*** The pronoun *He* has the antecedent *my brother*. This sort of English is perfectly fine, as long as it's clear what the pronoun refers to.

However, no Sentence Correction problem contains more than one sentence. So, on the GMAT, you need to match pronouns with antecedents in the same sentence.

Occasionally, a pronoun can legally come before the antecedent:

> CORRECT: Having finally put the pain behind her, Shilpa decided it was time to have a little fun.

The pronoun *her* occurs before the antecedent, *Shilpa*. This is perfectly acceptable as long as it's clear who *she* is.

Pop Quiz!

True or False: *You* and *it* can be both subject and object pronouns.

Answer is on page 131.

Drill 2.3 — Connect Pronouns with Antecedents

For each sentence, circle each pronoun or possessive adjective and make an arrow pointing back to its antecedent, if it has one.

Example: (Everyone) sacrificed to get the job done, so when Ellen attributed the project's success to (herself,) (she) lost a lot of friends.

1.   Can you finish it today?

2.   All of the cake was gone before we had a chance to try it.

3.   Marina joked about our security badges while ceremonially turning in hers—she said she would be certain to enjoy the fact that retired people no longer have to wear nametags.

4.   As soon as Davis saw me working on my project, he started plotting to take credit for it.

5.   It is clear that the dog loves the new toy that Joey bought for it, so much so that Joey is glad he didn't spend the money on himself.

Answers are on page 135.

A Special Note About the Pronoun "One"

Sometimes, *one* simply means "one of the things I just mentioned."

> CORRECT: Of all the corporate "green" policies, this is the **one** I find most disingenuous.

Here, *one* refers back to *policies* and means "one of the policies."

One can also mean *everyone* or *everyone in a certain group* or *the average person:*

2

CORRECT: **One** will benefit immensely from increasing *one's* verbal skills prior to taking the GMAT.

This usage is very common in British English. In American English, it is correct, but can sound formal or excessively fancy, especially when *one* is used multiple times (*If one wants to do well, one should do one's homework*).

In many situations in which *one* is used, *you* would also work:

CORRECT: If **you** want to do well, **you** should do **your** homework.

However, it is wrong to switch between *one* and *you:*

INCORRECT: **One** must be careful to account for all sources of income on **your** tax return.

In the above sentence, *one* and *one* would be fine, and *you* and *you* would also be fine, but we can't mix and match. *One* also doesn't mix with nouns that require the pronouns *he, they,* etc.:

INCORRECT: **People** who want to become politicians should keep **one's** reputation spotless.

Just as you would normally refer back to *people* with *they* or *their* (as in *People should pay their taxes*), you must do the same here.

Pop Quiz!

True or False: A pronoun may have an adjective as its antecedent.

Answer is on page 131.

The reflexive form of *one* is *oneself:*

CORRECT: Learning does not have to stop at graduation; **one** can educate **oneself** throughout life.

In general, if *one* appears as a pronoun on the GMAT, it is very likely that there is an error. One more example:

INCORRECT: Flawed in two ways, the earthquake detection system would often find a geological precursor event when **it** wasn't actually occurring and fail to find **one** when **it** was.

This complex sentence contains a string of pronouns: *it, one,* and *it.* Since you know that the pronoun *one* does not mix well with other pronouns, you should be suspicious of this sentence. Indeed, the problem is in the final part: *and fail to find* **one** *when* **it** *was.*

2

Here, *one* and *it* are referring back to the same thing (the *geological precursor event*, whatever that is). *One* cannot be used interchangeably with other pronouns when referring to the same thing, so the sentence is grammatically incorrect. The sentence could be fixed by replacing *one* with another *it*, as in:

CORRECT: Flawed in two ways, the earthquake detection system would often find a geological precursor event when **it** wasn't actually occurring and fail to find **it** when **it** was.

This does sound repetitive, but it is grammatically correct. All three uses of *it* refer back to the *geological precursor event*, which is a singular noun.

Try a drill.

Pronoun Drill 2.4 — Use the Pronoun *One*

Each sentence uses the pronoun *one*. Determine whether the sentence has an error and circle "Correct" or "Incorrect."

1. Fire is entrancing, but one should be careful with it. CORRECT/INCORRECT

2. Firefighters should always secure one's safety gear before rushing into a fire. CORRECT/INCORRECT

3. One who wishes to buy oneself a gift with funds from one's own company must first speak with one's accountant lest one run afoul of the law. CORRECT/INCORRECT

4. If you just can't wait to receive a letter in the mail, one can check one's admissions results by calling this number. CORRECT/INCORRECT

5. One of the zoo's foxes escaped from its cage. CORRECT/INCORRECT

Answers are on page 136.

Pronouns Wrap-Up

That was a long section on a lot of tiny words! However, recognizing and checking pronouns is one of the best skills you can develop for gaining points on GMAT Sentence Correction. Pronoun errors are *extremely common* on the exam, and the first step to recognizing those errors is spotting the pronouns.

You're making great progress! Next you'll learn about a new study strategy, making flashcards, and then move on to *Adjectives,* which are much simpler then *Pronouns.*

> ### Grade Yourself
>
> How did you do in this section?
>
> - ☐ **A** - I totally get this!
> - ☐ **B** - I'm okay with this. Maybe review later if there's time.
> - ☐ **C** - I'll make a note to review this later.

Making Flashcards

Now is a good time to introduce the idea of **flashcards**.

If you had trouble with any of the drill sentences in the last two sections, make a flashcard with the sentence on one side and the answer and explanation on the other.

Taking notes as you work through this book is also a fine strategy, of course. Flashcards are good because when you later review your flashcards, it will be very clear that you're supposed to *do* something with them. When people review notes, they tend to smile and nod (or maybe just nod). When people review flashcards, they actually solve problems in a more GMAT-like way.

You might just *look* at your notes. But when you pick up a flashcard, you actually answer the question. You might even take a risk and commit to an answer you're not sure of. Those are good skills to practice.

Here is a sample flashcard:

Firefighters should always secure one's safety gear before rushing into a fire.

FoV book page 36

2

> INCORRECT
>
> The pronoun "one" does not match the plural "firefighters" (correct pronoun is "their").

The example includes a source on the front of the flashcard ("FoV" for *Foundations of GMAT Verbal* plus a page number). You may wish to later make flashcards from *The Official Guide for GMAT Review, 13th Edition*, the *Manhattan GMAT Strategy Guides*, and practice exams from Manhattan GMAT or from mba.com. So it can be helpful to **note where the problem came from**.

Sentences like the one above will fit on any size card. But go ahead and **buy larger index cards** (4" × 6"). Later, you may wish to make flashcards for entire Sentence Correction, Critical Reasoning, or quantitative questions from the *Official Guide* and online exams, so using larger index cards is a good idea.

Adjectives

Adjectives describe or modify nouns or pronouns. They answer questions such as "What kind is it?", "Which one?", and "How many are there?" All of these are adjectives or can be used as adjectives:

red	annoying	75	third	a	an
patterned	utter	your	ten-minute	the	French

A, an, and *the* are sometimes called adjectives and sometimes called *articles*. This issue is not important on the GMAT, so you can lump them in with other adjectives.

Categories of Adjectives

Nouns can sometimes act as adjectives, as in the word *kitchen* in the phrase *kitchen floor*. (A "phrase" is just a group of words, by the way.) Similarly, the word *diamond* by itself is a noun, but in *diamond mine*, it is an adjective. A *diamond mine* is a kind of *mine*.

Proper adjectives are formed from proper nouns. Proper adjectives include *Japanese, Keynesian,* and *United Nations* (when used to describe nouns, as in the phrase *United Nations representative*).

Numbers are usually adjectives. In *100 is the number after 99*, both numbers are nouns. (Notice that they are not telling you how many of something *else* you have—100 and 99 actually are what the

2

sentence is about.) More commonly, however, you use numbers in this way: *The school has 250 first-year students.* Here, *250* is an adjective that answers the question, "How many first-year students?"

Compound adjectives (such as *first-year* in the previous sentence) contain more than one word and sometimes have hyphens. For example, a *twenty-minute workout* or an *egg-shaped jewel.* Many compound adjectives are hyphenated when placed before nouns, but not when on their own. For instance, *I am broken hearted* does not have a hyphen, but *She is a broken-hearted Justin Bieber fan* does. The hyphen in these cases makes the meaning clear. A *blue, fringed dress* (a dress that is blue and has fringe) is not the same as a *blue-fringed dress* (a dress that has blue fringe).

GMAT questions are not going to test you on hyphen placement, so don't freak out when you see a hyphen. Don't automatically cross off an answer that contains *an all-too-common refrain* or even *left-and right-handed people.* **Note:** The expression "freak out" is used elsewhere in this book. It is referring to what happens when students see an old-fashioned, formal, or unusual usage on the GMAT (such as *nonetheless* or *The company markets services more effectively **than does** its competitor*) and either panic or automatically cross it off because it "feels weird." Avoid these freak-outs by familiarizing yourself with formal, written American English, as you are now doing!

You already saw possessive adjectives in the section on pronouns (***his** car,* ***its** prey*). Several other pronouns—*whose, which, this, that, these, those, all, both, some*—can also be used as adjectives. Again, memorizing grammatical terms is not important for the GMAT. Just know that there is some overlap between adjectives and the "weird" pronouns. In general on the GMAT, don't stress over exactly what part of speech a word is. **Focus on the specific job the word is doing in the sentence.**

Pop Quiz!

True or False: In the sentence "7,919 is the one-thousandth prime number," 7,919 and *one-thousandth* are both adjectives.

Answer is on page 131.

Pronoun Errors Related to Adjectives

Overall, adjectives are pretty easy; there aren't many GMAT errors related to adjectives. The most important trick has to do with pronouns and compound nouns. Remember *diamond mine?* Because *diamond* is doing the work of an adjective, it is no longer a noun—meaning that it cannot be an antecedent for a pronoun. ProNOUNS can only refer back to NOUNS or other pronouns.

CORRECT: **The French** are insistent about the quality of their wines, and **they** produce the best in the world.

The pronoun is *they*. The antecedent is *The French*, which is a noun here (meaning "the French people"). Both *they* and *The French* are plural. The sentence is correct.

INCORRECT: I love **French** food because **they** really know how to make a good sauce.

Once again, the pronoun is *they*, but here *French* cannot be the antecedent. *French* is an adjective describing *food*. This error makes the sentence grammatically incorrect. You could fix it by writing *I love French food because **the French** really know how to make a good sauce.*

To tell whether a word is an adjective, try substituting other words that you know for sure are adjectives. If they fit, you're good. In the incorrect example above, you could easily switch in other adjectives: *I love **hot** food, I love **delicious** food.* This test makes it easy to see that *French* is an adjective in the sentence and therefore cannot be the antecedent of a pronoun.

In the correct version above, note that you *cannot* substitute in adjectives. ***Blue** are insistent? **Happy** are insistent?* You can see here that *The French* is a noun.

Drill 2.5 — Circle the Adjectives

Circle all the adjectives in the following sentences. You can leave out *a*, *an*, and *the*.

1. School hallways are a dangerous place in violent, overcrowded cities.

2. She felt that she was an utter failure, but her mother felt that she was a thoroughgoing success.

3. The Canadians were furious when their child came home from kindergarten with black-and-blue marks.

4. Danish queen Margrethe II is the first female monarch of Denmark since Margrethe I, who took the throne in 1388.

5. I know that this is a banausic concern, but six is my lucky number, so I am disappointed that I was only able to purchase five tickets for the raffle.

Answers are on page 136.

Absolute Adjectives

Absolute adjectives are adjectives that are not capable of being intensified. To *intensify* an adjective is to turn *intelligent* into *more intelligent* or *tall* into *taller.*

For instance, *smart* is not an absolute adjective. One person can be *smart,* but another person can be even *smarter.* However, *dead* IS an absolute adjective. You're either dead or you aren't. There is no such word as *deader. More dead* is also incorrect because it is illogical.

Other absolute adjectives include *square, essential, universal, immortal,* and the word *absolute* itself.

Traditionally, *unique* has been considered an absolute adjective, because it means "one-of-a-kind." Something is either one-of-a-kind or it isn't. The expression *more unique* is now common in everyday speech (many people simply use *unique* to mean *special*), but *more unique* should be avoided in formal English. Similarly, *circular* is an absolute adjective. People might casually describe one oval as *more circular* than another, but in formal speech, *more nearly circular* would be preferable.

The logic here is that *circular* indicates a 100% match with being a circle, and you can't go above 100%—thus, *more circular* is illogical. But *more nearly circular* means "closer to being a perfect circle than something else is." If two things are below 100%, one can be closer to 100% than the other one.

So don't freak out when you read that one disease is *more likely fatal* than another, for instance. Maybe one of them is fatal 0.01% of the time, and the other one is fatal 0.0001% of the time!

More likely fatal is correct. *More fatal* is not, because *fatal* is absolute. Remember, definitely do not just go for the shorter answer! Sometimes, these little "extra words" (such as *likely* in this case) are not extra at all.

Drill 2.6 — Find the Adjective Errors

Determine whether the sentence has an error and circle "Correct" or "Incorrect."

1. The chefs taught us to make delicious Chinese food, and they were always very nice about answering questions. CORRECT/INCORRECT

2. The Chinese army is the largest military force in the world; they have approximately 3 million members. CORRECT/INCORRECT

3. This liquor is a fifteen-year-old Scotch. CORRECT/INCORRECT

4. The college administrators have argued that it needs a larger budget to continue operating into the new year. CORRECT/INCORRECT

5. That professor never gives anyone an A, but he did tell me that my paper was more nearly perfect than any of my classmates' papers. CORRECT/INCORRECT

Answers are on page 136.

Adjectives Wrap-Up

You've now covered three very important parts of speech—*Nouns, Pronouns,* and *Adjectives.* You've also read about an important error to watch out for on the GMAT—a pronoun trying to refer back to an adjective, when it should refer back to a noun.

Notice that the last drill was more about pronouns than adjectives. You are starting to tie your learning together into usable skills!

> ### *Grade Yourself*
>
> How did you do in this section?
>
> ☐   **A** - I totally get this!
> ☐   **B** - I'm okay with this. Maybe review later if there's time.
> ☐   **C** - I'll make a note to review this later.

Chapter 3 *of*

Foundations of GMAT Verbal

Verbs & Adverbs

In This Chapter...

Chapter 3:
Verbs & Adverbs

Verbs

Verbs are a necessary part of all sentences. They express actions, events, or states of being.

ADVANCED TIP:

Did you know that *We left, Joe ran,* and *I do* are all complete sentences? Each has a subject and a verb.

Verbs are the critical part of any sentence's **predicate**. You'll see this term again soon, but for now, you can just think of a predicate as "everything besides the subject" in a simple sentence. All of the following are verbs:

is	decided	went
accomplishes	arose	forsook

Many verbs occur in combination with one another to express more information. These are **compound verbs**, such as the following:

will go	has been eating	is writing
had swollen	will have been broken	should have gone

Verbs occur in a variety of **tenses** (past, present, future, and many more complicated ones), **voices** (active and passive), and even **moods** (which have to do with the intention of what's being said).

Almost everything in English is in the **indicative** mood. *Indicative* means "indicating," and of course virtually all sentences indicate something. The **imperative** mood is for giving commands, as in ***Run faster!*** or ***Consider*** the case of the cassowary. The **subjunctive** mood is a special topic that will be discussed later. It is used to express a wish, an emotion, a possibility, or an action that has not yet occurred, as in *I wish you **were** mine* or *I suggest that you **be** on time.*

Categories of Verbs

Action verbs (such as *eat, disagreed, go*) express the action performed by a subject. The tense of an action verb (past, present, etc.) gives information about *when* the action was performed.

Linking verbs (such as *is, are, was, become, feel, seem*) "link" the subject to a noun or adjective:

Otto **is** a miniature bulldog.   He **seems** nice.

Don't worry about trying to tell action verbs from linking verbs.

Helping verbs (such as *is, was, has, does, will, should, can*) "help" other words to become complete compound verbs:

He **is planning** to attend.

Is is the helping verb. *Planning* is not quite a complete verb (you can't say *He planning to attend* in standard English), but together, *is planning* is a complete compound verb.

Notice that *planning* is made out of the verb *plan*. *Planning* is an "**-ing**" **word**. "-Ing" words need helping verbs to become complete compound verbs that could run a sentence:

She **will be leaving** shortly.

In this case, *will* and *be* are helping verbs. *Leaving* is an "-ing" word made out of the verb *leave*. Together, *will be leaving* is a complete compound verb. As you can see, a compound verb can have more than one helping verb.

It's fine to think of a phrase such as *is planning* or *will be leaving* as a single verb. Just keep in mind that sometimes another word (an adverb) can separate the individual verbs within a compound verb.

CORRECT: He **has** frequently **defaced** public property.

Here, you can say that *has defaced* is the verb (*frequently* is an adverb, telling you how often *has defaced* has happened). *Has* is the helping verb, and *defaced* is an "**-ed**" **word** created from the verb *deface*. Together, they make the compound verb *has defaced*.

Careful! You *can* use that "-ed" word as a complete past tense for many verbs, including *deface*. You are allowed to say *He frequently* **defaced** *public property*. However, this means something a little different from *He* **has** *frequently* **defaced** *public property*. A prosecutor would say *has defaced* to imply that the person in question is still doing these actions, or that he still is the type of person who would do them. A defense attorney would say *He defaced property, but...* to put the actions clearly in the past.

You'll get to those tense distinctions later—here's the point for now. To catch errors on the GMAT, **don't neglect the *has* if it's there.** If you think that *defaced* by itself were the verb in the example above, you might be okay with this sentence:

INCORRECT: He **has** frequently **defaced** public property and **went** to jail.

Those who do not catch the error in this sentence are probably imagining that *defaced* and *went* are both in the past tense and therefore "match."

However, *went* should be *gone*. Even though the helping verb *has* is written only once, it actually applies to both *defaced* and *gone*. That is, the two verbs are really *has defaced* and *has gone* (*has went* is never correct).

If you catch that the first verb is really *has defaced,* it is much more obvious that *has gone* matches *has defaced*:

CORRECT: He has frequently **defaced** public property and **gone** to jail.

Making parts of a sentence—especially those in a series or list—"match" is a topic that is discussed at more length in Chapter 6, which includes *parallelism*.

The individual verbs within a compound verb also can be separated from one another when the sentence is a question:

CORRECT: **Will** you **be taking** any leftovers home with you?

Here, the compound verb is *will be taking.*

Pop Quiz!

True or False: In the sentence "In 2034 when she is finally released from prison, she will have never so much as touched a cell phone," the main compound verb is *have touched.*

Answer is on page 132.

There is far more to say about verbs than will be covered in this book (or even than is tested on the GMAT). Complex situations can call for complex verb tenses. But you can figure them out—both the situations and the tenses.

CORRECT: By 2016, I will have been working on my Ph.D. for ten years.

This sentence is totally fine. The *will* expresses moving into the future, to 2016. *Have been working* expresses the action being performed *from the perspective of the speaker in 2016,* implying that, even in 2016, the action will be ongoing. In 2016, the speaker will not yet be finished with his or her Ph.D.

For a more in-depth discussion of complex verbs, see our *Sentence Correction GMAT Strategy Guide.*

3

Drill 3.1 — Find the Parts of the Verb

Circle all parts of each compound verb.

Example: I (have) always (wanted) to be an astronaut.

1. That rumor has been spreading like wildfire.

2. The pygmy marmoset has typically been found in the rainforest areas of South America.

3. I will run faster, jump higher, and play more aggressively this season.

4. The firm's executives had supported the eco-initiative until the financial crisis struck and they re-evaluated.

5. Are you going?

Answers are on page 137.

Gerunds

Identifying verbs can be tricky. There are many constructions that look like verbs, but aren't really. For instance, what part of speech is the word *losing*? It's been called an "-ing" word, but let's push further. Most people would say that the word *losing* is a verb. If so, then what's going on in this sentence?

EXAMPLE: Losing stinks.

While *stinks* is being used in a somewhat slang sense (in this case meaning that losing is no fun, not that it smells bad), this is a complete sentence. Certainly, then, *losing* and *stinks* can't both be verbs in this context. Two verbs in a row without a subject could never be a complete sentence.

As it turns out, *stinks* is the verb. *Losing* is what is performing the action of stinking. Thus, *losing* is the subject of the sentence. Although *losing* looks like a verb, it is acting like a noun. Subjects of sentences are always nouns or constructions such as this one that "act like nouns."

In *Losing stinks,* the word *losing* is called a **gerund**. A gerund is an "-ing" word used as a noun.

Gerunds can be subjects of sentences (***Overeating** causes weight gain*) or objects of verbs or prepositions (*I love **dancing**; This is a seminar about **writing***).

When looking for the main verb in a sentence, don't let yourself get distracted by gerunds. A good rule is this: **An "-ing" word without a helper verb isn't a real verb.**

If the "-ing" word is a gerund, you should be able to substitute in a noun in its place. For instance, in the sentence *Dating is tricky*, the word *dating* is a gerund. You can easily substitute a regular noun: *Algebra is tricky.* The sentence *I just adore dancing* works the same way: *I just adore cake. I just adore differential calculus.*

Here's how one "-ing" word can be used as three different parts of speech:

> *I am boxing.* The **compound verb** is *am boxing. Boxing* is part of the verb.

> *I love boxing.* The verb is *love* and *boxing* is a **gerund**, which effectively functions as a **noun**. Note that you could easily substitute another noun for *boxing* (*I love dogs* or *I love this book*).

> *I wish Christian Bale were my boxing coach.* The **adjective** *boxing* is describing the noun *coach.* Note that you can easily substitute an adjective for *boxing* (*I wish Christian Bale were my tall, handsome, famous coach*).

ADVANCED TIP:

To determine whether a word ending in "-ing" is a verb, look for helper verbs. If the "-ing" stands alone, it is not a verb.

Pop Quiz!

True or False: In the sentence "I hate smiling," *smiling* is a gerund, but in the sentence "I am smiling as big as I can," *am smiling* is the main verb.

Answer is on page 132.

Identifying gerunds will be an important skill later on when you need to match up a sentence's subject with its verb. A gerund may or may not be the subject, but it is not acting like a verb. Therefore, you can easily rule it out as being the main verb of the sentence.

Infinitives

As noted in the last section, identifying verbs can be tricky because some constructions look like verbs, but aren't really. Infinitives are a case in point.

An **infinitive** takes the form *to love, to defeat, to go.* These sure look like verbs! In some sense, infinitives are abstract versions of verbs. That's exactly what prevents them from being true working verbs. Infinitives look like verbs, but they do all sorts of *other* things. **An infinitive cannot be the main verb of a sentence.**

That's not to say that infinitives aren't handy! Like gerunds, they can act like nouns to some degree. Infinitives can be the subjects of sentences or the objects of verbs.

3

To love is divine.

To love is an infinitive and is the subject of the sentence. What *is divine*? *To love*, in other words, the act of loving.

I hate **to pay** taxes.

To pay is an infinitive and is the object of the verb *hate*. What do I hate? To pay taxes. That is the thing being hated.

You can test whether infinitives are acting like nouns just as you can with gerunds: **substitute a regular noun**.

~~To love~~ Music is divine.   I hate ~~to pay taxes~~ asparagus.

Infinitives can do other things as well. They can act like adjectives or adverbs too. *A friend **to call** would be nice.* Here, *to call* modifies the noun *friend*. *I went outside to sing.* Here, *to sing* modifies the verb *went*.

Identifying infinitives will be an important skill later on when we need to match up a sentence's subject with its verb. For now, recognize that an infinitive may or may not be the subject of a sentence, but it is not a true verb. It cannot run a sentence as its main verb.

Drill 3.2 — Find the Gerunds and Infinitives

Underline any gerunds or infinitives, and circle the main verb of the sentence.

Example: I (despise) watching television.

1. To be a ballerina is my lifelong dream.

2. The executive has been accused of embezzling funds.

3. Eating, praying, and loving are apparently author Elizabeth Gilbert's favorite activities.

4. To kill is to break the social contract.

5. Recovering from my accident is using all of my energy right now.

Answers are on page 137.

Subject–Verb Agreement

The most basic issue related to verbs on the GMAT is **subject–verb agreement**. Simply put, singular subjects go with singular verbs, and plural subjects go with plural verbs.

It is a bit weird that, in English, singular verbs generally end in -s, and plural verbs do not end in -s. Of course, some verbs are irregular (for instance, *is/are*).

Singular verbs (for *it, he, she*):	runs	differs	goes	has	is
Plural verbs (for *we, they*):	run	differ	go	have	are

3

In a short sentence, it's usually pretty easy to tell whether the subject and verb agree (that is, whether singular is matched with singular or plural is matched with plural).

> **Dogs bark.**   **It runs** well.   **The safety is** off.

You can sometimes run into difficulty with tricky subjects. For instance:

> *Everyone* is singular (we learned this in the section on Pronouns).

> *The Roman army* is singular (we learned this in the section on Nouns).

> This subject is plural: *The desire of our students to succeed and the guiding purpose of our teacher's union.* Some students mistakenly identify the singular *desire* or *union* as the subject, rather than the whole thing (subjects in the pattern *X and Y* are always plural, regardless of what is standing in for *X* and *Y*).

If you know intellectually that your subject is singular or plural, but you're still not sure whether the verb is correct, substitute *they* in your head for plural subjects and *it* for singular subjects. You'll figure out the verb in a flash:

> The Roman army is/are marching.
> (Say in your head, *IT is marching*).

> The desire of our students to succeed and the guiding purpose of our teacher's union sometimes seem/seems at odds.
> (Since *the desire and the purpose* are plural, say in your head *THEY seem at odds.*)

3

Drill 3.3 — Determine Subject–Verb Agreement

In each sentence, we have underlined the subject. Find the verb, determine whether the subject and verb agree, and circle "Correct" or "Incorrect."

1. Several new <u>species</u> were added to a list of endangered animals.
   CORRECT/INCORRECT

2. <u>Companies</u> that offer job-sharing policies or a flexible workday is lauded by
   Working Parents magazine. CORRECT/INCORRECT

3. <u>Every</u> one of our students was accepted to the college of his or her choice.
   CORRECT/INCORRECT

4. Our nation's legal <u>code</u> deem it illegal to use other people's creative and intellectual
   work without permission. CORRECT/INCORRECT

5. <u>The Philippines</u> offer an unparalleled vacation experience. CORRECT/INCORRECT

Answers are on page 138.

"Has/Have" Verbs

How are these two sentences different in meaning?

       It rained.   It has rained.

The first sentence describes an event in the past. The second sentence doesn't mean that it's *still* raining. If you wanted to say that the rain has been happening for some time and is still happening, you'd say, "It has been raining."

The difference between *It rained* and *It has rained* is that the second sentence implies that the rain extends into the present in its effects or consequences. That is, *It has rained* implies that it's still wet outside.

Has or *have* as helping verbs (I/you/they/we *have* danced, he/she/it *has* danced) create compound verbs in the **present perfect** tense.

Present perfect verbs are used to describe actions that occurred at an unspecified time before the present. You cannot use the present perfect with specific time expressions (*yesterday, last week,* etc.). The exact time of the action does not matter. What matters is the effect in the present:

       I **have danced** the tango.

MANHATTAN
GMAT

Google **has become** not just the top search engine, but one of the most important companies in the world.

Scientists **have mapped** the human genome.

In every case, the effect continues: I can still dance the tango (or I still remember having had the experience), Google is still the top search engine and one of the most important companies in the world, and the human genome is still mapped.

The present perfect can also be used in questions. In many questions, the parts of a compound verb are separated. For instance:

Has she **taken** ballet lessons for a long time?

If you make this question into a statement—*She has taken ballet lessons for a long time*—it is easier to see the present perfect.

Has and *have* are also used as helper verbs in more complex tenses. They still indicate that an action is ongoing or still relevant:

I **have been waiting** for an hour.

"Had" Verbs

The **"Had" verb** is an informal way to refer to a verb preceded by the helper verb *had*, as in *had danced, had eaten, had gone.*

Here's an example. What's wrong with this sentence?

INCORRECT: The jury had delivered a verdict of "guilty."

Had delivered? Why not just say *delivered?*

The regular past tense verb *delivered* would do the job nicely here. In fact, you can't even use a *had* verb by itself in this context. There has to be another past action that the *had* verb comes before.

> **MEMORIZE IT:**
> Don't use a complicated tense when the simple past tense will do.

"Had" verbs or **Past Perfect** verbs are used to express that something in the past occurred before something else in the past. That is, these verbs express the "double past"!

CORRECT: The judge **had spent** most of the trial convinced of the defendant's guilt, until the DNA test **proved** the defendant's innocence.

Here, two things happened in the past: the judge *had spent* and the DNA test *proved*. This sentence is correct—*had spent* happened first, and *proved* happened after that, but also in the past.

In a sentence with a "had" verb and a regular past tense verb, the sentence order can change, but that doesn't change which verb gets the *had*. It's the real-life order of events that is important. For instance, in both of the cases below, the *had* creates a compound verb with *eaten:*

> **MEMORIZE IT:**
>
> A verb with the helping verb *had* is used to express "the past of the past."

> CORRECT: I **had eaten** three pieces of cake when I **learned** that the cake was poisoned.

> CORRECT: By the time I **learned** that the cake was poisoned, I **had** already **eaten** three pieces.

In both cases, the action that happened first (in the past of something else in the past) gets the *had*.

A good way to check a "had" verb is to ask these questions of two events in the past:

> What happened first? (This one gets a *had*.)
> What happened after that? (This one does not get a *had*.)

The other requirement for using "had" verbs correctly is that the time order should be really important. Otherwise, just two regular past tense verbs will do:

> CORRECT: In my college years, I joined the sophomore pledge class at a fraternity and worked on the senior class homecoming float.

Here, the time order is not very important, even though the first thing (*sophomore pledging*) happened before the second thing (*senior float*). However, "had" verbs are often needed to express interrupted actions or changes in behavior:

> CORRECT: I had nearly exhausted my meager supply of food and water when help finally arrived.

Here, the sequence of events is super-important. The meaning of the sentence clearly indicates a change or interruption—if the speaker had not been rescued, he or she would have continued exhausting the supplies.

Drill 3.4 — Has/Have and Had Verbs

For each sentence, circle "Correct" or "Incorrect." If you circled "Incorrect," cross out the incorrect verbs and write a correction above or below.

1. My mother always warns me to stay away from the pet store, reminding me that I had been highly allergic to dogs and cats since childhood. CORRECT/INCORRECT

2. I worked there for twenty years when the company went out of business. CORRECT/INCORRECT

3.   When the company went out of business, I worked there for twenty years.
      CORRECT/INCORRECT

4.   The doctor told me I had a heart attack. CORRECT/INCORRECT

5.   I just began working at the circus when a clown stabbed me in the back.
      CORRECT/INCORRECT

Answers are on page 138.

Verbs Wrap-Up

This was the longest and most complicated section so far! Good job making it through *Verbs*! The rest of the parts of speech will be easier. Next up is *Adverbs*.

> ### Grade Yourself
>
> How did you do in this section?
>
> - ☐ **A** - I totally get this!
> - ☐ **B** - I'm okay with this. Maybe review later if there's time.
> - ☐ **C** - I'll make a note to review this later.

Adverbs

Adverbs are primarily used to modify verbs. They can also be used to describe adjectives and other adverbs. What they definitely do *not* do is describe nouns (that's the job of adjectives).

Many people think of adverbs as words that end in *-ly*, such as *slowly* and *suspiciously*. While these words certainly are adverbs, many adverbs do not end in *-ly*. All of the following are adverbs:

shyly	also	favorably	really	quite	badly
truly	agilely	wholly	duly	usually	simply

Also, the following words can be both adjectives and adverbs (there are others):

fast	early	late	hard	high	monthly

Here are some examples:

CORRECT: He eats raisin bran **daily**.

3

The adverb *daily* answers a question about the verb, *eats*. He eats raisin bran? Well, *when* does he eat it?

> CORRECT: "I'm free after the conference," she said **coyly**.

The adverb *coyly* (meaning "in a shy yet flirtatious way") modifies *said* and answers the question "*How* did she say it?"

Adverbs Modifying Adjectives and Other Adverbs

Adverbs can also modify adjectives:

> CORRECT: He is **very** tall.

Very is an adverb modifying the adjective *tall*.

> CORRECT: You are **quite** correct.

Quite is an adverb modifying the adjective *correct*.

> CORRECT: The employee you hired is **wholly** inadequate to the task.

The adverb *wholly* answers a question about the adjective *inadequate*. The employee is inadequate? *How* inadequate?

Finally, adverbs can modify other adverbs:

> CORRECT: The contestant danced **quite** awkwardly.

The verb is *danced*. *Awkwardly* is an adverb modifying *danced;* it answers the question, "*How* did he dance?" *Quite* is another adverb modifying *awkwardly;* it answers the question, "*How* awkwardly did he dance?"

The situation in which an adverb modifies another adverb is different from the situation in which there are simply two or more adverbs modifying something else:

> CORRECT: The child **drowsily** and **adorably** asked whether naptime had arrived.

Drowsily and *adorably* both correctly modify the verb *asked*.

Pop Quiz!

True or False: Adverbs can modify verbs, adjectives, or nouns.

Answers are on page 132.

> **NOTE:**
>
> In India, the word *timely* is used as an adverb, as in *Please do it timely*. In American English, this is NOT correct. While *timely* ends in "–ly," it is actually an adjective, so saying *Please do it timely* is incorrect, just as *Please do it quick* or *Please do it cheerful* are wrong. Instead, say *Please do it in a timely manner*. (The Indian way is certainly more concise. Perhaps this usage will make it into American English in the coming decades.)

Adverb Errors on the GMAT

Few errors on the GMAT are related solely to adverbs. Certainly it is incorrect to modify a verb with an adjective, rather than an adverb:

> INCORRECT: The company needs to move quick if it is to launch its new product before the holiday shopping season.

Quick should be *quickly*. In the corrected version, *quickly* (an adverb) would be modifying the verb *move*.

Note that *fast* is on the list of adverbs that are also adjectives. That is, you can have a *fast car* (*fast* is an adjective describing the noun *car*) or you can *run fast* (*fast* is an adverb describing the verb *run*).

If you have a word that does not end in *-ly* that is modifying a verb and you want to see whether it is correct, try asking, *Would this word make more sense with -ly on the end?*

> EXAMPLE: The boxer hit his opponent hard.

> TRY IT: The boxer hit his opponent *hardly*.

The original was correct. *Hard* is both an adjective and an adverb. *Hardly* is also a word, but has a different meaning (it means *not at all*, or *almost not*).

By the way, people often say *I feel badly* when what they mean is *I feel bad. Badly* is the adverb form of *bad*. When you say *I feel bad*, then the verb *feel* is a linking verb between the subject *I* and the adjective *bad*. The same pattern exists in *I feel smart* or *I feel pretty*, which of course are correct. *Smart* and *pretty* are adjectives! *I feel bad* matches this pattern and is just fine.

When you say *I feel badly*, the adverb *badly* is modifying the verb *feel*, which then turns into an action verb. *I feel badly* means that you are unskilled at the act of feeling. This would indeed be appropriate if you had burned your hands and no longer had a sense of touch, but no one ever means this.

Drill 3.5 — Find the Adverb Errors

Determine whether the sentence has an error and circle "Correct" or "Incorrect." If the sentence is correct, circle all adverbs, and draw an arrow from each adverb to the verb it modifies.

Example: (Slowly) and (thoughtfully), the child assembled a tower of blocks.
(CORRECT) / INCORRECT

1.   The new vendor did the job quite quick. CORRECT/INCORRECT

2.   I promise you that I can do the job well and fast. CORRECT/INCORRECT

3.   He woke up early and cheerfully did the dishes. CORRECT/INCORRECT

4.   The performer danced lively, delighting the children. CORRECT/INCORRECT

5.   I feel bad for doing the job so badly. CORRECT/INCORRECT

Answers are on page 138.

Adverbial Phrases

Some adjectives (*timely, friendly, lovely, lively, ugly, silly, holy*) that are *not* also adverbs end in *-ly*. If you want to use *friendly* to modify a verb, you can't say *friendlyly* (that's not a word). Instead, say *in a friendly manner* or *in a friendly way*.

You can use other adjectives in this manner as well—for instance, although the adjective *agile* (meaning "skilled") has an adverb form, *agilely,* many people find *agilely* very awkward to say. There's nothing wrong with saying *The quarterback moves down the field in such an agile way!*

Sometimes, phrases can do the job of adverbs:

> I will take control *quickly.*

> I will take control *on Tuesday.*

The adverb *quickly* is answering a question about the verb: *How will the speaker take control?* The phrase *on Tuesday* is also answering a question about the verb: *When will the speaker take control?* The phrase *on Tuesday* is doing the same job as the adverb *quickly.* They're both modifying the verb.

Pop Quiz!

True or False: An adverb has to "touch" (be placed next to) the verb it is modifying.

Answer on page 132.

Wrap-Up

Interestingly, *on* is a **preposition**, and *on Tuesday* is a **prepositional phrase**. The same things are true with *in* and *in such an agile way*. This is a nice transition—you're about to move into an entire section on prepositions. Now you already know that prepositional phrases can be used to do the job of adverbs.

You're making great progress! Time to move on.

> ### *Grade Yourself*
>
> How did you do in this section?
>
> ☐   **A** - I totally get this!
> ☐   **B** - I'm okay with this. Maybe review later if there's time.
> ☐   **C** - I'll make a note to review this later.

3

Chapter 4
of
Foundations of GMAT Verbal

Prepositions, Conjunctions, Mixed Drills

In This Chapter...

Chapter 4:
Prepositions, Conjunctions, Mixed Drills

Prepositions

Prepositions create relationships, usually having to do with location or time. The relationship that a preposition creates is between its **object** (what follows the preposition) and something else in the sentence.

There are more than 100 prepositions in English. Here are a few of the most common:

of	in	on
at	to	for

Many more words are (or can be) prepositions:

aboard	about	above	across
after	against	along	amid
among	around	as	at
before	behind	below	beneath
beside	besides	between	beyond
but	by	concerning	despite
down	during	except	for
from	in	inside	into
like	near	of	off
on	onto	opposite	out
outside	over	past	per
regarding	since	through	throughout
till	to	toward	under
underneath	until	up	upon
via	with	within	without

Study this list. It is important to be able to recognize prepositions immediately when they appear in GMAT sentences. Be careful—the word *to* can also do a few other jobs, such as being the first word in an infinitive. Similarly, the word *but* is usually a conjunction, but is a preposition when used to mean *except*, as in *All developed nations **but** the U.S. have some form of national health insurance.*

As you can see fromt the list, many prepositions give information about location. For example, any word you can logically put in the blank in this sentence is a preposition:

The cat hid _____ the house.

Depending on the type of house (and the abilities of the cat), a cat could hide *beneath, inside, beside, above, near, against, on, underneath, opposite, around, upon, at, within, behind, below,* or *in* the house. All of these prepositions answer the question, "Where did the cat hide *in relation to* the house?" Here, *house* is the object of the preposition.

Change *the house* to something plural, and you can use a few more prepositions in the blank:

The kittens hid _____ the tall weeds.

Throughout, amid, and *among* would all work nicely here.

Other prepositions give information about time and would fit into the blank in this sentence:

I exercised _____ noon.

Here, you could logically use *after, around, before, past, until,* or *till* (just a short verison of *until*). These all answer the question, "When did I exercise *in relation to* noon?" Here, *noon* is the object of the preposition.

Compound prepositions consist of two or more words, at least one of which is one of the prepositions in the list on the previous page:

according to	apart from	aside from
as for	in back of	instead of
out of	ahead of	because of
in case of	in front of	in view of
prior to	apart from	by means of
in place of	next to	as of
in addition to	in spite of	on account of

Drill 4.1 — Find the Prepositions

All of the words below are short, but not all of them are prepositions. Circle the words that are (or can be) prepositions, then check your answers.

or	despite	off
before	and	out
some	with	since
slow	beside	new
upon	to	into
now	during	outside
go	never	underneath
in	is	about

Answers are on page 139.

Prepositional Phrases

A **prepositional phrase** is a group of words with two major components: the preposition itself and the object. The object is almost always a noun or something acting like a noun (a pronoun, a gerund, even a clause). Don't worry—that sounds a lot more complicated than it is!

Here are some prepositional phrases:

into the garden	**besides** doing my homework	**under** the table	**of** them
until next Thursday	**from** him	**along** the rushing river	**at** a gallop
by committing murder	**between** a rock and a hard place	**beyond** good and evil	

Notice that each phrase begins with one of the words from the list of prepositions in this section of the book. After that, we have a variety of nouns (*garden, Thursday,* etc.), pronouns (*him, them*), and gerunds (*doing, committing*).

You might also note what *none* of the prepositional phrases contain—a true verb. Remember, a gerund is an "ing" word acting as a *noun*, so it doesn't count as a verb.

Moreover, the object in a prepositional phrase is just that: an object. It's a noun, but it cannot be the *subject*. What does all that mean? **You won't find the subject and the verb of a sentence in a prepositional phrase.**

In fact, when reading a GMAT sentence, you know a prepositional phrase is over when you hit a verb or the main subject of the sentence. Here is the above list of prepositional phrases in context:

She ran **into** the garden, hoping to hide in the bushes.

Besides doing my homework, I also have chores to complete before I am allowed to go out.

I'm sorry I couldn't figure out where to put all these cans and bottles—I didn't see your recycling station **under** the table. Maybe I'll take care **of** them myself.

I really don't care about the success of this project, because I'm only employed here **until** next Thursday.

I got a letter—maybe it's **from** him!

The stallions raced **along** the rushing river **at** a gallop.

By committing murder, she lost her chance to ever win a Nobel Peace Prize.

I find myself caught **between** a rock and a hard place, needing either to hurt a very nice person or else to confess that I've been seeing other people.

Nietzsche's book presented a system of ethics that he argued was **beyond** good and evil.

Pop Quiz!

True or False: In the sentence "He wants to go," the word *to* is not a preposition, but in the sentence "He went to the store," the word *to* is a preposition.

Answer is on page 132.

Recognizing prepositional phrases is very important—and not that hard! Most importantly, look for a preposition. There aren't too many of those in existence. In addition, the preposition should have an object, which will be a noun, pronoun, or gerund.

Most prepositional phrases are short, but it is perfectly possible to have more than one prepositional phrase in a row, taking up a lot of real estate in the sentence. You already saw the horses race *along the rushing river at a gallop*. Here's another example:

I walked **through** the valley **between** the two largest mountain ranges **in** South America.

The three underlined portions represent three prepositional phrases strung together. Valuable meaning is contained in those prepositional phrases, but they do not contain the subject or the verb. Once you

MANHATTAN
GMAT

recognize the prepositional phrases, you can temporarily ignore them in order to see the **core sentence**: *I walked.*

Drill 4.2 — Find the Prepositional Phrases

Underline the prepositional phrases. Once you have underlined the prepositional phrases, read the sentence back to yourself without the phrases—there should still be a "core sentence" containing at least a subject and a verb.

1. After a spell in the sun, a spot in the shade sounded delightful.

2. Seventy-five people with asthma marched in the parade.

3. In our club, to play by the rules is crucial.

4. The committee, which meets monthly for the purpose of discussing the fiscal management of the charitable fund, recommends passing the annual budget on Monday.

5. To run with the wolves on thirty consecutive cold winter mornings in Minsk, Belarus, is to truly strengthen your spirit in just one month; to drink nothing but cold mountain water and eat nothing but goat meat for thirty days in any of the former Soviet republics is to truly strengthen your character in a similarly spartan manner.

Answers are on page 139.

Prepositions Separating Subjects and Verbs

Why is it so important to be able to recognize prepositional phrases? So you can temporarily ignore them!

Prepositional phrases often separate a subject and verb, sometimes so much so that it is difficult to tell whether the subject and verb match. When multiple prepositional phrases or other "junk" separates the subject and verb, errors become difficult to find. For instance:

> The pies Mother cooled in the window on Christmas Day in the dead of a bleak winter in the 1990s after a long bout with an insidious form of tropical parasitic infection was delicious.

If you are reading this sentence in small chunks instead of mentally taking in the whole thing at once (a difficult task), then you might think that the core of the sentence is that last bit: *parasitic infection was delicious.* That sounds kind of gross, but not necessarily ungrammatical.

Cross out the prepositional phrases, though. Watch what happens:

The pies Mother cooled ~~in the window on Christmas Day in the dead of a bleak winter in the 1990s after a long bout with an insidious form of tropical parasitic infection~~ was delicious.

That was a series of *eight* consecutive prepositional phrases! Wow!

You're left with a simple core sentence: *The pies Mother cooled was delicious.*

It should now be obvious that this sentence is incorrect. The subject, *the pies,* is plural, while the verb, *was,* is singular. *Was* should be changed to *were.*

This was a fairly extreme example, but prepositional phrases are used widely on the GMAT to keep a subject and verb far apart—so far apart that you have a hard time matching them up mentally.

Pop Quiz!

True or False: Sometimes the main subject of a sentence is located inside a prepositional phrase.

Answer is on page 132.

Drill 4.3 — Cross Out the Prepositional Phrases

Cross out the prepositional phrases and then determine whether the sentence has an error. Circle "Correct" or "Incorrect" for each sentence.

1.   The trolls under the bridge really just want to be understood. CORRECT/INCORRECT

2.   The statistics from the study reveals that the United States is plagued by poor health. CORRECT/INCORRECT

3.   Each of the spouses of the victims have expressed their wish that a monument be constructed at the crash site. CORRECT/INCORRECT

4.   Each of the runners who chose to run this marathon in polyester is experiencing serious chafing. CORRECT/INCORRECT

5.   I ran over the bridge, through the woods, and into your arms. CORRECT/INCORRECT

Answers are on page 140.

Drill 4.4 — Cross Out More Prepositional Phrases

More practice with prepositions! Practice your skills from the previous drill on more GMAT-like sentences. Cross out the prepositional phrases and then determine whether the sentence has an error. Circle "Correct" or "Incorrect" for each sentence.

1. The editor of the newspaper would later make his reputation as a union firebrand. CORRECT/INCORRECT

2. Construction of the Parthenon, a temple in the Athenian Acropolis, began in 447 B.C. CORRECT/INCORRECT

3. Because provisions of the new international trade agreement specifies that imports must be inspected for drugs, international disputes have already begun over delayed shipments. CORRECT/INCORRECT

4. A company that specializes in the analysis of body language purports, from a one-minute video of a person's speech, to be able to ascertain numerous truths about the person. CORRECT/INCORRECT

5. Because the payment of interest is prohibited under Sharia law, some practicing Muslims in the U.K. and U.S. are able to obtain what is known in modern parlance as an "Islamic mortgage," often an arrangement in which a bank purchases a home outright and rents it to a tenant who pays down principal as he or she accumulates ownership. CORRECT/INCORRECT

Answers are on page 140.

Ending a Sentence with a Preposition

Some people say that it is not acceptable to end a sentence with a preposition. For instance, rather than *That is the mat I do yoga **on***, they would like you to say *That is the mat **on which** I do yoga*.

However, most grammarians agree that it is fine to end a sentence with a preposition; both versions above are fine. Thus, this issue is simply not tested on the GMAT.

While you should not use prepositions that don't add any meaning (for instance, *That is the house she went inside **of*** would be better as *That is the house she went inside*), it is often perfectly appropriate to end a sentence with a preposition (or even more than one preposition). For instance, say you spilled a glass of water—you could very reasonably ask, "What did I just knock that *over onto?*"

As a final note on this issue, take a look at Winston Churchill's famous reply to someone who suggested that he should not end a sentence with a preposition: "This is the sort of arrant pedantry up with which I will not put." *Arrant* means *complete* and *pedantry* means *excessive display of learning* or *slavish devotion to rules.* The joke, of course, is that the expression "put up with" sounds ridiculous when the words are put in a strange order to avoid ending the sentence with a preposition.

Prepositions Wrap-Up

Recognizing prepositional phrases has a high return on investment in GMAT grammar—it's not that hard to learn this skill, yet learning it will let you easily identify a Sentence Correction problem's core sentence and pinpoint relevant issues, such as subject-verb agreement. Thus, this was a very productive section!

You are almost done with the parts of speech! It's time to move on to *Conjunctions.*

> ### Grade Yourself
>
> How did you do in this section?
>
> ☐   **A** - I totally get this!
> ☐   **B** - I'm okay with this. Maybe review later if there's time.
> ☐   **C** - I'll make a note to review this later.

Conjunctions

Conjunctions link words, phrases, and clauses, making lists or contrasts. All of the following are conjunctions:

and	but
yet	either ... or
not only ... but also	if
when	because

There are only a few conjunctions in existence, but they're critically important to communication.

Following are the three types of conjunctions.

Coordinating Conjunctions

The **coordinating conjunctions** are *for, and, nor, but, or, yet,* and *so.* They can be remembered with the acronym FANBOYS. Without question, the most important coordinating conjunction is *and.* As was the case with pronouns, the biggest danger on Sentence Correction is that you will skip right past the conjunctions. Do not do that.

MANHATTAN
GMAT

The coordinating conjunctions can join anything from single words to entire sentences or complete ideas:

> Peanut butter **and** jelly go well together on a sandwich.

Here, the coordinating conjunction *and* joins two nouns:

> You will come with me to my mother's house for Mother's Day, **or** I will break up with you right now.

Here, the coordinating conjunction *or* joins two sentences to make a more complex sentence.

On the GMAT, you are tested on whether the *right* conjunction is being used. This is as much a question of meaning and logic as it is of grammar. For example:

> Many whale species are endangered, **but** they are overhunted.

Here, *but* simply doesn't make sense. Species are endangered, *but* they are overhunted? That seems less like a contrast and more like a causation type of relationship. *But* should be *because, since,* or *as.* Any of these three conjunctions would show the proper causal relationship between the two ideas. *Because, since,* and *as* fall into a different type of conjunction—*subordinating conjunctions*—which will be discussed soon.

Correlative Conjunctions

The **correlative conjunctions** are *either/or, neither/nor, both/and, whether/or,* and *not only/but also.* Occasionally, *not only/but also* occurs without the *also.*

Each correlative conjunction has two parts; after each part could be a noun, a phrase, or an entire simple sentence.

The GMAT does like to test errors related to correlative conjunctions. It is not that hard to catch these errors if you simply (1) watch out for the correlative conjunctions, and (2) test to make sure that the items after each of the two parts are the same part of speech or type of phrase.

Try to figure out why these two sentences are labeled "correct" and "incorrect":

> CORRECT: I like to eat **not only** steak **but also** ribs, pork chops, and chicken cutlets.

> INCORRECT: I like **not only** to eat steak **but also** ribs, pork chops, and chicken cutlets.

In the correct version, *not only* is followed by a noun (*steak*). The second part of the conjunction, *but also*, is followed by several nouns. Both parts answer the same question: "What do I like to eat?" This sentence is **parallel**. The parts are in harmony.

In the incorrect version, however, *not only* is followed by an infinitive (*to eat*), but *but also* is still followed by several nouns that are meant to be the object of the infinitive. The first part answers the question, "What do I like?" whereas the second part answers a different question, "What do I like *to eat?*" This sentence is NOT *parallel* and is incorrect.

Pop Quiz!

True or False: The sentence "The company's profits were outstanding, and it went bankrupt because of outrageously poor management" would be considered incorrect on the GMAT.

Answer is on page 133.

Here's another example:

> You can **either** wash these dishes **or** I will leave you forever.

Do the parts after *either* and *or* match? You need to analyze. After *either* is a verb (*wash*). After *or* is a pronoun (*I*). Also, *I will leave you forever* is a complete sentence, while the first part, *wash these dishes*, is not. This sentence is definitely not parallel. You can rearrange it so it is:

> Either you can wash these dishes, or I will leave you forever.

Now, *either* and *or* are both followed by pronouns. Even more importantly, *you can wash these dishes* and *I will leave you forever* are each complete sentences. The structure is now *Either [first sentence], or [second sentence]*. The new compound sentence is now parallel.

This idea about two parallel parts is most frequently tested with *not only/but also*. Be on the lookout for that pair.

You'll revisit this idea when you get to the section on parallelism in a couple of chapters.

Drill 4.5 — Find the Conjunction Errors

Circle the two parts of each correlative conjunction. Determine whether the sentence has an error and circle "Correct" or "Incorrect."

1. Critics allege that the company failed because of both market conditions and improper management. CORRECT/INCORRECT

2. Not only was the study flawed but also frivolous. CORRECT/INCORRECT

3.   The king wishes to express that he is neither a despot nor oblivious to the concerns of the people. CORRECT/INCORRECT

4.   The nation not only ranks very poorly in elementary education, but also trails every other nation in measures of child health. CORRECT/INCORRECT

5.   The speaker is both entertaining and an inspiration. CORRECT/INCORRECT

Answers are on page 140.

Subordinating Conjunctions

Subordinating conjunctions introduce **dependent clauses**. A *dependent clause* and a *subordinate clause* are the same thing. The word *subordinate* means *lower in position* or *submissive.*

A **clause** is a group of words that could stand alone as a complete sentence. For example, *Nearly 10% of children in the United States are without health insurance* is a complete sentence. So is *This health care bill will help millions of families.* The word *because* is a subordinating conjunction. You will use it to make the first sentence *subordinate* to the second:

> Because nearly 10% of children in the United States are without health insurance, this health care bill will help millions of families.

That is, a subordinating conjunction attaches two smaller sentences into a single sentence in a way that makes one the main part of the sentence and the other dependent on it. The subordinating conjunction also gives information about the relationship between the main part (known as the **main clause** or **independent clause**) and the dependent part.

Some of the most common subordinating conjunctions are:

after	although	as
as if	as long as	because
before	even though	how
if	if only	in order
once	since	so that
than	that	though
unless	until	when
where	whether	while

You may recognize some of these words from earlier in the book—a number of the subordinating conjunctions can also serve as prepositions. Here's a simple way to tell—if a word such as *until* is followed simply by a noun, pronoun, or gerund, it's a preposition, but if it introduces a clause, it's a subordinating conjunction.

4

I studied until midnight.

In the example above, *until midnight* is a prepositional phrase.

I intend to sleep until you wake me up.

In this second example, *until* is a subordinating conjunction and *you wake me up* is the subordinate clause.

Subordinating conjunctions are an important issue in understanding the structure of complex sentences. Students sometimes become confused when asked for the subject of a sentence, because it seems as though there are two or more subjects. If you can identify a *subordinate clause* and a *main clause,* it is much easier to figure out the *main* subject of the sentence. Also, if *until...* is a prepositional phrase, you can temporarily ignore it while looking at subject/verb issues, but if *until...* is a subordinate clause with its own subject and verb, you will need to check that subject and verb as well for agreement.

Drill 4.6 — Find the Dependent Clause

For each sentence, circle the subordinating conjunction. Then determine which clause is the dependent one—the first clause or the second one.

1.   The company's leadership began to falter after the board disagreed sharply over executive bonuses. FIRST/SECOND

2.   While freshly minted law school graduates greatly exceed the number of top law jobs available, prospective students continue to apply to law school in droves. FIRST/SECOND

3.   She ate as if she had been starved for weeks. FIRST/SECOND

4.   Unless you get your MBA, you cannot rise to the next level in this company. FIRST/SECOND

5.   I'll go if you do. FIRST/SECOND

Answers are on page 141.

Wrap-Up

You did it! Those are all the parts of speech that matter on the GMAT! Give yourself a pat on the back. Just for fun, below is one last part of speech that is *not* tested on the GMAT. That part of speech is **interjections**. These are words that you yell in pleasure, surprise, or pain. Not surprisingly, they don't obey the rules of grammar.

Ouch!   Hey!   Oh no!   Aww.   Holy cow!   Zounds!

You now know more about English grammar than 75% of Americans and a great many GMAT test-takers. Nice! (Interjection!) Now, it's time to move on to some drills to help solidify your new skills.

> ### Grade Yourself
>
> How did you do in this section?
>
> ☐ **A** - I totally get this!
> ☐ **B** - I'm okay with this. Maybe review later if there's time.
> ☐ **C** - I'll make a note to review this later.

Mixed Drills

Mixed Drill 4.7 — Match the Word with the Part of Speech

Label each word a noun, pronoun, adjective, verb, adverb, preposition, or conjunction. Some words can play more than one role.

1. each	_____	2. Scandinavian	_____
3. by	_____	4. really	_____
5. under	_____	6. yet	_____
7. an	_____	8. fly-by-night	_____
9. diverged	_____	10. primarily	_____
11. at	_____	12. equivalent	_____
13. no one	_____	14. into	_____
15. or	_____	16. the	_____
17. wrung	_____	18. so	_____
19. without	_____	20. finally	_____

Answers are on page 141.

Mixed Drill 4.8 — Identify Parts of Speech in Sentences

Label each underlined word a noun, pronoun, adjective, verb, adverb, preposition, or conjunction.

Example: <u>Many</u> <u>men</u> <u>feel</u> that <u>miniature</u> <u>poodles</u> <u>are</u> not <u>real</u> <u>dogs</u>.
        adj   *noun* *verb*   *adj*   *noun* *verb*   *adj* *noun*

1. <u>It</u> <u>may be</u> <u>true</u> that <u>Notre Dame</u> <u>alumni</u> <u>really</u> <u>care</u> <u>about</u> <u>football</u>, <u>but</u> <u>it</u> <u>is</u> <u>also</u> <u>true</u> that <u>they</u> <u>care</u> <u>about</u> <u>academics</u>.

2. <u>Thirty</u> <u>members</u> <u>of</u> <u>the</u> <u>marching band</u> <u>have voted</u> <u>to play</u> Lady Gaga's "Poker Face" <u>in</u> <u>the</u> <u>parade</u>.

3. <u>Russian</u> <u>players</u> <u>often</u> <u>beat</u> <u>the</u> <u>Americans</u> <u>in</u> <u>chess</u> <u>tournaments</u>.

4. <u>Class</u> <u>attendance</u> <u>and</u> <u>participation</u> <u>are</u> <u>important</u>, <u>but</u> <u>you</u> <u>cannot</u> <u>truly</u> <u>learn</u> <u>the</u> <u>material</u> <u>without</u> reading <u>primary</u> <u>sources</u>, <u>either</u> <u>in</u> <u>books</u> <u>or</u> <u>on</u> <u>the</u> <u>Internet</u>.

5. <u>The</u> <u>small</u> <u>boy</u> <u>was</u> <u>delighted</u>, <u>for</u> <u>he</u> <u>had received</u> <u>a</u> <u>jack-in-the-box</u> <u>for</u> <u>Hannukkah</u>.

Answers are on page 142.

Mixed Drill 4.9 — Identify Certain Kinds of Errors

Each sentence below contains one of these errors:

> A. A pronoun does not match its antecedent in number (that is, a singular pronoun refers back to a plural noun or vice-versa).
> B. A reflexive pronoun (such as *ourselves*) is used inappropriately.

Circle the error in the sentence and write A or B in the blank. (One answer is both A and B.)

1. It seems that everyone has brought loved ones to watch them graduate. _____

2. The area is rife with pickpockets, so a tourist should keep their handbag close. _____

3. The administration has amended their requirement that students who want to graduate on time must submit their theses one month before graduation. _____

4. Each of the children is going to sing a little song for your grandmother and myself. _____

5. All students must consider the options and decide for himself or herself. _____

Answers are on page 142.

MANHATTAN
GMAT

Mixed Drill 4.10 — Identify Certain Kinds of Errors

    A.   A pronoun refers back to an adjective.
    B.   The pronoun *one* is used incorrectly.
    C.   A subject and verb do not agree.
    D.   A verb is in the wrong tense.

Circle the error in the sentence and write A, B, C, or D in the blank.

1.   From 1971 to 1975, he earns his undergraduate degree at Villanova. _____

2.   The three employees who live in the townhouses by the river wants to move closer to work. _____

3.   One cannot help but wonder if you could float to the sky by holding on to a very large number of helium balloons. _____

4.   Dartmouth graduates often report years later that they loved it. _____

5.   The committee that controls the allocation of new funds and the dean often differs over policy. _____

Answers are on page 143.

Chapter 5
of
Foundations of GMAT Verbal

Subject/Predicate, Fragments & Run-ons, Punctuation

In This Chapter...

Chapter 5:

Subject/Predicate, Fragments & Run-ons, Punctuation

Subjects and Predicates

Every complete sentence contains a **subject** and a **predicate**. It is possible for a complete sentence to be only two words long:

> We went.

> Love hurts.

In both cases, the first word is the subject, and the second word is the predicate. Of course, most sentences are more complicated, but at minimum, **a predicate always includes a real verb**.

Sometimes, it is difficult to understand the meaning of a sentence without some background information, but that doesn't mean that the sentence isn't grammatically complete. For instance:

> They gave it to us.

Who is *they*? What did they give us? You have no idea. But the sentence is still complete—it has a subject (the pronoun *they*) and a predicate (*gave it to us*). The predicate contains a verb (*gave*), plus some additional information. On the GMAT, this sentence would be incorrect, because *they* and *it* lack antecedents, but again, the sentence is complete.

In a command, the subject *you* is implied:

> Go!

A "command" sentence that is more likely to appear in business or academic writing might look something like this:

> Consider the case of Watson and Crick.

Here, the sentence is understood to mean, "*You* consider the case of Watson and Crick." The subject is the pronoun *you*.

Subjects are generally nouns and pronouns (such as *we* and *love* in the examples above). As was discussed in the section on verbs, sometimes a gerund or infinitive can be a subject:

> *Dancing* is a great joy.

> *To die* for one's country is to pay the ultimate price.

Here, *dancing* is a gerund, and *to die* is an infinitive.

A group of words can be the subject of a sentence. Even a clause beginning with *that* can be the subject:

> *That forty people dropped out* is less a reason to condemn the program than to praise its rigor.

The subject is *That forty people dropped out*. That sounds like a very weird subject! You'd rarely hear such a construction in speech, but it's perfectly grammatical. You could also write the subject as *The fact that forty people dropped out*.

Now consider a much longer sentence:

> Each of us has saved for weeks to be able to attend the Madonna concert, where we will undoubtedly dance all night to Madonna's hits from the last twenty years, including "Papa Don't Preach," "Open Your Heart," "True Blue," "Express Yourself," "Ray of Light," "Beautiful Stranger," and "4 Minutes."

This rather silly example demonstrates how a *subject* is different from a *topic*.

What is the *topic* of this sentence? Perhaps "Madonna" or "some people who really love Madonna."

But what is the grammatical *subject*? It is the word *each*.

Please don't get angry. It is understandable that it seems a bit weird that the subject would be one of the least interesting, least descriptive words in the sentence.

To be clear—**the *subject* of a sentence is not the same as the *topic* of a sentence**. In some languages, the idea of a *subject* and a *topic* are interchangeable. In English, a *topic* is what you're really talking about. Two people could disagree about the topic of a sentence. A topic is a matter of opinion. A subject is not. A *subject* is a grammatical concept; it is not about the meaning or main idea of the sentence.

A **simple subject** is just one word—in this case, *each*. A **complete subject** is the simple subject plus the other words that help to identify the simple subject—in this case, *each of us*. Most of the time, you want the *simple subject* of the sentence so you can ask questions such as, "Does the subject match the verb?"

Here are some guidelines for locating the subject of a sentence:

- The subject is usually a noun or pronoun, but sometimes it's a gerund, infinitive, or a phrase or clause.

- One good way to find the main subject is to find the main verb and ask what or who is *doing* the action described by the verb.

- A subject can consist of two or more things joined by *and*. For instance, *Joe and Maria* could be a subject, or *Dancing, drinking, and eating*.

- The subject is NOT located in a prepositional phrase. This is why you spent so much time learning to identify prepositions and prepositional phrases—so you can rule them out when looking for the subject.

- If you have a subordinate clause joined to a sentence with a subordinating conjunction, you want the subject that is *not* in the subordinate clause—the "main" subject will be in the "main" clause of the sentence.

5

Pop Quiz!

True or False: The subject of a sentence can be a phrase beginning with *that* or *to*.

Answer is on page 133.

Here are some more examples and then try a drill.

> FIND THE SUBJECT: A big, fat, delicious chicken parmesan sandwich would be amazing right now.

The subject is *sandwich*. The adjectives *big, fat, delicious,* and *chicken parmesan* tell us more about the sandwich. The sandwich is performing the verb *would be*.

> FIND THE SUBJECT: Earth and the other planets in our solar system orbit around the Sun.

The subject is *Earth and the other planets. In our solar system* is a prepositional phrase. The subject *Earth and the other planets* is performing the verb *orbit*.

> FIND THE SUBJECT: None of the guests have arrived.

The subject is *none. Of the guests* is a prepositional phrase. The subject *none* is performing the verb *have arrived*.

> FIND THE SUBJECT: Although rapper Tupac Shakur died in 1996, his music has been released on no fewer than eight posthumous albums.

The subject is *music*. Note that most people would say that the *topic* of the sentence is Tupac Shakur. However, *Tupac Shakur* is located within a subordinate clause (*although* is a subordinating conjunction). The main clause of the sentence is *his music has been released on no fewer than eight posthumous albums*. The subject *music* is performing the verb *has been released*.

> FIND THE SUBJECT: Because his jokes were so offensive, we left before the show ended.

The subject is *we*. The first part of the sentence is the subordinate clause (*because* is a subordinating conjunction), and the second part, *we left before the show ended*, is the main clause. The subject *we* is performing the verb *left*.

> FIND THE SUBJECT: There are ten people waiting in the conference room.

In a sentence that begins with *there* and a form of *to be* (is, are, were…), the word *there* is NOT the subject—rather, the word *there* is a clue that the real subject will occur soon. Here, the subject is *people*. The subject *people* is performing the verb *are waiting*.

Notice that the compound verb is split up (*are* and *waiting* do not touch each other in the sentence). In this kind of sentence, it can be helpful to eliminate the word *there* and to put the sentence in a more normal order: *Ten people are waiting in the conference room*. This makes it pretty obvious that *people* is the subject and *are waiting* is the verb.

> FIND THE SUBJECT: Aside the highway was the wreckage from the crash.

A few sentences run backwards: *Here comes the sun*. It's the sun that comes, not "here" that comes.

The sentence in the example above begins with a prepositional phrase, *aside the highway*. Then there is a verb, *was*. Finally, the subject, *wreckage*. *From the crash* is another prepositional phrase. Put the sentence back in a more normal order to see the structure: *The wreckage from the crash was aside the highway*.

Drill 5.1 — Find the Subject

Circle the subject of each sentence.

1. Each of the women in the study said that her arthritis had gotten worse since beginning the therapy.

2. Only a thin sliver of the specimen is needed to perform the test.

3. All of us agree.

4. There are a bank, a nail salon, and a day care center in this shopping plaza.

5. Amid the weeds and trash was my lost kitten.

Answers are on page 143.

Some sentences have more than one subject-verb pair:

> I like game shows, but I hate those reality dating shows in which people hurt each others' feelings for money and prizes.

This sentence consists of two independent clauses joined by a coordinating conjunction, *but:*

> I like game shows,
> but
> I hate those reality dating shows in which people hurt each others' feelings for money and prizes.

In the first clause, the subject *I* is performing the verb *like.* In the second clause, the subject *I* is performing the verb *hate.* Simple.

> Although *Ailurus fulgens* is commonly called the "red panda," the species is only distantly related to the giant panda and is actually more closely related to weasels and raccoons.

Ailurus fulgens is the subject of the first part of the sentence. Its verb is *is* or *is called.*

The species is the subject of the second part of the sentence. Its verbs are *is* and *is,* or *is related* and *is related.*

If you wanted to mark up the subjects and verbs visually (a process you want to be able to do mentally on the real GMAT), you could do so as follows:

Although (Ailurus fulgens) is commonly called the "red panda," the (species) is only distantly related to the giant panda and is actually more closely related to weasels and raccoons.

Here subjects are highlighted with curved rectangles and verbs with underlining. It doesn't exactly matter how you do the mark-ups. If you are making flashcards, though, try to be consistent. Don't mark every part of speech; focus on whatever's important in the sentence you're dealing with.

By the way, when a sentence has more than one subject-verb pair, it is not terribly important for GMAT purposes to decide which subject-verb pair is the "main" one. After all, a mistake could exist anywhere in the sentence.

Pop Quiz!

True or False: In the sentence "Although Italy is famous for pasta, noodles were invented by the Chinese," the dependent clause has the subject *Italy* and the independent clause has the subject *the Chinese.*

Answer is on page 133.

MANHATTAN
GMAT

Subject/Predicate Wrap-Up

Good work so far! Matching up subjects and verbs is a very important topic on the GMAT. For more review, you might want to return to the section on Verbs in Chapter 3.

> ### Grade Yourself
>
> How did you do in this section?
>
> ☐   **A** - I totally get this!
> ☐   **B** - I'm okay with this. Maybe review later if there's time.
> ☐   **C** - I'll make a note to review this later.

Sentence Fragments & Run-on Sentences

A **sentence fragment** is a group of words that cannot stand alone. It is not a complete thought; it does not contain an independent clause. Sentence fragments trying to stand alone are always wrong.

All of the following are sentence fragments:

> Under the bridge at the edge of town.

> While it's lovely that you came to visit.

> If it's true that Chandler was responsible for the project's failure.

> The Japanese medal given for bravery.

> Rushing the field during the football game.

These fragments are not complete sentences and cannot stand alone, but they would all be fine as part of larger sentences that include independent clauses:

> The drug dealer was arrested <u>under the bridge at the edge of town.</u>

> <u>While it's lovely that you came to visit</u>, I do think it's time you headed back home.

> <u>If it's true that Chandler was responsible for the project's failure</u>, he will probably be fired.

> The *bukosho*, <u>the Japanese medal given for bravery</u>, was instituted in 1944 by Imperial edict.

<u>Rushing the field during the football game</u> is strictly forbidden.

Note that in every example but the last one, the non-underlined part of the sentence can stand alone without the underlined portion. In the last example, *Rushing the field during the football game* is actually the subject of the sentence (specifically, *rushing* is the simple subject).

If a group of words lacks a verb, it is a sentence fragment. As you learned in the last section, all good sentences contain, at minimum, a subject and verb. Note that *rushing* does not count as a verb; it is a gerund.

> **REMINDER:**
> To determine whether a word ending in "-ing" is a verb, look for helper verbs. If the "-ing" stands alone, it is not a verb.

Just one word can make the difference between being a complete sentence and being a fragment. In fact, you can make a perfectly good sentence a fragment by *adding* a word, such as *who* or *since* (a subordinating conjunction).

5

COMPLETE: My brother broke his foot.   INCOMPLETE: My brother **who** broke
                                                                                              his foot.
                                                          INCOMPLETE: **Since** my brother broke
                                                                                              his foot.

Notice that the words on the right do not feel like complete thoughts. If someone said either one aloud, you would wait impatiently for the person to continue speaking and finish his or her thought. The GMAT will try to make you accept a fragment as a sentence by using lots of long words. Don't be fooled. **Demand complete thoughts!**

A **run-on sentence** consists of two (or more) independent clauses joined without appropriate punctuation or a conjunction. For instance:

I pronounce "tomato" one way, you pronounce it a completely different way.

This so-called "sentence" consists of two independent clauses joined by only a comma. This specific kind of run-on sentence is called a **comma splice**. Run-on sentences, including comma splices, are always wrong.

To make this a real sentence, you need a conjunction or a semicolon (semicolons are discussed in the next section):

CORRECT: I pronounce "tomato" one way, **while** you pronounce it a completely
                   different way.

CORRECT: I pronounce "tomato" one way**;** you pronounce it a completely
                   different way.

Drill 5.2 — Find Fragments and Run-Ons

For each sentence, circle "Complete Sentence," "Fragment," or "Run-On."

1. Scott Fitzgerald, planning, writing, and revising *The Great Gatsby* from 1922 to 1925 in Great Neck, Long Island. COMPLETE SENTENCE/FRAGMENT/RUN-ON

2. That the charge was true was the worst part. COMPLETE SENTENCE/FRAGMENT/ RUN-ON

3. There are only seven of us because the twins couldn't make it. COMPLETE SENTENCE/FRAGMENT/RUN-ON

4. The decorated war general, who stormed the beach in Normandy in 1944. COMPLETE SENTENCE/FRAGMENT/RUN-ON

5. The company sold off its machine parts and chemicals divisions, they hadn't made a profit in the last five years. COMPLETE SENTENCE/FRAGMENT/RUN-ON

Answers are on page 143.

Fragments & Run-ons Wrap-Up

Great! You've just covered two major sources of errors on GMAT Sentence Correction. Next you'll learn about one way to fix mistakes with run-ons—with punctuation.

> *Grade Yourself*
>
> How did you do in this section?
>
> ☐   **A** - I totally get this!
> ☐   **B** - I'm okay with this. Maybe review later if there's time.
> ☐   **C** - I'll make a note to review this later.

Punctuation

The English language contains many punctuation marks: commas, periods, question marks, quotation marks, exclamation points, parentheses, hyphens, a couple different kinds of dashes....

Fortunately, there are very few punctuation marks you need to care about for the GMAT. Perhaps most importantly, no one is going to test you on precise comma placement. (Note: The four periods at the end of the previous sentence are made up of one ellipsis—three periods in a row—followed by a regular period to mark the end of a sentence. If you'd put an ellipsis in the middle of a sentence... you'd have just used three periods.)

On the GMAT, commas can sometimes serve as a clue, helping us understand sentence structure. So don't ignore commas entirely. But you will never mark an answer choice wrong because of a misplaced comma. In real life, the rules of comma placement also involve quite a few judgment calls; while sometimes commas are mandatory, such as the ones in this sentence, in many cases the decision to use a comma or not is more a matter of style.

Do you have a strong opinion about whether another comma belongs in this sentence?

> Please buy eggs, bread and milk.

The comma that many people (including most Americans, as well as the GMAT writers) would put after *bread* is called the *serial comma* or the *Oxford comma*. Even experts disagree about it. So, don't worry about it; it's not tested.

Three punctuation marks are discussed next: colons, semicolons, and dashes.

The Colon (:)

The colon goes before a list or explanation:

> CORRECT: This recipe requires only three ingredients: sardines, tomato sauce, and
> olive oil.

There is an important rule that must be followed here: the part of the sentence before the colon must be able to stand alone (that is, it must be an independent clause).

> INCORRECT: I am going to the store to get: sardines, tomato sauce, and olive oil.

I am going to the store to get is not able to stand alone as a complete sentence. The example sentence is thus incorrect. It can be fixed by simply removing the colon. A good rule is that, if you don't need *any* punctuation there at all, a colon is wrong.

> **MEMORIZE IT:**
>
> The part of a sentence before a colon must be an independent clause.

Sometimes, a list contains only one item. This is completely fine.

CORRECT: I only like one kind of music: hip-hop.

Finally, colons are *not just for going before lists*. **Colons can also go before explanations, rules, or examples**. Some students freak out when they see a correct sentence such as this one:

CORRECT: I was fired today: my boss caught me trying to steal a laser printer.

This sentence is completely correct. The first part is able to stand alone. The second part (stealing) *explains* the first part (getting fired).

Drill 5.3 — Examine the Colon

Determine whether the sentence has an error and circle "Correct" or "Incorrect."

1.   I have really enjoyed hearing you lecture about: grammar, punctuation, and sentence structure. CORRECT/INCORRECT

2.   We will do a soft launch of our new product in two markets: Los Angeles and New York. CORRECT/INCORRECT

3.   It can hardly be said that the nation's government was negligent in planning for such a disaster: there had never been volcanic eruption in the region in the whole of recorded history. CORRECT/INCORRECT

4.   The protest was effective, but not without cost: sixteen people died. CORRECT/INCORRECT

5.   He said something absolutely outrageous: "Shut up, Mr. President." CORRECT/INCORRECT

Answers are on page 144.

The Semicolon (;)

A semicolon connects two independent clauses. That is, the two parts on either side of the semicolon must be able to stand alone; they must also be closely related in meaning.

CORRECT: I have to admit that I hate spending Christmas with your parents; they always give me a ridiculous sweater and expect me to wear it.

MEMORIZE IT:

The two parts on either side of a semicolon must be able to stand alone and must be closely related in meaning.

What does it mean to be "closely related in meaning"? Everyone agrees that *I like milk; my husband prefers cola* is correct. But what about *I like milk; my husband likes bicycling*? That sentence looks very strange, but the question of whether the two parts are "closely related" is related to context. If someone had just asked the couple,

"What are your very favorite things in the world?", then *I like milk; my husband likes bicycling* could indeed be a sensible answer.

When you worry about clauses being closely related in meaning on the GMAT, what you are really trying to avoid is this:

> INCORRECT: The volcano devastated the town; there was still hope.

This sentence violates the "closely related in meaning" rule because it needs a word such as *although, but,* or *however.* The contrasting meaning of the two clauses demands a contrasting conjunction. This rule is not specific to sentences containing semicolons. In *any* sentence, if *but, however,* or an equivalent word is needed, it is incorrect to leave it out.

> **MEMORIZE IT:**
>
> Do NOT use a semicolon before *and* or *but.* Use a semicolon before *however* and a comma after. In every case, the parts before and after the semicolon must be able to stand alone.

Here is another important rule: do not use a semicolon before *and* or *but.* A simple comma will do. For example:

> INCORRECT: He applied to Harvard Business School; but he forgot to send his GMAT score.

> INCORRECT: I like beer; and my grandmother likes bourbon.

In both cases, a comma should be used instead. Some people would use nothing at all in the second case, since the sentence is so short—this is a matter of style.

You *do* use a semicolon before *however.* The two parts of the sentence must still be independent clauses. A comma also comes after *however*:

> CORRECT: Raw oysters are delicious; however, you should be careful where you buy them.

You may have realized that, because colons can go before explanations, either a colon or a semicolon would work in some sentences. Both of these examples are correct:

> Bill was tormented; the Packers lost again.
> Bill was tormented: the Packers lost again.

Grammar experts would say that using a colon would actually give more information, because the colon would make it clear that the Packers' loss was the *cause* of Bill's torment, whereas the semicolon just joins two related ideas, without being as clear about how the ideas are related.

> **ADVANCED TIP:**
>
> Words like *thus, therefore, moreover,* and *nevertheless* can also be used after semicolons in the way that *however* is used above. These words are all conjunctions, but they are *not* the "FANBOYS" conjunctions (*for, and, nor, but, or, yet, so*) we learned about earlier on. When the "FANBOYS" conjunctions join two independent clauses, they are generally separated by a comma, or occasionally by nothing at all. FANBOYS get commas; the rest of the conjunctions have to use semicolons.

On the GMAT, you will never have to decide between using a semicolon and using a colon, with everything else exactly the same. Just don't freak out about either one.

Pop Quiz!

True or False: The sentence "The dog asked for a treat; he gave it one" correctly uses a semicolon to join two independent clauses.

Answers are on page 133.

Finally, there are a few other uses of semicolons, such as punctuating a list in which the individual items already have commas (*Our firm will be opening offices in Portland, Maine; Detroit, Michigan; and Tampa, Florida.*)

Drill 5.4 — Correct the Punctuation Errors

Determine whether the sentence has an error and circle "Correct" or "Incorrect."

1. The cobblestone streets lent a certain historic charm; but they cost the city a mint to maintain. CORRECT/INCORRECT

2. I was offended; we left. CORRECT/INCORRECT

3. The 1950s in America were a period of prosperity and consumerism; programs such as *The Donna Reed Show, Leave it to Beaver,* and *Father Knows Best* portrayed comfortable suburban lifestyles made easier by modern appliances. CORRECT/INCORRECT

4. Although he won the election by a landslide; international bodies suspect serious irregularities in the voting process. CORRECT/INCORRECT

5. He needs a kidney transplant; without it, he'll die. CORRECT/INCORRECT

Answers are on page 144.

Drill 5.5 — Correct More Punctuation Errors

Each sentence below has a blank within the text. Circle your answer based on which would be correct in that spot: a colon, a semicolon, either a colon or a semicolon, or nothing at all.

1. I have always loved hockey ___ my dad is from Canada. COLON/SEMICOLON/EITHER/ NOTHING

2. The investors are demanding that the board be replaced ___ however, we think we can convince the major players otherwise. COLON/SEMICOLON/EITHER/NOTHING

3.   The administration has introduced numerous cost-saving measures, such as ___ cutting less popular classes, reducing opening hours in libraries and other buildings, and using work-study labor wherever possible. COLON/SEMICOLON/EITHER/NOTHING

4.   I only need one thing from you ___ silence. COLON/SEMICOLON/EITHER/NOTHING

5.   Many law school graduates are having serious trouble finding suitable employment ___ law schools are being criticized for a lack of transparency in releasing informa-tion about the employment rates of previous years' graduates. COLON/SEMICOLON/ EITHER/NOTHING

Answers are on page 145.

Dashes

In the section on Adjectives, also discussed are hyphens, which occur in compound adjectives like *fifteen-year-old.* Hyphens are *not* the same as dashes. Hyphens (-) are shorter. They join words together with no spaces before or after the hyphen.

Dashes (—) are longer, and come in two varieties, the *en dash* (the width of a letter n) and the *em dash* (the width of a letter m). The *en dash* is used for things such as "pages 15–34." You don't really care about this for purposes of the GMAT. Let's talk about the *em dash.* (For the rest of this book, when we say *dash,* we mean *em dash.*)

5

NOTE:
Ever notice that when you type a hyphen in Microsoft Word and hit return, the "hyphen" gets longer? That's the program correcting your hyphen to a dash.

A dash adds an additional thought to an independent clause. A set of two dashes is used in much the same way as you use a set of commas or pair of parentheses to include an interrupting thought. Used for this purpose, dashes are considered stronger than commas or parentheses:

> CORRECT: The preacher gave an entire sermon against eating beans—I think he's gone mad!

> CORRECT: The company leadership is faltering—the CEO embarrassed himself on the news just last night—and the investors are restless.

A set of dashes can also insert a list into the middle of an independent clause:

> CORRECT: The wives of Henry VIII—Catherine of Aragon, Anne Boleyn, Jane Seymour, Anne of Cleves, Kathryn Howard, and Katherine Parr—were wed to a dangerous monarch who was not afraid to execute his enemies.

You don't need to be too concerned about dashes on the GMAT. First, when you see them, don't freak out. It's actually fairly difficult for dashes themselves to be incorrect, since their very purpose is to allow one thought to interrupt another (*My mother is coming—Oh no!—and I haven't cleaned the house*). On the GMAT, phrases in dashes are often there to provide a huge distraction that keeps you from seeing the real grammatical issues in the sentence.

When you are given a sentence using a set of dashes, you should attempt to **remove the dashes and whatever is in between them** and see whether the sentence still makes sense (it's fine if the sentence needs a comma once you've mentally removed all that text). Here's the example from above:

> CORRECT: The company leadership is faltering—the CEO embarrassed himself on the news just last night—and the investors are restless.

> TEST IT: The company leadership is faltering and the investors are restless.

This sentence works very nicely without the dashes and the content between them. Try this sentence:

> CORRECT OR INCORRECT? Every one of the researchers—none of whom has ever accomplished anything of merit—have introduced errors and irregularities into the data.

> TEST IT: Every one of the researchers have introduced errors and irregularities into the data.

This sentence is wrong! The subject is **every one**, which is singular and cannot take the plural verb *have*. The completed sentence should read:

> CORRECT: Every one of the researchers—none of whom has ever accomplished anything of merit—has introduced errors and irregularities into the data.

Note that the problem was not with the dashes themselves. The dashes were merely masking one of the types of grammatical errors you've already learned about.

Pop Quiz!

True or False: A colon is not needed when a list is introduced with the word *including*.

Answer is on page 133.

Punctuation Wrap-Up

You now know more about punctuation than the vast majority of English speakers! And you certainly know enough to succeed on the GMAT. Well done!

If you are especially interested in punctuation, you may enjoy the bestselling book *Eats, Shoots & Leaves,* by Lynne Truss.

If you are not especially interested in punctuation, that is totally understandable. In the next chapter, you'll move on to a few more crucial topics on the GMAT—Modifiers, Parallelism, and Comparisons.

> *Grade Yourself*
>
> How did you do in this section?
>
> ☐ **A** - I totally get this!
> ☐ **B** - I'm okay with this. Maybe review later if there's time.
> ☐ **C** - I'll make a note to review this later.

5

Chapter *of* 6

Foundations of GMAT Verbal

Modifiers, Parallelism, Comparisons

In This Chapter...

Modifiers

Parallelism & Comparisons

Chapter 6:

Modifiers, Parallelism, Comparisons

Modifiers

A modifier describes or **modifies** something else in the sentence. It is not part of the core sentence. All prepositional phrases are modifiers, and there are also many other kinds of modifiers.

All of the underlined portions below are modifiers:

> Ptolemy, <u>an accomplished mathematician</u>, used a symbol for zero as far back as 130 A.D.

> The students <u>who go to my school</u> are hardworking.

> Please complete this task <u>in a timely manner</u>.

Modifiers are one of the most difficult topics in GMAT Sentence Correction, and for more advanced study refer to our *Sentence Correction GMAT Strategy Guide*. However, there are a few common modifier errors that you can easily learn to spot right now.

Pop Quiz!

True or False: It can be helpful to ignore modifiers temporarily in order to help match up subjects and verbs.

Answer is on page 134.

Introductory Modifiers or "Warmups"

When a sentence begins with what is often called a "warmup" followed by a comma, the thing being described should come directly after the comma.

What is a warmup? It is a phrase that begins a sentence but doesn't have a subject. For instance:

> Full of one million tons of trash, …   (WHAT is full of trash?)

> Hiking through the woods, …   (WHO is hiking?)

Whatever is "full of trash" or "hiking" should come directly after the comma. Consider the following:

> <u>Full of one million tons of trash, the mayor</u> suggested that a new landfill be built.

> <u>Hiking through the woods, my backpack</u> was stolen by bears.

Now, what's full of trash? The mayor!

What's hiking? My backpack!

This is a type of grammar error that is often unintentionally hilarious. There are several ways you could rewrite these sentences in order to fix them, but say you are only allowed to change the second part:

> <u>Full of one million tons of trash, the landfill</u> was cited by the mayor as sorely in need of expansion.

> <u>Hiking through the woods, I</u> had my backpack stolen by bears.

Sometimes, even introductory modifiers ("warmups") used correctly sound a bit weird, because people almost never use this sentence pattern when speaking aloud.

> CORRECT: <u>Accomplished mathematicians and astronomers, the ancient Babylonians</u> used a base-60 number system and were able to measure the length of the solar year with a high degree of accuracy.

The warmup creates a question—**who** are the *accomplished mathematicians and astronomers*? The question is answered right after the comma—*the ancient Babylonians*.

This sentence may sound odd, but it's fine.

That, Who, When, and Where

Here are some simple rules that won't be hard to memorize. They make perfect sense when you think about them:

> Don't use **that** or **which** for people—instead, use **who**. Use **when** only for times. Use **where** only for places

Easy enough, right? Here are some examples:

INCORRECT: Young professionals **that** go to business school hope to increase their salary prospects.

Do not use *that* for people. Some experts disagree with the GMAT on this issue, but from our perspective, GMAT wins. The sentence should say *Young professionals who....*

INCORRECT: First-degree murder is **when** the killing was premeditated.

First-degree murder is not a time. You don't have to figure out on your own how to fix this sentence; you just need to know that it's wrong. Here is one correction: *One criterion for first-degree murder is that the killing was premeditated.*

INCORRECT: Algebra II was **where** I learned to factor.

Algebra II is not a place. Algebra II probably took place in classroom, and you could say *Room 201 is where I learned to factor.* But physical location isn't really the point of the sentence above. One correction: *Algebra II was the class in which I learned to factor.*

> **ADVANCED TIP:**
>
> While *who* is only for people, *whose* can actually be used with objects. For instance, it is fine to say *I am going to fix all the tables whose legs are broken.*

Drill 6.1 — Find the Modifier Errors

Determine whether the sentence has an error and circle "Correct" or "Incorrect."

1. The two companies made an illegal agreement where they agreed to raise prices significantly on the first of the year. CORRECT/INCORRECT

2. Running the final mile of the marathon, Jeff doubted that he would be able to keep going. CORRECT/INCORRECT

3. Although Balaji managed to eat 75 hot dogs with incredible speed, the hot-dog-eating contest trophy ultimately went to another competitor. CORRECT/INCORRECT

4. A good haircut is when you leave the salon feeling great. CORRECT/INCORRECT

5. Once rivaling the Great Pyramids, an earthquake snapped the Colossus of Rhodes, a statue of the Greek god Helios, at the knees. CORRECT/INCORRECT

Answers are on page 145.

Modifiers Wrap-Up

As previously mentioned, modifiers can get pretty complicated. However, you've just knocked out several serious modifier errors in one short section! Well done! Later, you'll want to check out the *Sentence Correction GMAT Strategy Guide* for more on this important topic.

Parallelism and Comparisons

When you list or compare two or more things, make sure your lists and comparisons are both logically and grammatically parallel.

Parallelism

First, consider a list:

> INCORRECT: The charges against him include financial crimes, human rights abuses, and that he murdered international aid workers.

What are the items in the list?

1.   financial crimes
2.   human rights abuses
3.   that he murdered international aid workers

Note that in #1 and #2, the main words are *nouns*: *crimes* and *abuses*. #3 in the list is an entire clause beginning with *that*. These items are not in the same format. You'll need to correct #3:

> CORRECT: The charges against him include financial crimes, human rights abuses, and **the murders of** international aid workers.

Another example:

> INCORRECT: The college cut expenses by laying off staff and it stopped work on a new library.

This list has only two items:

1.   laying off staff
2.   it stopped work on a new library

MANHATTAN
GMAT

What on earth is that *it* doing there? You already know that the college is what is performing both actions. Also, *laying off* and *stopped* do not match, so you need to put them in the same format:

> CORRECT: The college cut expenses by laying off staff and **stopping** work on a new library.

Laying and *stopping* match both logically and grammatically.

Here is one more example:

> TRY IT: You can purchase tickets by phone or on the Web.

What are the two things in the list?

1. by phone
2. on the Web

Remember how *laying off* and *stopping* were considered parallel in the sentence above? Here, *by* and *on* are also parallel—the items in the list just have to be the same part of speech, not the exact same word. *By phone* and *on the Web* are both prepositional phrases, telling you *how* to purchase tickets.

You use different expressions for telephones and the Internet, so each item in the list needs a different preposition. The sentence is correct. Prepositional phrases that are in parallel don't have to have the same preposition.

Comparisons

Now, consider a comparison:

> INCORRECT: Stuyvesant's math team beat Bronx Science.

Both *Stuyvesant* and *Bronx Science* are nouns, but the comparison is illogical—presumably, Stuyvesant's math team beat Bronx Science's *math team* (not the whole school!). There are several ways to fix the problem:

> CORRECT: Stuyvesant's **math team** beat Bronx Science**'s math team**.

> CORRECT: Stuyvesant's **math team** beat Bronx Science**'s**.

> CORRECT: Stuyvesant's **math team** beat **that of** Bronx Science.

In the last example, the word *that* stands in for *math team* and creates a logical comparison. Here is a similar example that matches a format used frequently on the GMAT:

> INCORRECT: The theories of astronomer Johannes Kepler superseded his teacher and colleague, Tycho Brahe.

What was just compared?

1. The theories of astronomer Johannes Kepler
2. his teacher and colleague, Tycho Brahe

You just compared a person's *theories* with *another person*. You need to compare *theories* to *theories* and *people* to *people*:

> CORRECT: The **theories** of astronomer Johannes Kepler superseded **those of** his teacher and colleague, Tycho Brahe.

Pop Quiz!

True or False: It is not parallel to put singular nouns and plural nouns in the same list, or to compare them with one another.

Answer is on page 134.

Now consider an example with a different problem:

> INCORRECT: I hate having to work late even more than to have to do what my horrible boss demands.

Here, working late and having to follow orders are logically the same kind of thing, but the way they are phrased in the sentence (*having to* and *to have to*) makes them a *grammatical* mismatch. This is really just a problem with parallelism, which you just practiced in the previous section. Here is the fixed sentence:

> CORRECT: I hate having to work late even more than having to do what my horrible boss demands.

Phrases Beginning with "That" and "When"

Here's a special case that the GMAT likes to test:

> INCORRECT: I liked the birthday cake you made me better than when you called me names.

Okay, that sentence is pretty silly, but that's not the problem. Look at the two things being compared:

1. the birthday cake you made me
2. **when** you called me names

> **MEMORIZE IT:**
>
> Do not compare a phrase that starts with *that* to one that starts with *when, where, which,* or *who.*

It is wrong to compare a thing (cake) with a period of time (*when* something happened). To correct the error, you can eliminate *when* or use *when* for both parts:

> CORRECT: I liked the birthday cake you made me better than the name-calling.

> CORRECT: I liked when you made me a birthday cake better than when you called me names.

Note that in the first correction, *when you called me names* was changed to *the name-calling* in order to create a noun, since *cake* is a noun and the two things being compared need to be grammatically parallel. A little bit of meaning was lost when that was done (*who* is doing the name-calling?). The second correction might be a bit better because it preserves the original meaning more closely.

Now try to spot a similar problem in a more GMAT-like example:

> INCORRECT: Cell-phone customers are much more likely to become incensed over additional charges they view as punitive than when obscure service fees are added to their monthly bills.

Did you find the error? Ask yourself, "What are the two things being compared?"

1.   additional charges they view as punitive
2.   **when** obscure service fees are added to their monthly bills

Once again, the sentence is comparing a thing (charges) with a time (WHEN fees are added). The correct GMAT answer could use *when* for both parts of the sentence, but will probably just eliminate *when*, since the idea of a time isn't really important to the sentence:

> POSSIBLE CORRECT ANSWER: Cell-phone customers are much more likely to become incensed **when** additional charges they view as punitive are applied to their accounts than **when** obscure service fees are added to their monthly bills.

> MORE LIKELY CORRECT ANSWER: Cell-phone customers are much more likely to become incensed over **additional charges** they view as punitive than over **obscure service fees** that are added to their monthly bills.

One more related example—do not compare a phrase that starts with *that* to one that starts with *when, where, which,* or *who:*

> INCORRECT: Liechtenstein is the only European nation that still has a monarchy with real—rather than largely ceremonial or diplomatic—power, and where the power given to the sovereign has actually increased in the current millennium.

What are the two things being compared?

> Liechtenstein is the only European nation…

1. THAT still has a monarchy…

    and

2. WHERE the power given to the sovereign…

Here, *that* has the correct meaning and should be used in both spots:

CORRECT: Liechtenstein is the only European nation that still has a monarchy with real—rather than largely ceremonial or diplomatic—power, and that has actually increased the sovereign's power in the current millennium.

In the cases above in which you're given more than one possible correction, the GMAT would only ever give you *one* of those correct answers—you will not have to choose between two correct answers that differ only in matters of style.

Drill 6.2 — Find the Parallelism/Comparison Errors

Determine whether the sentence has an error and circle "Correct" or "Incorrect."

1. New York City's population is greater than Montana, Wyoming, Vermont, North Dakota, South Dakota, Delaware, and Rhode Island all added together. CORRECT/INCORRECT

2. While we think of our state parks as pristine stretches of nature, some parklands actually cost more than maintaining busy city streets. CORRECT/INCORRECT

3. Although the people revolted when their leader was found fixing election results, they scarcely made a sound when the same ruler was discovered siphoning campaign funds for personal use. CORRECT/INCORRECT

4. While the age at which Americans become parents has been steadily rising over past decades, most young people still say that parenthood is an important milestone in life, much as it was for their own progenitors. CORRECT/INCORRECT

5. Despite the contributions of many great American novelists and playwrights, Shakespeare's plays are still taught in schools more frequently and deeply than any American writer. CORRECT/INCORRECT

Answer is on page 145.

Parallelism & Comparisons Wrap-Up

Comparisons wasn't so hard, was it? Especially after you made it through the really hard stuff (remember Verbs way back towards the beginning?). There are some more complicated issues in parallelism (sometimes lists can involve some pretty long and strange items) that you'll want to study in *Sentence Correction*, but you've already come a long way! You're almost done with Sentence Correction. If your brain hurts a bit, you can relax—the next section talks about figures of speech that can simply be memorized.

> ### Grade Yourself
>
> How did you do in this section?
>
> - ☐ **A** - I totally get this!
> - ☐ **B** - I'm okay with this. Maybe review later if there's time.
> - ☐ **C** - I'll make a note to review this later.

6

Chapter 7
of

Foundations of GMAT Verbal

Idioms, Subjunctive, Wrap-Up

In This Chapter...

Chapter 7:
Idioms, Subjunctive, Wrap-Up

Idioms

Idioms are expressions or figures of speech, such as *pushing up the daisies* (a cute reference to being dead—the person is pushing up flowers from under the ground).

On the GMAT, it rarely *rains cats and dogs,* and no one is described as *under the weather.* Idioms on the GMAT are a bit more subtle. For instance:

> INCORRECT: The meeting devolved into a fight between the marketing team with the sales team.

Many GMAT idiom errors are related to using the wrong preposition. In this case, the error concerns the preposition that goes with the word *between:*

> Incorrect pattern: between X with Y

> Correct pattern: between X and Y

The sentence should read *The meeting devolved into a fight between the marketing team AND the sales team.* Some of these patterns are not logical—that's why they're idioms. For instance, compare these two examples:

> I prohibit you <u>from leaving</u> school grounds.   I forbid you <u>to leave</u> school grounds.

Both sentences are correct and mean the same thing. *Prohibit* and *forbid* mean the same thing. Why does *prohibit* go with the preposition *from* plus a gerund (*leaving*), while *forbid* goes with the infinitive form (*to leave*)? No reason. Idioms simply must be memorized.

> *Idioms in Sentence Correction versus Idioms in Reading Comprehension:* There is a section on *Idioms* in the Reading Comprehension portion of this book, but that section is more about understanding the *meaning* of idioms when you read. This section is about identifying idioms that have been used incorrectly in Sentence Correction problems. There is certainly some overlap between the two sections, and understanding the meaning of idioms can be helpful in recognizing logical errors in Sentence Correction problems.

Some of the most common Sentence Correction idioms are covered here. Many more can be found in the Idioms section in the *Sentence Correction GMAT Strategy Guide*.

ABILITY

RIGHT: I value my ABILITY TO SING.

(Note: I CAN SING is preferred to I HAVE THE ABILITY TO SING.)

WRONG: I value my ABILITY OF SINGING.

I value my ABILITY FOR SINGING.

I value the ABILITY FOR me TO SING.

ALLOW

RIGHT: The holiday ALLOWS Maria TO WATCH the movie today. (= permits)

Maria WAS ALLOWED TO WATCH the movie.

The demolition of the old building ALLOWS FOR new construction.

(= permits the existence of)

WRONG: The holiday ALLOWED FOR Maria TO WATCH the movie.

The holiday ALLOWED Maria the WATCHING OF the movie.

The holiday ALLOWS THAT homework BE done (or CAN BE done).

Homework is ALLOWED FOR DOING BY Maria.

The ALLOWING OF shopping TO DO (or TO BE DONE).

AND

RIGHT: We are concerned about the forests AND the oceans.

We are concerned about the forests, the oceans, AND the mountains.

We work all night, AND we sleep all day. (Note the comma before AND.)

SUSPECT: We are concerned about the forests AND ALSO the oceans.

We work all night AND we sleep all day. (The GMAT usually links 2 clauses with comma + AND.)

WRONG: We are concerned about the forests, ALSO the oceans.

AS

RIGHT: AS I walked, I became more nervous. (= during)

AS I had already paid, I was unconcerned. (= because, since)

AS we did last year, we will win this year. (= in the same way)

JUST AS we did last year, we will win this year. (= in the same way)

AS the president of the company, she works hard. (= in the role of)

AS a child, I delivered newspapers. (= in the stage of being)

My first job was an apprenticeship AS a sketch artist.

AS PART OF the arrangement, he received severance.

SUSPECT: AS A PART OF the arrangement, he received severance.

WRONG: My first job was an apprenticeship OF a sketch artist.

They worked AS a sketch artist. (Needs to agree in number.)

WHILE BEING a child, I delivered newspapers.

AS BEING a child, I delivered newspapers.

WHILE IN childhood, I delivered newspapers.

AS... AS

RIGHT: Cheese is AS GREAT AS people say.

Cheese is NOT AS great AS people say.

We have AS MANY apples AS need to be cooked.

We have THREE TIMES AS MANY pears AS you.

We have AT LEAST AS MANY apples AS you.

We have ten apples, ABOUT AS MANY AS we picked yesterday.

His knowledge springs AS MUCH from experience AS from schooling.

His knowledge springs NOT SO MUCH from experience AS from schooling.

He wins frequently, AS MUCH because he plays SO hard AS because he cheats.

SUSPECT: Cheese is NOT SO great AS people say.

We have AS MANY apples AS OR MORE apples THAN you.

We have AS MANY apples AS THERE need to be cooked.

He wins frequently, AS MUCH because he plays AS hard AS because he cheats.

WRONG: Cheese is SO great AS people say.

Cheese is SO great THAT people say.

Cheese is AS great THAT people say.

We have AS MANY apples THAN you.

We have SO MANY apples AS you.

We have AS MANY OR MORE apples THAN you.

We have THREE TIMES AS MANY MORE pears AS you.

We have ten apples, ABOUT EQUIVALENT TO what we picked yesterday.

His knowledge springs NOT from experience AS from schooling.

BEING

RIGHT: BEING infected does not make you sick.

The judges saw the horses BEING led to the stables.

SUSPECT: BEING an advocate of reform, I would like to make a different proposal.

Note: The word BEING is often *wordy or awkward. However, having caught on to the*

"BEING is wrong" shortcut, the GMAT problem writers have created a few problems that force you to choose BEING. BEING appears in many more wrong answers than right ones. But BEING can be used correctly as a gerund or as a participle. In the end, you should pick a BEING answer only if you are 100% sure that the other answer choices are wrong for clear grammatical reasons.

BECAUSE

RIGHT:	BECAUSE the sun SHINES, plants grow.
	Plants grow BECAUSE the sun SHINES.
	BECAUSE OF the sun, plants grow.
	BY SHINING, the sun makes plants grow.
	Plants grow, FOR the sun shines. (Grammatically correct but very formal.)
SUSPECT:	Plants grow BECAUSE OF the sun, WHICH SHINES.
	Plants are amazing IN THAT they grow in the sun. (Correct but wordy.)
	The growth of plants IS EXPLAINED BY THE FACT THAT the sun shines. (Correct but wordy.)
WRONG:	Plants grow BECAUSE OF the sun SHINING.
	Plants grow AS A RESULT OF the sun SHINING.
	BECAUSE OF SHINING, the sun makes plants grow.
	ON ACCOUNT OF SHINING or ITS SHINING, the sun makes plants grow.
	BECAUSE the sun SHINES IS the REASON that plants grow.
	The ABILITY OF plants TO grow IS BECAUSE the sun shines.
	BEING THAT the sun shines, plants grow.
	The growth of plants IS EXPLAINED BECAUSE OF the shining of the sun.
	The growth of plants IS EXPLAINED BECAUSE the sun shines.

BELIEVE

RIGHT:	She BELIEVES THAT Gary IS right.
	She BELIEVES Gary TO BE right.
	IT IS BELIEVED THAT Gary IS right.
	Gary IS BELIEVED TO BE right.
SUSPECT:	Gary IS BELIEVED BY her TO BE right.

BOTH... AND

RIGHT:	She was interested BOTH in plants AND in animals.
	She was interested in BOTH plants AND animals.
WRONG:	She was interested BOTH in plants AND animals.
	She was interested BOTH in plants AS WELL AS in animals.
	She was interested BOTH in plants BUT ALSO in animals.

BUT

RIGHT: I STUDY hard BUT TAKE breaks.

I STUDY hard, BUT I TAKE breaks.

ALTHOUGH I TAKE frequent naps, I STUDY effectively.

DESPITE TAKING frequent naps, I STUDY effectively.

I TAKE frequent naps, YET I STUDY effectively.

SUSPECT: DESPITE THE FACT THAT I TAKE frequent naps, I STUDY effectively.

ALTHOUGH a frequent napper, I STUDY effectively.

Note: ALTHOUGH should generally be followed by a clause.

WRONG: I STUDY effectively ALTHOUGH TAKING frequent naps.

ALTHOUGH I TAKE frequent naps, YET I STUDY effectively.

ALTHOUGH I TAKE frequent naps, AND I STUDY effectively.

DESPITE TAKING frequent naps, YET I STUDY effectively.

CAN

RIGHT: The manager CAN RUN the plant.

The plant CAN CAUSE damage.

SUSPECT: The manager IS ABLE TO RUN the plant.

The manager IS CAPABLE OF RUNNING the plant.

The manager HAS THE ABILITY TO RUN the plant.

The manager HAS THE CAPABILITY OF RUNNING the plant.

It is POSSIBLE FOR the plant TO CAUSE damage.

The plant POSSIBLY CAUSES damage.

The plant HAS THE POSSIBILITY OF CAUSING damage.

Note: ALL of these suspect forms are grammatically correct but wordier than CAN.

CONSIDER

RIGHT: I CONSIDER her a friend. I CONSIDER her intelligent.

Note: You can switch the order of the two objects, if one is long.

I CONSIDER illegal the law passed last week by the new regime.

The law IS CONSIDERED illegal.

SUSPECT: The judge CONSIDERS the law TO BE illegal.

WRONG: The judge CONSIDERS the law AS illegal (or AS BEING illegal).

The judge CONSIDERS the law SHOULD BE illegal.

The judge CONSIDERS the law AS IF IT WERE illegal.

ENOUGH See also SO/THAT

RIGHT: The book was SHORT ENOUGH TO READ in a night.

The book was SHORT ENOUGH FOR me TO READ in a night.

SUSPECT: The power plant has found a way to generate energy at an unprecedented scale,

ENOUGH FOR powering and entire city.

WRONG: The book was SHORT ENOUGH THAT I could read it in a night.

The book was SHORT ENOUGH FOR IT TO BE read in a night.

The book was SHORT ENOUGH SO THAT I could read it in a night.

The book was SHORT ENOUGH AS TO BE read in a night.

EXPECT

RIGHT: We EXPECT the price TO FALL. The price IS EXPECTED TO FALL.

We EXPECT THAT the price WILL FALL.

IT IS EXPECTED THAT the price WILL FALL.

Inflation rose more than we EXPECTED.

There IS an EXPECTATION THAT the price will fall.

SUSPECT: There IS an EXPECTATION the price WILL FALL.

There IS an EXPECTATION OF the price FALLING.

Inflation rose more than we EXPECTED IT TO.

Inflation rose more than we EXPECTED IT WOULD.

WRONG: The price IS EXPECTED FOR IT TO FALL.

IT IS EXPECTED THAT the price SHOULD FALL.

IN ORDER TO

RIGHT: She drank coffee IN ORDER TO STAY awake.

She drank coffee TO STAY awake. (Infinitive TO STAY indicates purpose.)

SUSPECT: She drank coffee IN ORDER THAT (*or SO THAT*) she MIGHT stay awake.

She drank coffee SO AS TO STAY awake.

WRONG: She drank coffee FOR STAYING awake.

Coffee was drunk by her IN ORDER TO STAY awake (*or* TO STAY awake).

Note: The subject COFFEE is not trying TO STAY awake.

INDICATE

RIGHT: A report INDICATES THAT unique bacteria LIVE on our skin.

SUSPECT: A report INDICATES the presence of unique bacteria on our skin.

Note: This correct form seems to be avoided in right answers.

A report IS INDICATIVE OF the presence of unique bacteria on our skin.

WRONG: A report INDICATES unique bacteria LIVE on our skin. (THAT is needed)

A report IS INDICATIVE THAT unique bacteria LIVE on our skin.

A report INDICATES unique bacteria AS present on our skin.

A report INDICATES unique bacteria TO LIVE on our skin.

LIKE	*See also SUCH AS.*
RIGHT:	LIKE his sister, Matt drives fast cars. (= both drive fast cars)
	Matt drives fast cars LIKE his sister.
	(= both drive fast cars, *OR* both drive fast cars in the same way)
	Matt drives fast cars LIKE his sister's.
	(= both drive *similar* cars; he does *not* drive his sister's car)

WRONG:	Matt drives fast cars LIKE his sister does.
	LIKE his sister, SO Matt drives fast cars.

LIKELY	
RIGHT:	My friend IS LIKELY TO EAT worms.
	IT IS LIKELY THAT my friend WILL EAT worms.
	My friend is MORE LIKELY THAN my enemy [is] TO EAT worms.
	My friend is TWICE AS LIKELY AS my enemy [is] TO EAT worms.
	MORE THAN LIKELY, my friend WILL EAT worms.

WRONG:	My friend IS LIKELY THAT he WILL EAT worms.
	RATHER THAN my enemy, my friend is THE MORE LIKELY to EAT worms.

NOT... BUT	
RIGHT:	She DID NOT EAT mangoes BUT ATE other kinds of fruit.
	She DID NOT EAT mangoes BUT LIKED other kinds of fruit AND later BEGAN to like kiwis, too.
	A tomato is NOT a vegetable BUT a fruit.
	A tomato is NOT a vegetable BUT RATHER a fruit.
	The agency is NOT a fully independent entity BUT INSTEAD derives its authority from Congress. *Note: The verbs "is" and "derives" are parallel.*
	She DID NOT EAT mangoes; INSTEAD, she ate other kinds of fruit.

WRONG:	She DID NOT EAT mangoes BUT other kinds of fruit.
	She DID NOT EAT mangoes; RATHER other kinds of fruit.

NOT ONLY... BUT ALSO	
RIGHT:	We wore NOT ONLY boots BUT ALSO sandals.
	We wore NOT ONLY boots, BUT ALSO sandals. (Comma is optional.)
	We wore NOT JUST boots BUT ALSO sandals.

SUSPECT:	We wore NOT ONLY boots BUT sandals.
	*Note: The GMAT has **used this construction in correct answers.***
	We wore NOT ONLY boots BUT sandals AS WELL.
	We wore boots AND ALSO sandals.

WRONG:	We wore NOT ONLY boots AND ALSO sandals.
	We wore NOT ONLY boots BUT, AS WELL, sandals.

7

ONLY

RIGHT: Her performance is exceeded ONLY by theirs. (Modifies by theirs.)

WRONG: Her performance is ONLY exceeded by theirs. (Technically modifies exceeded.)
Note: ONLY should be placed just before the words it is meant to modify. In both speech and writing, ONLY is often placed before the verb, but this placement is generally wrong, according to the GMAT, since it is rarely meant that the verb is the only action ever performed by the subject.

ORDER

RIGHT: The state ORDERS THAT the agency COLLECT taxes. (subjunctive)

The state ORDERS the agency TO COLLECT taxes.

WRONG: The state ORDERS THAT the agency SHOULD COLLECT taxes.

The state ORDERS the agency SHOULD (*or* WOULD) COLLECT taxes.

The state ORDERS the agency COLLECTING taxes.

The state ORDERS the agency the COLLECTION OF taxes.

The state ORDERS the COLLECTION OF taxes BY the agency.

The state ORDERS taxes collected.

REQUIRE

RIGHT: She REQUIRES time TO WRITE (*or* IN ORDER TO WRITE).

She REQUIRES her friend TO DO work.

Her friend IS REQUIRED TO DO work.

She REQUIRES THAT her friend DO work. (subjunctive)

She REQUIRES OF her friend THAT work BE done. (subjunctive)

SUSPECT: In this hostel, there is a REQUIREMENT OF work.

There is a REQUIREMENT THAT work BE done.

WRONG: She REQUIRES her friend DO work (*or* MUST DO) work.

She REQUIRES her friend TO HAVE TO DO work.

She REQUIRES OF her friend TO DO work.

She REQUIRES THAT her friend DOES work (*or* SHOULD DO) work.

She REQUIRES THAT her friend IS TO DO work.

She REQUIRES DOING work (*or* THE DOING OF work).

She REQUIRES her friend DOING work.

In this hostel, there is a REQUIREMENT OF work BY guests.

RESULT

RIGHT: Wealth RESULTS FROM work.

Work RESULTS IN wealth.

Wealth IS A RESULT OF work.

Wealth grows AS A RESULT OF work.

AS A RESULT OF our work, our wealth grew.

MANHATTAN
GMAT

7

The RESULT OF our work WAS THAT our wealth grew.

WRONG: We worked WITH THE RESULT OF wealth.

We worked WITH A RESULTING growth of wealth.

RESULTING FROM our work, our wealth grew.

BECAUSE OF THE RESULT OF our work, our wealth grew.

The RESULT OF our work WAS our wealth grew. (THAT is needed.)

The growth of wealth RESULTS.

SEEM

RIGHT: This result SEEMS TO DEMONSTRATE the new theory.

IT SEEMS THAT this result DEMONSTRATES the new theory.

IT SEEMS AS IF this result DEMONSTRATES the new theory.

SUSPECT: This result SEEMS TO BE A DEMONSTRATION OF the new theory.

This result SEEMS DEMONSTRATIVE OF the new theory.

This result SEEMS LIKE A DEMONSTRATION OF the new theory.

WRONG: This result SEEMS AS IF IT DEMONSTRATES the new theory.

This result SEEMS LIKE IT DEMONSTRATES the new theory.

SO... THAT

See also ENOUGH.

RIGHT: The book was SO SHORT THAT I could read it in one night.

The book was SHORT ENOUGH FOR me TO READ in one night.

Note: These two expressions have slightly different emphases, but it is unlikely that you will need to choose an answer solely on this basis.

SUSPECT: The book was SO SHORT I could read it. (THAT is preferred.)

The book was OF SUCH SHORTNESS THAT I could read it.

The book had SO MUCH SHORTNESS THAT I could read it.

SUCH was the SHORTNESS of the book THAT I could read it.

WRONG: The book was OF SUCH SHORTNESS, I could read it.

The book was SHORT TO SUCH A DEGREE AS TO ALLOW me to read it.

SO THAT

RIGHT: She gave money SO THAT the school could offer scholarships. (= purpose)

SUSPECT: She gave money, SO the school was grateful. (= result)

WRONG: She gave money SO the school could offer scholarships.

SUCH AS

RIGHT: Matt drives fast cars, SUCH AS Ferraris. (= example)

Matt enjoys driving SUCH cars AS Ferraris.

Matt enjoys intense activities, SUCH AS DRIVING fast cars.

WRONG: Matt drives fast cars LIKE Ferraris. (= similar to, but "example" is implied)

Matt drives Ferraris AND THE LIKE.

Matt drives Ferraris AND OTHER cars SUCH AS THESE.

Matt trains in many ways SUCH AS BY DRIVING on racetracks.

Matt enjoys intense activities, SUCH AS TO DRIVE fast cars.

THAN

RIGHT: His books are MORE impressive THAN those of other writers.

This paper is LESS impressive THAN that one.

This paper is NO LESS impressive THAN that one.

This newspaper cost 50 cents MORE THAN that one.

MORE THAN 250 newspapers are published here.

Sales are HIGHER this year THAN last year.

WRONG: His books are MORE impressive AS those of other writers.

This paper is MORE impressive RATHER THAN that one.

This paper is MORE impressive INSTEAD OF that one.

This paper is NO LESS impressive AS that one.

This paper is NONE THE LESS impressive THAN that one.

This newspaper cost 50 cents AS MUCH AS that one.

AS MANY AS OR MORE THAN 250 newspapers are published here.

Sales are HIGHER this year OVER last year.

TO + verb   *See IN ORDER TO.*

UNLIKE   *See also CONTRAST.*

RIGHT: UNLIKE the spiny anteater, the aardvark is docile.

WRONG: UNLIKE WITH the spiny anteater, the aardvark is docile.

Drill 7.1 — Find the Idioms Errors

Find and attempt to correct the errors in each of the following sentences. Every sentence has at least one error.

1.   Although I have the ability of doing gymnastics well, this time I fell off of the balance beam.

2.   The ostensible reason for Anne Boleyn's execution was because of adultery, although the charges were almost certainly fabricated wholesale.

3.   Because she has deep relationships with the unions like other leaders have, there is an expectation of her being appointed as chairperson.

4.   The study indicates more men are working in education, traditionally considered as a "female" profession.

5.   The company is likely that it will gain market share.

Answers are on page 146.

Idioms Wrap-Up

Great, you've learned the most commonly tested idioms on the GMAT!

There are many more to learn (see *Sentence Correction*), but it's pretty straightforward to memorize idioms—you can make flashcards, for instance.

You can also test your knowledge of idioms and other simple grammatical issues with the free downloadable flashcards (use online, in print, or on the iPhone) available at http://www.manhattangmat.com/gmat-flashcards.cfm.

Pop Quiz!

True or False: The sentence "I prohibit you from breaking up the fight between Jared and Bill" is correct.

Answer is on page 134.

> *Grade Yourself*
>
> How did you do in this section?
>
> ☐   **A** - I totally get this!
> ☐   **B** - I'm okay with this. Maybe review later if there's time.
> ☐   **C** - I'll make a note to review this later.

The Subjunctive

The **subjunctive mood** falls under the category of verbs. If you have learned British or Indian English, please pay careful attention to this section.

In the beginning of Chapter 3, it was noted:

> Almost everything in English is in the **indicative** mood. *Indicative* means "indicating," and of course virtually all sentences indicate something. The **imperative** mood is for giving commands, as in **Run** *faster!* or **Consider** *the case of the cassowary.* The **subjunctive** mood is a special topic that will be discussed later. It is used to express a wish, an emotion, a possibility, or an action that has not yet occurred, as in *I wish you* **were** *mine* or *I suggest that you* **be** *on time.*

Here is a sentence in the subjunctive mood (specifically, the **command subjunctive**, the subjunctive mood issue most frequently tested on the GMAT):

CORRECT: The security chief <u>demanded</u> <u>that</u> the leak <u>be found and stopped</u>.

Here the security chief is expressing an action that has not taken place. The verb is *demanded.* "Bossy" verbs such as *demand, suggest,* and *recommend* tell you that you need to follow a sentence pattern like the one above.

The next important part of the above sentence is *that.* The word *that* is mandatory: I demand *that* you do it. I suggest *that* you attend.

The final important part of the example sentence is the verb: *be found and stopped.* In this sentence pattern, you need to use the *command* form of the verb. For the verb *to be,* that is always *be,* just as you would yell at someone *Be here! Be on time!*

The verb in this sentence pattern does not conjugate—it does not change based on whether the subject is singular or plural. For instance, you would use the same verb form in *I demanded that he run faster* and *I demanded that they run faster.* The reason is that, when you order someone to run, you always say *Run!* You never order anyone to *Runs!*

Pop Quiz!

True or False: The sentence pattern *I demand that you ARE (adjective)* cannot be correct.

Answer is on page 134.

Here is another example with the relevant parts underlined:

CORRECT: I <u>suggest</u> <u>that</u> you <u>arrive</u> on time.

INCORRECT: I <u>suggest</u> <u>that</u> you should <u>arrive</u> on time.

In British English, it is common to add the word *should,* as in *I suggest that you should arrive on time.* In American English, this is always incorrect. Do not add the word *should.*

Here is a sentence that is very common in Indian English:

I requested him to get it done.

This is incorrect in American English. *Request* is a "bossy verb" that demands the subjunctive sentence pattern you learned above.

I <u>requested</u> <u>that</u> he <u>get</u> it done.

In American English, you cannot *request* a person to do something. To *request* a person means to choose that person, as in *I requested Samantha as my lab partner.* If you asked Samantha to do something, you would say *I requested that Samantha compile our data.*

> **BY THE WAY:**
>
> There is one other issue related to the subjunctive, although this issue doesn't occur often on the GMAT. After *if* or *wish,* use *were* instead of *was.*
>
> For instance, *I wish I was rich* should be *I wish I **were** rich.*
>
> *If I was qualified, I would definitely apply* should be *If I **were** qualified, I would definitely apply.*

Drill 7.2

Determine whether the sentence has an error and circle "Correct" or "Incorrect."

1. I suggested him to study earlier in the evening, before he gets tired. CORRECT/INCORRECT

2. In order to ensure the effective functioning of our organization, the president asks that everyone vacate the meeting room directly following a meeting's scheduled end time. CORRECT/INCORRECT

3. The CEO demanded that everyone be prompt, dress appropriately, and follow regulations. CORRECT/INCORRECT

4. We hope that you will be available on weekends. CORRECT/INCORRECT

5. The board suggests that our budget ought to be revised. CORRECT/INCORRECT

Answers are on page 146.

Subjunctive Wrap-Up

The command subjunctive might have been new to you, but fortunately, there is just a single sentence pattern to memorize. Not so bad!

Congratulations! You've made it through all of the grammar issues in this book!

You're now ready to wrap Sentence Correction up as a whole.

Grade Yourself

How did you do in this section?

- ☐ **A** - I totally get this!
- ☐ **B** - I'm okay with this. Maybe review later if there's time.
- ☐ **C** - I'll make a note to review this later.

Sentence Correction Wrap-Up

You've covered a lot of ground. Now you've got to apply all this knowledge to Sentence Correction problems.

The table below gives a recap of what you already know about the parts of speech. It's not important that you draw these shapes, or any particular shapes at all, when you write out and analyze your own sentences. However, you do want to indicate the key issues somehow, such as the connection between a pronoun and its antecedent.

7

Parts of Speech

N	Noun	*dog, happiness, production*	Represents a thing, person, or idea.	Count noun: *one dog, two dogs* Mass noun: *happiness, bread*
Pro	Pronoun	*they, it, its*	Stands for a noun.	I found the [dog] after [it] ran away.
Adj	Adjective	*green, expensive*	Modifies a noun.	The *green* [hat] was *expensive*. The [dog] chased *its* [tail].
V	Verb	*chased, bark, was*	Shows what a noun does or is.	Dogs—(bark). That [hat]—(was) expensive.
Adv	Adverb	*quickly, very*	Modifies a verb, adjective or adverb.	Dogs—(bark) loudly.

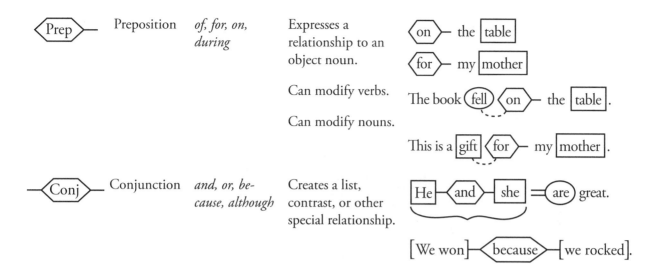

Sentence Structure

Likewise, you now know a ton about sentence structure.

The table below captures the basic forms of a sentence and some variations. Take a few minutes and look over these templates. Again, it is not important that you draw them out yourself. But they do illustrate the point of grammar: that words in a sentence fit together according to rules.

Basic Templates

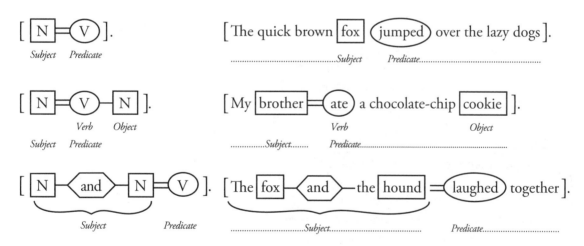

Combinations

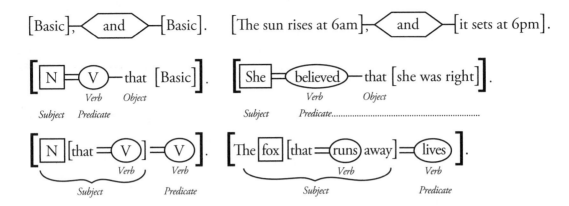

Drill 7.3

The following are complete GMAT-style Sentence Correction problems testing issues discussed in this book. Note that answer choice (A) is always identical to the original. For each question, write A B C D E on your paper and practice process of elimination. After making your way through so much of this book, you now know better than to try to pick the answer that "sounds the best." Instead, cross off all of the answers that have mistakes. The remaining choice is correct.

1. Avgolemono, or "egg lemon," is a soup or sauce made by mixing egg, lemon juice, and broth and <u>heat the mixture until it will thicken</u>.

    (A) heat the mixture until it will thicken
    (B) heat the mixture until it thickens
    (C) heating the mixture until it will thicken
    (D) heating the mixture until it thickens
    (E) heating the mixture until it had thickened

2. Soldier ants are sterile, wingless females that serve many roles within a colony, from <u>serving as sentinels and sound</u> a warning when danger is near.

    (A) serving as sentinels and sound
    (B) serving as sentinels and sounding
    (C) to serve as sentinels and to sound
    (D) serving as sentinels to sound
    (E) serving as sentinels to sounding

3. <u>That the consumer products division lacks credible leadership cannot be blamed</u> for the company's troubles.

    (A) That the consumer products division lacks credible leadership cannot be blamed
    (B) That the consumer products division has a lack in credible leadership cannot be blamed
    (C) The consumer products division lacks credible leadership cannot be blamed
    (D) The lack of credible leadership of the consumer products division is not blaming
    (E) It is not blameworthy that the consumer products division lacks credible leadership

4. Many small businesses <u>are finding that it can avoid the fees associated with credit card merchant accounts, using</u> Internet-based credit card processing services, which typically take a percentage of sales but charge no setup fee or monthly service fee.

    (A) are finding that it can avoid the fees associated with credit card merchant accounts, using
    (B) are finding that they can avoid the fees associating with credit card merchant accounts, using
    (C) are finding that they can avoid the fees associated with credit card merchant accounts by using
    (D) had found that they can avoid the fees associated with credit card merchant accounts by the use of
    (E) have founded that they can avoid the fees associated with credit card merchant accounts by using

5. Confounded by the seemingly contradictory data, <u>the experiment was suggested by the scientist to be re-run by his graduate students.</u>

    (A) the experiment was suggested by the scientist to be re-run by his graduate students
    (B) the graduate students were suggested by the scientist to re-run the experiment
    (C) the scientist suggested his graduate students to re-run the experiment
    (D) the scientist had suggested his graduate students should re-run the experiment
    (E) the scientist suggested that his graduate students re-run the experiment

7

6.   The agency's top creative team — each member of which <u>was asked to submit at least three ideas — remain</u> stymied in the development of a new campaign.

   (A)   was asked to submit at least three ideas — remain
   (B)   was asked to submit at least three ideas — remains
   (C)   were asked to submit at least three ideas — remain
   (D)   were asked to submit at least three ideas — remains
   (E)   asked to submit at least three ideas — remains

7.   The peanut, or groundnut, <u>a legume probably</u> first cultivated as long as 7,600 years ago in the valleys of Peru.

   (A)   a legume probably
   (B)   a legume was probably
   (C)   is a legume probably
   (D)   probably is a legume
   (E)   the legume probably

8.   The Paris Commune, hailed by many as an assumption of power by the working class, <u>a government in 1871 that ruled France for less than two months</u>.

   (A)   a government in 1871 that ruled France for less than two months
   (B)   a government that ruled France for less than two months in 1871
   (C)   were a government that ruled France for less than two months in 1871
   (D)   was a government that ruled France for less than two months in 1871
   (E)   was a French government in 1871 that ruled for less than two months

9.   Communards, or leaders of the Paris Commune, <u>once mistook the painter Renoir, painting on the banks of the Seine River, for</u> a spy.

   (A)   once mistook the painter Renoir, painting on the banks of the Seine River, for
   (B)   once mistook the painter Renoir, painting on the banks of the Seine River, as
   (C)   once mistook the painter Renoir, painting on the banks of the Seine River, to be
   (D)   once were mistaken of the painter Renoir, painting on the banks of the Seine River, for
   (E)   once mistaked the painter Renoir, a painter on the banks of the Seine River, to be

10. The king's guests <u>had had plenty of time to glut themselves at the feast by the time the rebels broke into the castle, and thus they</u> were too stupefied, drunk, and startled to react effectively.

   (A) had had plenty of time to glut themselves at the feast by the time the rebels broke into the castle, and thus they

   (B) had plenty of time to glut themselves at the feast by the time the rebels broke into the castle, and thus they

   (C) had plenty of time to glut themselves at the feast by the time the rebels had broken into the castle, and thus the guests

   (D) had had plenty of time to glut themselves at the feast by the time the rebels broke into the castle, and thus the guests

   (E) had plenty of time to glut themselves at the feast by the time the rebels were breaking into the castle, and furthermore they

Answers are on page 147.

<u>Grade Yourself</u>

How did you do in this section?

- ❑ **A** - I totally get this!
- ❑ **B** - I'm okay with this. Maybe review later if there's time.
- ❑ **C** - I'll make a note to review this later.

Now Go and Do Likewise

If you purchased this book or received it as part of a package of materials from Manhattan GMAT, you have free access to an online bank of GMAT-style verbal problems written expressly to supplement this book. Extensive explanations for each problem will help ensure that you understand why the right answer is right and the wrong answers are wrong. It is recommended that you begin working out of *The Official Guide for GMAT Review, 13th Edition,* and out of our *Sentence Correction GMAT Strategy Guide.*

Now, turn to the next part on Critical Reasoning!

Answers to Pop Quizzes

Nouns, page **29**

The sentence, "I have a great amount of homework and a great amount of deadlines," is correct.

FALSE! *Homework* is not countable (it is a mass noun), so the first *amount* is correct. But *deadlines* are countable, so the second part of the sentence should read *a great NUMBER of deadlines.*

Pronouns, page **34**

You and *it* can be both subject and object pronouns.

TRUE! Think of a sentence like "*She* threw the ball to *him.*" *She* is a subject pronoun (the corresponding object pronoun is *her*). *Him* is an object pronoun (the corresponding subject pronoun is *he*). In the case of *you* and *it,* however, there is no "other version"—both *you* and *it* can go in either spot. *You* gave *it* a cat toy. *It* gave *you* a nasty bite on the arm.

Pronouns, page **35**

A pronoun may have an adjective as its antecedent.

FALSE! A proNOUN refers back to a NOUN (or, technically, to a phrase or clause, although this is an advanced topic you don't need to worry about right now).

The incorrect example on page **37**, "I love *French* food because *they* really know how to make a good sauce," is an example of a pronoun *(they)* incorrectly attempting to refer back to an adjective *(French).*

Adjectives, page **39**

In the sentence, "7,919 is the one-thousandth prime number," *7,919* and *one-thou-sandth* are both adjectives.

FALSE! *One-thousandth* is an adjective describing *prime number,* but *7,919* is serving as the subject of the sentence. It is a noun. (It would be perfectly possible for *7,919* to be an adjective in a different sentence, such as *I have 7,919 reasons not to date you, thank you very much.*)

7

Verbs, page **47**

In the sentence, "In 2034 when she is released from prison, she will have never so much as touched a cell phone," the compound verb is *have touched*.

FALSE! The compound verb is *will have touched*. (*Never* is an adverb.) Make sure you catch all the parts of a compound verb!

Verbs, page **49**

In the sentence, "I hate smiling," *smiling* is a gerund, but in the sentence, "*I am smiling as big as I can*," *am smiling* is the main verb.

TRUE! The first use of *smiling* could easily be replaced with a noun *(I hate pizza),* but the second cannot. Also, the second use of *smiling* has a helper verb.

Adverbs, page **56**

Adverbs can modify verbs, adjectives, or nouns.

FALSE! Adverbs can modify verbs, adjectives, or other adverbs—NOT nouns! Use *adjectives* to modify nouns.

Adverbs, page **58**

An adverb has to "touch" (be placed next to) the verb it is modifying.

FALSE! As long as it is clear what verb an adverb is modifying, an adverb does not have to touch the verb. For instance, *He walked slowly to school, He slowly walked to school* and *Slowly, he walked to school* are all correct.

Prepositions, page **66**

In the sentence, "He wants to go," the word *to* is not a preposition, but in the sentence, "He went to the store," the word *to* is a preposition.

TRUE! *To* just before a verb is part of an infinitive (*to go*), but *to* followed by a noun (*to the store*) is a prepositional phrase.

Prepositions, page **68**

Sometimes the main subject of a sentence is located inside a prepositional phrase.

FALSE! The reason you are learning to identify prepositional phrases is so you can temporarily ignore them for the purpose of matching up subjects and verbs. The subject of the sentence will never be located inside a prepositional phrase. (There are a couple of exceptions that the *Manhattan GMAT Sentence Correction Strategy Guide* goes into.)

Conjunctions, page 72

The sentence, "The company's profits were outstanding, and it went bankrupt because of outrageously poor management," would be considered incorrect on the GMAT.

TRUE! For this sentence to make sense, *and* should be *but* (or *yet*, etc.).

Subjects and Predicates, page 83

The subject of a sentence can be a phrase beginning with *that* or *to.*

TRUE! Here are examples: *That the architecture is so lovely is why I chose Yale. To love is the purpose of life.*

Subjects and Predicates, page 85

In the sentence, "Although Italy is famous for pasta, noodles were invented by the Chinese," the dependent clause has the subject *Italy* and the independent clause has the subject *the Chinese.*

FALSE! The dependent clause is *Italy is famous for pasta* and its subject is indeed *Italy.* The independent clause is *noodles were invented by the Chinese.* Its subject is *noodles.* The verb is *were invented. By the Chinese* is a prepositional phrase.

Punctuation, page 92

The sentence, "The dog asked for a treat; he gave it one," correctly uses a semicolon to join two independent clauses.

TRUE! Some students are thrown off by *he gave it one* as a complete clause, but it has a subject and a verb and can stand alone. A good rule here might be that "pronouns are just as good as nouns in determining whether you have a complete sentence. The sentence is correct.

Punctuation, page 94

A colon is not needed when a list is introduced with the word *including.*

TRUE! Only use a colon when the first part of the sentence can stand alone. (If the first part ends with *including*, it is not a stand-alone sentence.)

Modifiers, page **99**

> It can be helpful to ignore modifiers temporarily in order to help match up subjects and verbs.

> **TRUE!** Remember, prepositional phrases are modifiers, and one of the reasons you spent so much time on prepositional phrases was so you could learn to temporarily ignore them in order to get down to a "core sentence" that you can check for subject-verb agreement.

Parallelism and Comparisons, **104**

> It is not parallel to put singular nouns and plural nouns in the same list, or to compare them with one another.

> **FALSE!** As long as the items in a list or comparison are all nouns, some can be singular and some plural. Of course, it's fine to say *I'm going to the store to buy rice, vegetables, and a carton of milk.*

Idioms, **121**

> The sentence, "I prohibit you from breaking up the fight between Jared and Bill," is correct.

> **TRUE!** Both these idioms were covered at the beginning of the chapter. *Prohibit* goes with *from* and *between* goes with *and.*

The Subjunctive, **122**

> The sentence pattern *I demand that you ARE (adjective)* cannot be correct.

> **TRUE!** The correct pattern for the subjunctive is *I demand that you BE (adjective),* as in *Our mother demanded that we be polite.*

Answers to Drill Sets

Answers to Drill 2.1 — Find the Nouns

1. companies, United States, protections, imports

2. Jane Austen, *Pride and Prejudice,* novel, 2005, film, Keira Knightley

3. purpose, passage, explanation, fact

4. study, support, theory, origin, fruit bat

5. happiness

Answers to Drill 2.2 — Find the Pronouns

1. it, everyone, his (possessive adjective)

2. one, one, mine

3. everybody, each

4. he, most (Note that *most* is a pronoun in this sentence because it stands in for a noun: *most people.*)

5. who, me, myself

Answers to Drill 2.3 — Connect Pronouns with Antecedents

1. Can (you) finish (it) today?

2. (All) of the cake was gone before (we) had a chance to try (it).

3. Marina joked about (our) security badges while ceremonially turning in (hers)— (she) said (she) would be certain to enjoy the fact that retired people no longer have to wear nametags.

4. As soon as Davis saw (me) working on (my) project, (he) started plotting to take credit for (it).

5. (It) is clear that the dog loves the new toy that Joey bought for (it) so much so that Joey is glad (he) didn't spend the money on (himself).

Answers to Pronoun Drill 2.4 — Use the Pronoun *One*

1. CORRECT. Here *one* has the sense of "everyone," and *it* clearly refers back to *fire*. It is fine to use *one* in a sentence with other pronouns when those other pronouns are referring to different things.

2. INCORRECT. *Firefighters* is plural and cannot mix with *one's*. A correct version would say *their safety gear*.

3. CORRECT. This sentence sounds very old-fashioned and formal, but it is perfectly correct.

4. INCORRECT. *You* and *one* cannot mix here (they are clearly both referring to the same person, the reader).

5. CORRECT. *One* here is simply a number, as in *one fox*. A fox is singular and is correctly referred to with the pronoun *it*.

Answers to Drill 2.5 — Circle the Adjectives

1. School, dangerous, violent, overcrowded. Note that *school* is usually a noun (*I have always enjoyed school*), but here it is an adjective because it is modifying "hallways." Remember, you can test whether a word is an adjective by trying to replace it with other adjectives—*long* hallways, *cold* hallways, etc.

2. Utter, thoroughgoing. *Thoroughgoing* is an adjective that means "thorough, complete." Even when you do not know the meaning of a word, you can often tell its part of speech by substituting other words—in this case, adjectives—to see whether they fit (*big success, minor success*).

3. Furious, black-and-blue. Note that *Canadian* can sometimes be an adjective (*Canadian waterways*), but here, *The Canadians* is a noun.

4. Danish, first, female

5. Banausic, lucky, disappointed, five. Here, an extremely obscure word was chosen—*banausic*—that you most likely will never see again in your entire life (and certainly not on the GMAT). The important point is that you don't need to know this word to analyze the sentence—you can easily tell that it's an adjective (the *-ic* ending is a good clue) by substituting *small concern, silly concern*. Note that *six* is being used as a noun, but *five* is describing *tickets*, and so it is an adjective.

Answers to Drill 2.6 — Find the Adjective Errors

1. CORRECT. The pronoun *they* refers back to *chefs*. Both are plural, and the meaning is clear. *Chinese* is used as an adjective describing *food*. There is no problem here.

2. INCORRECT. Here, *Chinese* is used as an adjective describing *army*. The pronoun *they* is attempting to refer back to either *Chinese* or *army*. The sentence is incorrect either way—*Chinese* is an adjective

and *army* is singular, so the plural pronoun *they* cannot refer back to either word. (In a different sentence, *they* could refer back to something like *soldiers* or *the Chinese*, both of which are plural nouns.)

3. CORRECT. *Fifteen-year-old* is a hyphenated adjective. The hyphens are appropriate here because the Scotch is not *fifteen*, and *year*, and *old* (the way we would say *tight, shiny pants*). *Fifteen-year-old* is just one adjective.

4. INCORRECT. The pronoun *it* cannot refer back to *college,* which is being used as an adjective describing the *administrators.*

5. CORRECT. *More nearly perfect* is a good way to describe being closer to perfect than something else. Some language experts say that *perfect* is an absolute adjective (like *dead*) and that it is not possible to be *more perfect.* However, the phrase *more perfect union* appears in the U.S. Constitution, so obviously there is a debate. For the GMAT, just know that *more nearly perfect* is fine.

Answers to Drill 3.1 — Find the Parts of the Verb

1. has been spreading

2. has been found

3. will run, jump, play (Note that the *will* applies to all three verbs—the meaning is *will run, will jump, and will play.*)

4. had supported, struck, re-evaluated (Note that the *had* does NOT apply to all three verbs. The executives *had supported* a plan in the distant past, but then sometime after that, crisis *struck* and they *re-evaluated.*)

5. are going

Answers to Drill 3.2 — Find the Gerunds and Infinitives

1. To be a ballerina (is) my lifelong dream.

2. The executive (has been) accused of embezzling funds.

3. Eating, praying, and loving (are) apparently author Elizabeth Gilbert's favorite activities.

4. To kill (is) to break the social contract.

5. Recovering from my accident (is using) all of my energy right now.

Answers to Drill 3.3 — Determine Subject–Verb Agreement

1. CORRECT. *Species* can be singular or plural, but the word *several* tells us that it is plural in this sentence. The matching verb is *were.*

2. INCORRECT. The subject *companies* is plural. The verb *is* should be *are.*

3. CORRECT. *Every* is singular. The verb is *was.*

4. INCORRECT. *Code* is singular. The verb *deem* is plural and should be *deems.* (To *deem* is to judge or consider.)

5. INCORRECT. *The Philippines* certainly sounds plural, but country names are singular. Say in your head, *IT offers….*

Answers to Drill 3.4 — Has/Have and Had Verbs

1. INCORRECT. *Had been* should be *have been.* The speaker is saying that he or she started being allergic in the past and is still allergic.

2. INCORRECT. *Worked* should be *had worked.* Two things happened in the past, and *had worked* happened before *went out of business.* The word *when* does not clarify the order, so we need the past perfect.

3. INCORRECT. This sentence has the same meaning as the sentence in #2, but the two halves of the sentence are presented in the opposite order. This does not change the fact that *worked* should be *had worked.* The placement of *had* before one of the verbs is based on the order in which the events happened in real life, not the order of the sentence.

4. INCORRECT. *Had* should be *had had.* The speaker *had had* a heart attack before the doctor *told* him or her about it. You can test *had had* by substituting another verb; here, *had had* means *had suffered.*

5. INCORRECT. *Just began* should be *had just begun.* Two things happened in the past, and *had just begun* happened before *stabbed.*

Answers to Drill 3.5 — Find the Adverb Errors

1. INCORRECT. *Quick* should be *quickly.* In the corrected sentence, "The new vendor did the job quite quickly," *quickly* would be an adverb modifying the verb *did,* and the adverb *quite* would be modifying *quickly.*

2. CORRECT. The adverbs are *well* and *fast.* Both adverbs modify the verb *do.*

3. CORRECT. The adverbs are *early* and *cheerfully.* *Early* modifies *woke* and *cheerfully* modifies *did.*

4. INCORRECT. *Lively* is an adjective, not an adverb, and is thus incorrect. Since *livelyly* is not a word, a phrase such as *in a lively manner* could be used, or another word (*spiritedly, enthusiastically*) could be substituted.

5. CORRECT. The adverb is *badly*. *Bad* is an adjective correctly modifying the subject *I* and joined with the linking verb *feel*. *Badly* is an adverb modifying *doing*.

Answers to Drill 4.1 — Find the Prepositions

The following words are (or can be) prepositions:

despite	off	before	out	with
since	beside	upon	to	into
during	outside	underneath	in	about

The remaining words in the drill are *not* prepositions:

Or and **and** are conjunctions.   **Some** can be an adjective, pronoun, or adverb.
Slow and **new** are adjectives.   **Now** can be an adverb, noun, or conjunction.
Never is an adverb.   **Go** and **is** are verbs.

Answers to Drill 4.2 — Find the Prepositional Phrases

1. **after a spell, in the sun, in the shade**. The sentence minus its prepositional phrases reads *A spot sounded delightful.*

2. **with asthma, in the parade**. The sentence minus its prepositional phrases reads *Seventy-five people marched.*

3. **in our club, by the rules**. The sentence minus its prepositional phrases reads *To play is crucial.*

4. **for the purpose, of discussing the fiscal management, of the charitable fund, on Monday**. The sentence minus its prepositional phrases reads *The committee, which meets monthly, recommends passing the annual budget.*

5. **with the wolves, on thirty consecutive cold winter mornings, in Minsk, Belarus, in just one month, but cold mountain water, but goat meat, for thirty days, in any, of the former Soviet Republics, in a similarly spartan manner**. The sentence minus its prepositional phrases reads *To run is truly to strengthen your spirit; to drink nothing and eat nothing is to truly strengthen your character.*

Answers to Drill 4.3 — Cross Out the Prepositional Phrases

1. The trolls ~~under the bridge~~ really just want to be understood. **CORRECT.**

2. The statistics ~~from the study~~ reveals that the United States is plagued ~~by poor health~~. **INCORRECT.** *Reveals* should be *reveal*.

3. Each ~~of the spouses of the victims~~ have expressed their wish that a monument be constructed ~~at the crash site~~. **INCORRECT.** *Have* should be *has* to match the singular subject *each*. Also, *their* should be *his or her*.

4. Each ~~of the runners~~ who chose to run this marathon ~~in polyester~~ is experiencing serious chafing. **CORRECT.**

5. I ran ~~over the bridge~~, ~~through the woods~~, and ~~into your arms~~. **CORRECT.** The *and* isn't technically canceled out, but that's okay. It was only there to link the three prepositional phrases together.

Answers to Drill 4.4 — Cross Out More Prepositional Phrases

1. of the newspaper, as a union firebrand. **CORRECT.**

2. of the Parthenon, in the Athenian Acropolis, in 447 B.C. **CORRECT.**

3. of the new international trade agreement, for drugs, over delayed shipments. **INCORRECT.** *Specifies* should be *specify* in order to match the subject *provisions*.

4. in the analysis, of body language, from a one-minute video, of a person's speech, about the person. **CORRECT.**

5. of interest, under Sharia law, in the U.K. and U.S., in modern parlance, as an "Islamic mortgage," to a tenant. **CORRECT.**

Answers to Drill 4.5 — Find the Conjunction Errors

1. CORRECT. The parts following *both/and* are *market conditions* and *improper management*.

2. INCORRECT. *Not only* is followed by the verb *was,* whereas *but also* is followed by the adjective *frivolous.* A correct version could read *The study was not only flawed but also frivolous.*

3. INCORRECT. *Neither* is followed by *a despot* (*despot* is a noun) and *nor* is followed by *oblivious* (an adjective). A correct version could read *neither despotic nor oblivious.*

4. CORRECT. *Ranks* and *trails* are both verbs; the two parts of the sentence match nicely.

5. INCORRECT. *Entertaining* is an adjective and *inspiration* is a noun. A correct version could read *The speaker is both entertaining and inspiring.*

Answers to Drill 4.6 — Find the Dependent Clause

1. **After.** The **second** clause, *the board disagreed sharply over executive bonuses*, is dependent.

2. **While.** The **first** clause, *freshly minted law school graduates greatly exceed the number of top law jobs available*, is dependent.

3. **As if.** The **second** clause, *she had been starved for weeks*, is dependent.

4. **Unless.** The **first** clause, *you get your MBA*, is dependent.

5. **If.** The **second** clause, *you do,* is dependent.

Answers to Mixed Drill 4.7 — Match the Word with the Part of Speech

1.   pronoun (Can also be used as an adjective, as in *Each cell phone should be turned off.*)
2.   adjective (Can also be used as a noun, as in *A Scandinavian came into the store.*)
3.   preposition (Can also be used as an adverb, as in *He drove by.*)
4.   adverb
5.   preposition (Can also be used as an adverb, as in *He went under.*)
6.   conjunction
7.   adjective (or article)
8.   adjective
9.   verb
10.   adverb
11.   preposition
12.   adjective (Can be used as a noun, as in *This is an equivalent to an iPod.*)
13.   pronoun
14.   preposition
15.   conjunction
16.   adjective (or article)
17.   verb (*Wrung* is the past tense of *wring,* as in *He wrung out the wet towel.*)
18.   conjunction (Can also be used as an adverb, as in *She is so tall that she can touch the ceiling.*)
19.   preposition
20.   adverb

7

Answers to Mixed Drill 4.8 — Identify Parts of Speech in Sentences

1. It   may be   true that Notre Dame alumni really care about football, but   it   is
pronoun verb adj   *adj*   *noun adv verb prep noun conj pronoun verb*

    also true that they   care about academics.
    adv adj   *pronoun verb prep noun*

2. Thirty members of the marching band have voted to play Lady Gaga's
adj noun prep adj adj noun verb noun (infinitive)

    "Poker Face" in the parade.
    prep adj noun

3. Russian players often beat the Americans in chess tournaments.
adj noun adv verb adj noun prep adj noun

4. Class attendance and participation are important, but   you   cannot truly learn the
adj noun conj noun verb adj conj pronoun verb adv verb adj

    material without reading primary sources, either in books or on the Internet.
    noun prep adj noun conj prep noun conj prep adj noun

5. The small boy was delighted, for   he   had received a jack-in-the-box for Hanukkah.
adj adj noun verb adj conj pronoun verb adj noun prep noun

Answers to Mixed Drill 4.9 — Identify Certain Kinds of Errors

1. A. *Them* is plural and does not match with *everyone,* which is singular. Fix this sentence by saying, "It seems that everyone has brought loved ones to watch *him or her* graduate," or the less awkward, "It seems that *all of the seniors have* brought loved ones to watch them graduate."

2. A. *A tourist* is singular. So the phrase should be *his or her handbag.*

3. A. *Administration* is singular and does not match *their.* The sentence should say, "has amended *its* requirement." (The second *their* is correct—it refers to *students.*)

4. B. *Myself* should be replaced with the object pronoun *me.* There is no reason here to use the reflexive.

5. Both A & B. The students must decide for *themselves.* The reflexive pronouns *himself* and *herself* were used incorrectly, in that they did not agree with the antecedent (*All students*).

Answers to Mixed Drill 4.10 — Identify Certain Kinds of Errors

1. D. Since the action occurred between 1971 and 1975, it is in the past. The verb should be *earned*.

2. C. The *employees … wants?* The word *employees* is plural and requires the plural verb *want*.

3. B. *One* and *you* cannot be mixed and matched.

4. A. The pronoun *it* seems to mean *Dartmouth*. By itself, *Dartmouth* is a noun, but in this sentence, *Dartmouth* is an adjective modifying *graduates*. Fix the sentence by saying, "*Graduates of Dartmouth* often report years later that they loved it" or "*Dartmouth graduates* often report years later that they loved *their time at the school*." Phrases such as *their time at the school* can be substituted in to avoid the repetitive "Dartmouth graduates often report years later that they loved *Dartmouth*."

5. C. The subject is *The committee that controls the allocation of new funds and the dean*. You can shorten this in your head as *The committee and the dean*. (You could read the sentence to mean that the committee controls the dean, but that's an unlikely reading.) The subject is clearly plural; it requires the plural verb *differ*.

Note: As this book's author was writing the ten incorrect sentences in the previous two drills, Microsoft Word's grammar check only caught 1 out of 10 errors! You cannot depend on computers to fix your writing.

Answers to Drill 5.1 — Find the Subject

1. **Each.** *Of the women* is a prepositional phrase. The subject *each* is performing the verb *said*.

2. **Sliver.** *Of the specimen* is a prepositional phrase. The subject *sliver* is performing the verb *is needed*.

3. **All.** *Of us* is a prepositional phrase. The subject *all* is performing the verb *agree*.

4. **A bank, a nail salon, and a day care center.** *In this shopping plaza* is a prepositional phrase. Omit *there* and put the sentence in a more normal order to make the structure clear: *A bank, a nail salon, and a day care center are in this shopping plaza.*

5. **Kitten.** This sentence is backwards: it begins with a prepositional phrase and puts the subject after the verb. *Amid the weeds and trash* is a prepositional phrase. The verb is *was. Kitten* is performing the verb *was*. Put the sentence back in a more normal order to make the structure clear: *My lost kitten was amid the weeds and trash.*

Answers to Drill 5.2 — Find Fragments and Run-ons

1. FRAGMENT. Remember, words ending in *-ing* aren't verbs unless accompanied by helper verbs (for instance, *is planning* is a compound verb, but *planning, writing,* and *revising* alone are not verbs). This fragment lacks a true verb.

2. COMPLETE SENTENCE. The subject is *That the charge was true.*

3. COMPLETE SENTENCE. *There are only seven of us* and *the twins couldn't make it* are both independent clauses, correctly joined with the conjunction *because.*

4. FRAGMENT. This sentence lacks a main verb. *1944* should be followed by a comma and then the verb that matches with *The decorated war general.*

5. RUN-ON. The two parts of the sentence should be joined with a conjunction (*since, because, as*) or a semicolon.

Answers to Drill 5.3 — Examine the Colon

1. INCORRECT. The first part of the sentence cannot stand alone. The colon should simply be removed.

2. CORRECT. The first part is an independent clause, and the second part is a list of two items.

3. CORRECT. The first part is an independent clause, and the second part is an explanation for the first.

4. CORRECT. The first part is an independent clause, and the second part is an explanation for the first.

5. CORRECT. The first part is an independent clause, and the second part is a "list of one item." Generally, a comma sets off a quote, but it is perfectly common and correct to use a colon when the quote is being used as a list item and the other rules of colons are followed.

Note: Four out of five of the examples above have been deliberately made correct. Students tend to freak out when they see colons that are not before lists of three or more items. Colons are much more versatile than most people think!

For example, you may have also noticed colons used throughout this book, such as after the words "CORRECT" and "INCORRECT" in the indented examples. Colons also traditionally follow greetings (*To Whom It May Concern:*) in business letters. While these uses are common in real life, they are not of concern to us for purposes of the GMAT.

Answers to Drill 5.4 — Correct the Punctuation Errors

1. INCORRECT. Do not use a semicolon before "but." A comma would be correct here instead.

2. CORRECT. Although "we left" is very short, it has a subject and verb; both sides are independent clauses.

3. CORRECT. Both sides of the sentence are independent clauses.

4. INCORRECT. The first part of the sentence is a *dependent* clause. *Although he won the election by a landslide* cannot stand alone. The sentence could be fixed by removing the word *although* OR by replacing the semicolon with a comma (but not both).

5. CORRECT. Both sides of the sentence are independent clauses.

Answers to Drill 5.5 — Correct More Punctuation Errors

1. EITHER. Both parts of the sentence are independent clauses, so a semicolon is fine. The second part is a plausible explanation for the first, thus making a colon fine as well.

2. SEMICOLON. Both parts of the sentence are independent clauses, but the second part is not an explanation, rule, or example; in fact, it is in opposition to the first part.

3. NOTHING. No punctuation is needed here, and adding any would make the sentence wrong.

4. COLON. The first part can stand alone, but not the second. The second part is a "list of one thing."

5. SEMICOLON. Both parts of the sentence are independent clauses, but the second part is not an explanation, rule, or example. In fact, it seems as though the *first* part is an explanation for the *second* part.

Answers to Drill 6.1 — Find the Modifier Errors

1. INCORRECT. An agreement is not a place, so *where* cannot be used.

2. CORRECT. Who is *running the final mile of the marathon*? The answer, *Jeff*, is correctly placed directly after the comma.

3. CORRECT. While this sentence might sound a bit strange, it is fine. The first part is NOT a warmup because it actually answers its own question—*who* managed to eat 75 hot dogs? Balaji. Therefore, there is no requirement that any special word go directly after the comma.

4. INCORRECT. A haircut is not a time, so *when* cannot be used. *X is when...* is generally a poor way to write any definition.

5. INCORRECT. *Once rivaling the Great Pyramids* is a warmup that raises a question—*what* was once rivaling the Great Pyramids? The answer to that question is *the Colossus of Rhodes*, which needs to come directly after the comma. Right now, the sentence is illogically saying that the earthquake once rivaled the Great Pyramids.

Answers to Drill 6.2 — Find the Parallelism/Comparison Errors

1. INCORRECT. New York City's *population* is being compared to *Montana, Wyoming, Vermont, North Dakota, South Dakota, Delaware, and Rhode Island all added together* (if you add all those states together, the answer is seven—seven states, that is, which is clearly not the point of this sentence). Corrected version: *New York City's population is greater than THOSE OF Montana, Wyoming, Vermont, North Dakota, South Dakota, Delaware, and Rhode Island all added together.*

2. INCORRECT. *Parklands* is being compared to *maintaining* busy city streets. Corrected version: *...some parklands actually cost more to maintain than do busy city streets.* OR, *...the maintenance of some parklands actually costs more than that of busy city streets.*

3. CORRECT. The people *revolted*, and later they scarcely *made* a sound (*revolted* and *made* are both past tense verbs). The leader was *found fixing election results* and later was *discovered siphoning campaign funds*. These two actions match both grammatically and logically.

4. CORRECT. Parenthood is an important milestone in life for young people, much as *it* was for their own progenitors. The *it* stands for parenthood and the comparison is both grammatical and logical.

5. INCORRECT. *Shakespeare's plays* are being compared to *any American writer*. Do not compare plays to people! Corrected version: *...Shakespeare's plays are still taught in schools more frequently and deeply than are the works of any American writer.*

Note that #5 in this drill was very much like the example about Johannes Kepler and Tycho Brahe from earlier in the section. Whenever two people and their creative work are being compared, watch out for this error!

Answers to Drill 7.1 — Find the Idioms Errors

1. **Ability of doing** and **off of** are wrong. Corrected sentence: *Although I can do* (or *am able to do*, or *have the ability to do*) *gymnastics well, this time I fell off the balance beam.*

2. **Reason ... because** is wrong. Corrected sentence: *The ostensible reason for Anne Boleyn's execution was adultery....*

3. **Like, there is an expectation of her being appointed,** and **appointed as** are wrong. Corrected sentence: *Because she has deep relationships with the unions as other leaders have, it is expected that she will be appointed chairperson.*

4. **Indicates** ought to be followed by **that**, and **considered as** is wrong. Corrected sentence: *The study indicates that more men are working in education, traditionally considered a "female" profession.*

5. **Is likely that it will** is wrong. Corrected sentence: *The company is likely to gain market share.*

Answers to Drill 7.2

1. INCORRECT. The sentence should read *I suggested that he study....*

2. CORRECT. The core sentence follows the pattern: *The president asks that everyone vacate.*

3. CORRECT. The core sentence follows the pattern: *The CEO demanded that everyone be, dress, and follow.*

4. CORRECT. The verb *hope* isn't very bossy (it doesn't demand the subjunctive), but this sentence still follows the correct pattern: *We hope that you will be available.*

MANHATTAN
GMAT

5. INCORRECT. Just as you should not insert *should* into a command subjunctive sentence, do not insert *ought to* or any other phrase that means *should*. The idea of *should* is already included in the subjunctive pattern itself. The sentence should read *The board suggests that our budget be revised.*

Answers to Drill 7.3

1. **(D)**

Issues tested: Parallelism, Verb Tense

Avgolemono is a soup or sauce made by MIXING and HEATING. "Mixing" and "heating" are two steps in the same process and must be in the same format. Eliminate answers (A) and (B).

Choice (C) incorrectly changes to a future tense, and choice (E) incorrectly changes to the past perfect.

In general, when we want to describe a general process (an if/then situation that is true regardless of the time period, such as *To achieve X, do Y*, or *When it rains, my roof leaks*), use the present tense. The answer is (D).

2. **(E)**

Issues tested: Parallelism, Idioms

Soldier ants serve many roles FROM serving TO sounding.

The pattern from X to Y is correct and cannot be replaced with from X and Y, so eliminate (A), (B), and (C).

Finally, the ants are doing two things that must be parallel: serving and sounding. The answer is (E).

3. **(A)**

Issues tested: Idioms, Meaning

Choice (A) is correct as written. "That the consumer products division lacks credible leadership" is the subject of the sentence. The subject is performing the action *cannot be blamed*. This is a complete sentence.

In choice (B), *has a lack in* is not a correct idiom (we *lack* something, have *a lack of* something, or *are lacking in* something).

Choice (C) incorrectly eliminates the word "that" at the beginning of the sentence, which is both grammatically incorrect and makes the meaning unclear. (Read choice (C)—*what* cannot be blamed?)

Choices (D) and (E) change the meaning entirely. Choice (D) says that *the lack* is not *blaming*. Blaming whom?

Choice (E) says that the lack itself is not blameworthy—that is, the original sentence says that the lack of credible leadership (which sounds bad) isn't responsible for the company's troubles, but choice (E) says it's totally okay that the consumer products division has terrible leadership!

Do not change the meaning of a GMAT sentence unless the original sentence did not make sense. The answer is (A).

4. **(C)**

Issues tested: Verb tense, Pronouns, Meaning

Are finding is the correct verb tense to describe something that is happening continuously in the present. (While it make take an individual small business only a moment to "find" that it can save money, different small businesses are finding this out all the time.) Eliminate (D) and (E).

Note that (D) and (E) also have other errors. In (D), "by the use of" is not a correct idiom, and in (E), "founded" is actually a completely different verb—"founded" is the past tense of *found*, meaning *to establish* (She *founded* a new club at school).

Choice (A) incorrectly refers to *small businesses* as *it*, whereas (B) and (C) correctly use *they*. Eliminate (A). (Note that a single *small business* would indeed be singular and take the pronoun *it*, but multiple *small businesses* are plural and take the pronoun *they*.)

(B) has two problems—*associating* should be *associated*, and the comma before *using* does not express the causal relationship. That is, (B) does not make it clear that people are avoiding fees BY using Internet-based services.

(C) corrects these problems—fees *associated with* is the correct idiom, and the use of *by* correctly expresses exactly *how* small businesses are avoiding fees. The answer is (C).

5. **(E)**

Issues tested: Modifiers, Verb Tense, Subjunctive Mood

Note that the introductory modifier *Confounded by the seemingly contradictory data* does not have a subject. *Who is confounded?* You must answer this question by placing directly after the comma the word or phrase for whoever was confounded. In this case, that is *the scientist*. Kill (A) and (B).

Among (C), (D), and (E), only choice (D) inserts the word *had*. This creates a verb tense error. Remember, only use a *had* verb to express the "double past"—that is, to indicate action that is in the past of other action in the sentence that is also in the past (*I HAD BEEN WORKING there for ten years by the time I WAS promoted*). You need only the simple past here. Kill (D).

Between (C) and (E), the deciding issue is the Command Subjunctive. The correct pattern is *I demand THAT you DO something*. In other words, the scientist *suggested THAT his graduate students RE-RUN the experiment*. (C) is missing the necessary word *that* and inserts the incorrect word *to*.

(E), however, matches the subjunctive pattern perfectly. The answer is (E).

6. **(B)**

Issues tested: Subject–Verb Agreement

This type of sentence is confusing to some people because at one point in the sentence the *team* is referred to as a group and at another point in the sentence *each member* of the team is referred to. There is nothing wrong with this. Just make sure that the verb for *team* is singular and makes logical sense, and that the verb for *each member* is also singular and makes logical sense.

Mentally eliminate the part within the dashes to see the core sentence: *The team remain stymied.* Because *team* is singular, you need the singular verb *remains*. Eliminate (A) and (C).

Now go back to the part within the dashes. *Each member* is singular, so you need *was*, not *were*. Eliminate (D).

Notice that choice (E) completely changes the meaning and is therefore wrong. Each member *was asked* to submit three ideas—that is, someone else asked each member to do something. Choice (E) says that each member *asked* to submit ideas.

The answer is (B).

7. **(C)**

Issues tested: Sentence Fragments, Meaning

The original sentence is incorrect because it does not contain a main verb. It is a sentence fragment (much like *Hemingway, a writer* or *The cantaloupe, a popular melon in the United States*). Our main subject *peanut* needs a verb. Since (A) and (E) do not contain any verbs, eliminate those choices.

(B) changes the meaning. *A legume was probably cultivated?* What legume? The sentence seems to imply that all legumes are peanuts (or you can just say that the sentence makes no sense at all).

(D) also changes the meaning by misplacing the word *probably*. You want to say that peanuts are definitely a legume and that they were *probably* first cultivated in Peru a long time ago. (D) says that peanuts are *probably* a legume.

The answer is (C).

8. **(D):**

Issues tested: Sentence Fragments, Subject–Verb Agreement, Modifiers

Choices (A) and (B) are sentence fragments—the main subject, *The Paris Commune*, lacks a verb.

The Paris Commune is definitely singular, so kill choice (C). You need the singular verb *was*.

Choice (E) incorrectly places the modifier *in 1871* next to *government*; it should instead be modifying *two months*. Also, choice (D)'s *a government that ruled France* is very clear, whereas *a French government in 1871 that ruled* leaves open the question, What did they rule? (French governments have certainly ruled things outside of France.)

The answer is (D).

9. **(A)**

Issues tested: Idioms

The first "split" in the choices is between *mistook, were mistaken,* and *mistaked*. Most obviously, *mistaked* is not a word. Kill (E).

People certainly can *be mistaken about* something, but *were mistaken of* in choice (D) is not a correct idiom, so kill (D) as well.

Finally, the correct preposition for the verb *mistake* or *mistook* is *for* (as in, *I mistook you for the actor Tony Leung!*).

The answer is (A).

10. **(D)**

Issues tested: Verb Tense, Pronouns

The first "split" in the answer choices is whether you need *had had* or just *had*. Remember, you put a *had* before a verb when that verb is in the past of other action in the sentence that is also in the past. And it certainly is possible to say *had had*—if the original verb in the sentence was had, but that action happens before other action in the past, had will need another had before it. Check to see if that's the case here.

What really happened in this story? The guests *had* plenty of time. And then the rebels *broke* into the castle. Certainly *had plenty of time* is the earlier action and *broke into the castle* is the later action. Both actions are in the past, and the time order is certainly important (time order is always important when one action interrupts the previous action). Thus, the first verb needs a *had*, so *had had* is correct.

The answer must therefore be (A) or (D). The only difference between the two choices is *they* in (A) versus the *guests* in (D). What is the antecedent of the pronoun *they*? It's the guests, right? Oh wait—the pronoun *they* is also suspiciously close to the rebels, which is also plural. The pronoun is ambiguous. Kill choice (A).

The answer is (D).

Chapter 8

of

Foundations of GMAT Verbal
Part 2: *Critical Reasoning*

Arguments & Conclusions

In This Chapter...

Chapter 8:
Arguments & Conclusions

Have you ever witnessed or even taken part in the following kind of discussion?

Person A	Person B
– Makes a statement of some kind.	
	– Says something that doesn't address what Person A just said.
– Responds with a random thought that popped into his head.	
	– Confidently states an opinion as if it were a fact.
– Talks in circles, leaving his true position unspoken.	
	– Makes a mistaken assumption about what Person A wants.
– Can't articulate what he really thinks.	
– Winds up frustrated.	– Winds up frustrated.

This sort of exchange is typical. In real life, people are generally bad at arguing.

Even folks who try to be fair-minded can be fuzzy in their thinking. For instance, people will hear both sides of an issue and then say, "Well, I need more information to decide." But they can't tell you what information they need. They can't identify specific flaws in the chains of logic they've heard, so they have no idea how to fix those flaws.

It doesn't have to be this way! GMAT Critical Reasoning questions force you to really understand **arguments**. In the context of the GMAT, the word *argument* doesn't usually mean "a verbal scuffle or debate" (*I had an argument with my significant other last night*). Rather, it means **"a set of logically connected statements that put forth an assertion of some kind"** (*She made the argument that we should replace the refrigerator*).

You "have" the first kind of argument, which is the verbal scuffle. In contrast, you "make" the second kind of argument, which is a case for some position.

As you study GMAT arguments—as you delve into their structure, their purpose, their flaws, and possible cures for those flaws—you will start to come across similar arguments all around you.

Most arguments on the GMAT are flawed in some fashion. So are most arguments in the real world.

Be warned: Once your eyes are opened, there's no going back to blind acceptance of the self-serving arguments of some salesperson or politician. But that's not a bad thing, right?

In short, improving on Critical Reasoning will make you better at **critical reasoning** in general. That's a pretty useful side effect of your preparation for the GMAT.

A Critical Reasoning problem looks something like this:

> Ostrich meat, which is low in fat and cholesterol, is becoming popular in the United States among dieters and those concerned with health. However, ostriches are an endangered species. If the popularity of ostrich meat continues to grow at the present rate, ostriches will inevitably become extinct.
>
> Which of the following, if true, most seriously weakens the argument above?
>
> (A)   Ostrich meat is not any healthier than lean beef, which is available everywhere and less expensive.
> (B)   Ostrich meat is considered by many to be a gourmet food, suitable only for special occasions.
> (C)   Concerns about avian flu, although spurious, have caused many consumers to avoid ostrich meat.
> (D)   An increased demand for ostrich meat will lead to increased ostrich farming, thus increasing the number of ostriches.
> (E)   Ostriches are killed more frequently for their feathers and for the making of leather than they are for meat.

The initial paragraph (*Ostrich meat... ostriches will inevitably become extinct*) is the **argument** itself.

The specific question you're asked (*Which of the following, if true, most seriously weakens the argument above?*) is called the **question stem**.

The rest of the problem consists of five answer choices. You have to pick the best one, of course.

As with all GMAT problem types, the problems are displayed on a computer, requiring you to take notes or do other scratchwork on paper (when you're practicing) or on an erasable noteboard (on the real exam). Because the Verbal part of the exam consists of 41 problems in 75 minutes, you should aim for a little under 2 minutes per problem.

Notice that the question stem contains the phrase *if true*. What an interesting little bit of verbiage!

Questions involving *if true* can cause us to perform a bit of mental gymnastics. You may have to suspend judgment as to whether something is really true, and consider what the consequences would be if it *were* true.

In real life, you rarely throw *if true* into your debates. It would not be wise to initiate a conversation with one's spouse by asking, "Which of the following, if true, would cause you to divorce me?"

In GMAT Critical Reasoning, on the other hand, an argument can be based on strange-sounding or unproven claims, but still have a conclusion that follows logically from those claims.

By the way, what do you think the answer is to the problem at the top of the page? Read on when you're ready.

According to the argument, ostriches will *inevitably* become extinct if demand for ostrich meat continues to rise the same way. Won't free enterprise kick in, though? Won't some entrepreneurial types try to breed these very valuable animals and make serious money from these flightless golden geese? The possibility of increasing supply undermines the claim that ostriches will definitely disappear under the given conditions. The correct answer is (D).

Valid Arguments versus Sound Arguments

Every complete argument has two components written down on paper:

- **Premises**—supporting statements

- **Conclusion**—the main point or biggest claim of the argument

A **sound argument** is successful on every level: the premises are true, and the conclusion logically follows from the premises. When a conclusion follows logically from true premises, that conclusion is therefore true.

A **valid argument** is one in which the conclusion follows logically from the premises—but the premises may or may not be true. In a valid argument, *if* the premises are true, *then* the conclusion will also be true.

On the GMAT, many arguments deal with made-up countries or mention outside facts that you don't have the ability to evaluate the truth of. So, while soundness is the goal in real-life reasoning, GMAT questions tend to be more about validity.

Every sound argument is valid. But an argument can be valid but not sound. That is, it can have a good structure while being based on false statements. This can take some getting used to. For instance:

8

Premise: Circles have four sides.

Obviously, this premise is completely false. It cannot be part of a sound argument, but it might be part of a valid one. Let's continue.

Premise: All four-sided things taste like cinnamon.

Oh, come on! That's just ridiculous.

Conclusion: Therefore, circles taste like cinnamon.

This argument looks like nonsense. However, you cannot deny that IF circles had four sides and IF four-sided things tasted like cinnamon, then indeed, circles would taste like cinnamon. The argument is quite silly in the real world, but it is valid.

On the GMAT, **avoid challenging the truth of the premises themselves.** You are not meant to evaluate whether circles really have four sides, or whether all four-sided things taste like cinnamon, as you would in a real-life debate. Rather, you should focus on whether the premises *as given* join together to establish the conclusion definitively. That is, **focus on whether the argument is valid.**

The circle-cinnamon argument follows a pattern that always makes valid arguments:

A = B	Circles = four-sided
B = C	Four-sided = cinnamon taste
Therefore, A = C	Therefore, circles = cinnamon taste

This pattern should look familiar—from math! It is the **transitive property**.

Logic has much in common with math and the sciences. In fact, some universities teach courses on logic that are shared between the philosophy and the computer science departments. (This is not suggesting that the phil and comp sci majors actually hang out afterwards or anything.)

If you develop the skill of finding the underlying structure of arguments, you can make arguments more like math problems. Math problems have definite answers; they are very concrete. GMAT Critical Reasoning problems are more concrete than you may think.

Consider this crazy argument. What would be needed to make it valid?

Squares are blue. Therefore, squares explode within seven days.

If you match to the pattern on the previous page, you can see that you have A = B and A = C, so you must be missing B = C. The missing premise is this: *Everything blue explodes within seven days.*

The Structure of Arguments

In a good, valid argument, the premises lead to the conclusion in a direct way. They provide enough evidence to guarantee the truth of the conclusion (which is occasionally implied rather than stated explicitly).

Look at an example:

> To be considered a form of cardiovascular exercise, an activity must raise the heart rate and keep it elevated for at least 20 minutes. Skydiving cannot properly be considered a form of cardiovascular exercise. While skydiving certainly does elevate a person's heart rate, the skydiver only experiences freefall for 60–70 seconds, followed by 5–6 minutes under a parachute—and, of course, it is not possible to string multiple dives back-to-back.

What is the conclusion of this argument? Is it the last statement, *it is not possible to string multiple dives back-to-back?* That doesn't really seem like the main point, of course, and conclusions are rarely preceded by *of course*, which is a wink from the author: "We both know this is true, right?"

Sometimes, the conclusion is hiding in the middle. In the paragraph above, it is doing just that:

> Skydiving cannot properly be considered a form of cardiovascular exercise.

Everything else consists of the premises. By the way, you might have noticed that this argument isn't airtight. The author assumes that the elevated heart rate doesn't persist past the jump itself. Who knows, your heart might beat faster for hours after you land. So the premises as given don't guarantee the conclusion.

For now, just try to restate the argument more simply and in a better order, building from premises to conclusion:

8

Cardio exercise has 2 requirements:
    1. high heart rate
    2. rate stays high over a period of time

Skydiving meets first requirement but not second.

Therefore, skydiving isn't cardio.

The conclusion of an argument should be the speaker's main point. Some other clues are these:

- The conclusion should be the *biggest* claim—the statement that needs the most proof.

- You can think of the conclusion as coming last in a *chain* of ordered statements such as the one above about skydiving. Every statement must link to the next, and the chain ends with the conclusion.

Drill 8.1 — Find the Conclusion

Locate the conclusion in each of the arguments. In the first four, you will be able to simply *underline* the conclusion. For the last argument, you will have to rephrase the conclusion yourself.

Underline the conclusion:

1. Quoting sources in your papers without attributing the quotes to those sources is forbidden on this campus. Plagiarism is strictly forbidden by our code of conduct, and quoting without attribution is a form of plagiarism.

2. The difference between a weed and a garden plant depends entirely on the opinion of the person who owns the land. Thus, it is impossible to develop a flawless garden "weed-killer" that kills all types of weeds and leaves all types of garden plants un-harmed. The Vytex Company's attempt to develop a perfect garden weed-killer will fail.

3. An anti-smoking policy would cause a loss of revenue to our town's bars. Since we are a small town, smokers would likely just drive an extra couple of miles to bars in any of the neighboring towns, none of which have anti-smoking policies.

4. The city parks are overcrowded, leading to long wait times for athletic fields and courts and lessening citizens' enjoyment of the parks. A new park should be built at the southern tip of the city, which does not have its own park. Because the heavily populated south of the city lacks a park, residents regularly travel to other parts of the city to use those parks, thus leading to overcrowding.

Rephrase the conclusion on the lines below:

5.   Some say that Saddlebrook College provides the best value in our state. Yet, this simply isn't true: students at our state's Tunbridge College pay less, enjoy newer buildings and smaller class sizes, and make more after graduation.

Conclusion: _____

_____

Answers can be found on page 233.

Grade Yourself

How did you do in this section?

- ☐ **A** - I totally get this!
- ☐ **B** - I'm okay with this. Maybe review later if there's time.
- ☐ **C** - I'll make a note to review this later.

Getting Rid of Extras

Some arguments contain background information, definitions, etc. that help you understand the content of the premises better. For purposes of argument structure, this background information isn't really part of the argument.

Some arguments also contain irrelevant information, snarky comments, or repetitive language. You will want to put aside all this extra information to boil the argument down to its real premises and conclusion.

Here is a lengthy example:

> One of our company's investors has accused the company president of financial impropriety. The company president did make a $50,000 payment to his son, allowing the son to close on a house in Brookhurst, a wealthy and respectable part of town. It is doubtful that the investor was really seeking the facts when he supposedly investigated the matter, but let it be known that the president's son has long been a consultant to the company, providing over $150,000 per year in services. The $50,000 was an advance on future billings, and well within established company practice: in the last year, the company provided a similar advance to a supplier seeking to upgrade to a larger production facility.

8

Wow, that was long! There is clearly some unnecessary background information (it hardly matters that Brookhurst is a nice place to live, or even what the son spent the money on—even if he used it to take orphans to Disneyworld, that wouldn't change whether his father had committed financial impropriety). The speaker also issues an insult to the investor: *It is doubtful that the investor was really seeking the facts when he supposedly investigated the matter.* This is a personal attack that can be disregarded.

Try this simpler version:

> *Company president paid $50,000 to son.*
>
> *Investor's conclusion: company president guilty of impropriety.*
>
> *BUT*
>
> *$50,000 was an advance to a contractor, and such advances are normal.*
>
> *THEREFORE…*

Notice that the speaker did not explicitly state a conclusion. What do you think the logical conclusion is? Since the speaker is arguing against the investor, the investor's conclusion is a valuable clue.

In fact, the speaker's conclusion is the opposite of the investor's:

> *The company president is **not** guilty of financial impropriety.*

You should not stretch as you articulate an implied conclusion. Draw from the text you're given, and don't go too far. Avoid making the conclusion any more assertive or extreme than is justified by the premises.

The following will help you practice stating a speaker's implied conclusion.

Drill 8.2 — State the Implied Conclusion

Each of the arguments below strongly hints at a conclusion, but doesn't state it explicitly. Write the argument's implied conclusion on the line below.

Remember, don't make a conclusion any "bigger" than it has to be. For instance, consider the argument: *Some people think Jack Jones is the best in the world at fencing, but there are two lesser-known competitors from Asia whose records are superior to his.* The implied conclusion is simply that Jack Jones is *not* the best—not that he's actually bad at fencing!

1. Any college that has produced more than ten Rhodes Scholars throughout its history is a good college. Van Hoyt College has produced at least one Rhodes Scholar per year for the past decade. Therefore:

    _____

2. The female arkbird will lay eggs only when a suitable quantity of nesting material is available, and the climate is suitably moderate. This winter is the coldest on record, but the temperature change has actually increased the amount of nesting material as trees and plants die, shedding twigs and leaves. All the same, although nesting material is abundant:

    _____

3. John Doe pleaded not guilty to the charge of second-degree murder, but was convicted after a video of his brutal crime was revealed. In the state in which he was convicted, however, the only crime punishable by the death penalty is first-degree murder. Therefore:

    _____

4. Some doctors have been performing extreme body modification procedures—such as creating a snakelike forking by surgically cutting the tongue down the middle— solely for cosmetic or lifestyle reasons. Harming a healthy body part is against the Hippocratic Oath, which doctors have sworn to uphold. Therefore:

    _____

5. The school board has responded to the new school lunch guidelines by replacing French fried potatoes with fruit in a standard meal option that includes a beef hamburger and milk as well. However, the guidelines specifically require that vegetables, not fruits, be included in every meal option. Therefore:

    _____

Answers can be found on page 233.

> ### Grade Yourself
>
> How did you do in this section?
>
> - ☐ **A** - I totally get this!
> - ☐ **B** - I'm okay with this. Maybe review later if there's time.
> - ☐ **C** - I'll make a note to review this later.

8

Chapter 9
of
Foundations of GMAT Verbal

Patterns & Flaws

In This Chapter...

Chapter 9:

Patterns & Flaws

How GMAT Critical Reasoning Is Unlike Real-World Decision Making

Many students make errors in Critical Reasoning when they confuse *real-life concerns* with *the argument actually being made.* Take this argument from the drill:

> The school board has responded to the new school lunch guidelines by replacing French fried potatoes with fruit in a standard meal option that includes a beef hamburger and milk as well. However, the guidelines specifically require that vegetables, not fruits, be included in every meal option. Therefore, the school board is not following the new school lunch guidelines.

In real life, you might say, "Who cares? The kids are eating fruit—that's just as good." Or maybe, "It's the parents' job to feed the kids vegetables—let them eat whatever they want at school." Or, more practically, "Kids like fruit more than they like vegetables, so fruit is a smart choice because the kids will be more likely to actually eat it."

All of these are fine points—in real life. If you were a parent of a child affected by this policy, you might reasonably mention these considerations at a school board meeting.

But the argument's conclusion doesn't say, "The new school lunch is unhealthy" or "Vegetables are best in school lunches." It says, "The school board is not following the new school lunch guidelines." That is 100%, undeniably true.

Maybe the guidelines are stupid, but the conclusion is correct: the school board is not following the guidelines.

Stick to the argument presented. Many considerations in real-life decision making often simply do not affect whether an argument's premises support its conclusion. Again, **focus on validity**.

Consider another example:

> Our company currently spends millions of dollars disposing of industrial waste. Since our shareholders are demanding that expenses be slashed by the end of the year, I propose that we dump the waste in rivers instead. The waste is highly toxic, although healthy adults can survive repeated exposure to it. The cost of bribing government officials to cover up the dumping will be more than outweighed by the cost savings. Therefore, illegally dumping toxic waste in rivers will provide the short-term cost savings demanded by our shareholders.

Whoa! This argument is morally horrifying! Did you notice the part about how "healthy adults" can survive the toxic waste? That strongly implies that children will die. (And even people who "survive" can suffer serious health consequences.) Surely this toxic waste will also kill fish and cause environmental damage all up and down the path of the river. Moreover, the person proposing this plan can (and should) go to prison! If your boss made these statements to you, you should be worried that you could be implicated in a crime.

All of that is true—and all of that is irrelevant to whether the argument supports its own conclusion.

Note that the conclusion is very modest: *illegally dumping toxic waste will provide the short-term cost savings.* Yes, it probably will.

None of the very real moral objections to this argument logically weaken its conclusion. To undermine this fairly well-supported conclusion, you would have to attack a "gap" between the plan and short-term savings. Consider a GMAT-like question using the same argument, with three answer choices:

> Our company currently spends millions of dollars disposing of industrial waste. Since our shareholders are demanding that expenses be slashed by the end of the year, I propose that we dump the waste in rivers instead. The waste is highly toxic, although healthy adults can survive repeated exposure to it. The cost of bribing government officials to cover up the dumping will be more than outweighed by the cost savings. Therefore, illegally dumping toxic waste in rivers will provide the short-term cost savings demanded by our shareholders.

Which of the following most weakens the argument?

(A) Executives convicted of bribing government officials are receiving much harsher sentences than have white-collar criminals in the past.

(B) An environmental group tests the river water daily and is prepared to notify the media immediately if it identifies any industrial contaminants.

(C) A former competitor, Chemical West, was forced into bankruptcy after a similar dumping scheme was eventually exposed.

Note that choices (A) and (C) are about bad consequences of the illegal dumping plan: harsh criminal sentences and "eventual" bankruptcy. These things don't affect whether the plan would result in *short-term cost savings*. Choices (A) and (C) are off-topic. However, answer choice (B) directly contradicts the idea that it's possible to cover up the dumping with bribes—if the dumping would *immediately* be exposed, then it is very unlikely that even a short-term profit could be achieved. The answer is (B).

Real GMAT arguments rarely involve issues of morality to this extent, but they do drag in real-life, off-topic considerations to try to distract you. If someone proposes a plan to save money, it's normal for others to say, "But these other bad things will happen." People's brains are designed to make connections and to go beyond the arguer's conclusion.

On the GMAT, however, you should **note the speaker's conclusion precisely**. You are asked to evaluate the argument in front of you—not whether the plan or idea is good or bad in general. The conclusion often contains a very specific goal or measurement of success (e.g., *short-term cost savings*). Never lose sight of that goal.

Grade Yourself

How did you do in this section?

- ☐ **A** - I totally get this!
- ☐ **B** - I'm okay with this. Maybe review later if there's time.
- ☐ **C** - I'll make a note to review this later.

Identifying Patterns in Arguments

You don't need to be a philosopher or a logician to do well on the GMAT. But you should get some exposure to **the study of logic**. This is rocket science for the mind, and it's been around for centuries.

Don't worry—formal logic terms are not used on the GMAT. But most mistakes in logic have been made many times before. Many of the logical mistakes, or fallacies, that are made on the GMAT are the same ones that Aristotle (the founder of the study of logic) complained about over 2,000 years ago!

In fact, you will see the same argument, or the same mistake, over and over again. It will just be dressed up in different clothes. In other words, these mistakes fall into certain recognizable **patterns**. For instance:

> EXAMPLE 1: People who eat diets rich in tropical fruits rate higher in surveys of happiness. Therefore, a diet rich in tropical fruit is a cause of happiness.

EXAMPLE 2: Company X implemented a new time-tracking system and profits went up 10%. Therefore, the time-tracking system has caused the company to profit.

Initially, it may seem as though these arguments are about totally different things—tropical fruit and time tracking. However, the arguments share a common pattern:

PATTERN: Two things happened at roughly the same time. Therefore, one of them caused the other one.

When put that way, it sounds a bit ridiculous, doesn't it?

Using this pattern, you could also say:

EXAMPLE 3: I have a runny nose and a stomachache. Therefore, the runny nose caused the stomachache.

EXAMPLE 4: All of the cancer patients in our hospital drank soda. Therefore, soda causes cancer.

EXAMPLE 5: People who eat more ice cream have more heart attacks. Therefore, a genetic predisposition to heart attacks causes a love of ice cream.

These examples are getting absurd. But *why* are they so absurd, and how can you recognize this mistake when the examples are dressed up in boring, respectable clothes (like the example about time tracking)?

You can break this down a little more. In the given examples, the premise indicates that two things often occur together. In fancier language, you can say that the two things are **correlated**. In even fancier language, there is a **correlation** between X and Y, the two phenomena under consideration. By the way, you will learn much more about correlation in business school. (This is a GMAT subject that actually *correlates* with the curriculum of business school. Get it?)

The argument concludes that X causes Y. This causation *could* be true. That is, it is possible that tropical fruit causes happiness, or soda causes cancer. But the arguer has not given us enough reason to believe that this is the case. **Correlation does *not* guarantee causation.**

Lots can go wrong in between "X and Y happen at the same time" and "X causes Y." For instance:

Maybe the causality runs in reverse. That is, Y might be the cause of X. This certainly seems probable in the case of ice cream and heart attacks. In reality, it is more likely that eating ice cream contributes to heart attacks than the other way around.

Maybe both things are caused by a separate, outside cause. In other words, maybe Z causes both X and Y. This is probably the case with the runny nose and the stomachache. It is very likely that neither the runny nose nor the stomachache is causing the other, but rather that an outside influence—influenza, for instance—is causing both symptoms. Likewise, people who eat a lot of tropical fruit probably live in tropical climates. The weather or the culture of such places might lead both to happiness and to consumption of tropical fruit.

Maybe it's all just a coincidence. X and Y just happen to occur together in the chosen sample. This is probably the case with the soda and the cancer patients. Almost everybody drinks soda. Some people get cancer. Maybe it doesn't mean anything at all, as in the argument, "Murderers breathe air. Therefore, air causes murder." Ridiculous, right? The case of the time-tracking software and the increase in profits—while less ridiculous sounding—may also be a case of a mere coincidence. Perhaps many changes occurred in the company around the same time, or perhaps the fluctuation in profits was simply due to the holiday shopping season, etc.

While this logical flaw may seem transparent (at least after reading the above), it occurs all the time in real life, especially in pop-cultural articles about health and medicine. "A study of villagers in a remote corner of the Amazon jungle has shown a high consumption of Brazil nuts and a low rate of Alzheimer's. Therefore, we should all eat Brazil nuts." This correlation, while perhaps providing an opening for further study, by itself doesn't prove that Brazil nuts actually lower the rate of Alzheimer's.

Satirist Bobby Henderson, poking fun at the argument made by some folks that bad things in the world correlate with a lack of respect towards some particular deity, once pointed out that "global warming, earthquakes, hurricanes, and other natural disasters are a direct effect of the shrinking numbers of pirates since the 1800s." He even presented a graph showing a steady inverse relationship between a decrease in pirates and an increase in global warming. Obviously, if two things happen at the same time, they must be related, right?

Fortunately, as a GMAT test-taker, you don't have to try to figure out what the real story is. It's the job of the arguer to prove his or her case to *you* by building a sound argument backed by appropriate evidence. Your job is simply to recognize flaws and omissions.

Not all logical flaws on the GMAT are about causality. This is just one fallacy of many. Soon, you'll learn about other types of flaws.

First, practice recognizing the same argument in different clothes.

9

Drill 9.1 — Match Analogous Arguments

Six arguments are presented below. Not all arguments are complete—some lack conclusions.

Match each argument with a partner—that is, an argument that uses the same pattern or shares the same problem. You should wind up with three pairs of arguments.

1. **Running Study:** A study was conducted to research the effects of running for exercise. Volunteers ran 5 miles per day, six days a week, for three months. At the end of the study, volunteers were shown to have a much lower rate of nearly all illnesses than is present in the general population. Thus, the researchers recommend that everyone begin daily 5-mile runs.

2. **Freight Trains:** In a survey of working freight trains, a recent study found that engines built before 1960 had better tolerances and higher-grade steel than engines built since 1960. Therefore, freight train engines were constructed according to higher quality standards before 1960 than afterward.

3. **New Product:** To make a profit this quarter, we must increase sales of our old product while also introducing a new product that is as profitable as the old one. Whenever our company introduces a new product, sales of the old product drop sharply.

4. **Heart Murmurs:** At our veterinary clinic, we see more potentially fatal heart murmurs in puppies than in dogs over fifteen years old. Thus, we believe that the diet and care given to dogs must have declined over the last fifteen years.

5. **Peacekeeping Force:** For the violence in Kirkenberg to be stopped, the majority of surrounding nations must vote to send in a peacekeeping force, and the wealthy nation of Nandia must provide funding. If Nandia becomes involved in any way regarding Kirkenberg, at least half of the nations surrounding Kirkenberg will vote against intervening in Kirkenberg.

6. **Diversity Training:** Company G offered an optional diversity training at five of its fifteen job sites, and over 100 employees signed up. At the end of the four-week program, the participants in the diversity training rated much higher than coworkers who didn't participate in the training on a test of sensitivity and multicultural knowledge. Therefore, the training was effective, and the company should extend the training to its remaining job sites.

The pairs are: ____ & ____, ____ & ____, and ____ & ____.

Describe the pattern for each pair.

Pair A:

Pair B:

Pair C:

Answers can be found on page 234.

Grade Yourself

How did you do in this section?

☐   **A** - I totally get this!
☐   **B** - I'm okay with this. Maybe review later if
      there's time.
☐   **C** - I'll make a note to review this later.

Logical Flaws on the GMAT

Learning to spot some common flaws will make your Critical Reasoning process much faster and easier, so be sure to learn the list of twelve flaws that will be described over the next several pages.

Plenty of arguments can be categorized as having more than one flaw. For instance:

> Elite cyclists perform best while consuming 5,000 calories per day. Thus, professional ballerinas would also benefit from consuming 5,000 calories per day

You could say that this argument makes a **Troubled Analogy**: these two groups of people are not necessarily directly comparable. Or you could say that the argument **Assumes Shared Beliefs**, in that both elite cyclists and professional ballerinas are extremely athletic, and therefore you might assume that they have enough in common to warrant the same diet. These flaws overlap somewhat; it doesn't really matter. This isn't a full course in formal logic. What's more important is that you **understand the typical version of each flaw**. This way, you can spot any of them on the test.

After the description of each flaw, you'll be asked to write your own argument using that flaw. That's right—you need to write bad arguments as practice! Feel free to use examples from your own knowledge and background. For instance, in practicing the flaw **Draws Extreme Conclusion**, you might write something such as this:

> Exercise and dieting are an even more effective way to lose weight than dieting alone. Therefore, exercise is necessary to lose weight.

The problem here is the word *necessary*: the conclusion is too strong to be supported by the premise. It takes serious effort to make a specific logical mistake on purpose. Doing so in your own terms is an excellent way to make sure that you grasp the error fully.

The twelve flaws listed on the following pages are grouped into five major categories:

> A. **Unjustified Assumptions**—the most general kind of error involving a hole in the argument

B. **Causation Errors**—specific kinds of unjustified assumptions around causality

C. **Comparison Errors**—flawed or unjustified comparisons between two groups, situations, etc.

D. **Math Errors**—bad or missing numbers

E. **Communication Errors**—in a debate, missing the point of the other side

A. Unjustified Assumptions

Unjustified Assumptions are by far the most common logical mistake on the GMAT, occurring in more than half of all arguments.

An argument with this sort of flaw requires an **unspoken and unsupported premise**—that is, the author is depending on a premise that he or she didn't write down and hasn't proven. Thus, the conclusion can't be validated unless the assumption can be proven.

Several varieties of Unjustified Assumptions can be roughly distinguished. Again, it's not important to make narrow distinctions. What you need is a set of memorable examples, whether or not they overlap a little.

1. Assumes Shared Beliefs

Here, the arguer assumes that the listener will share certain basic beliefs—some of which are mere impressions, prejudices, and so on. Here is an example:

> Smalltown Cinemas currently prohibits movie attendance by unaccompanied teenagers under age 16. If this restriction is lifted, the theater's operating expenses will increase because of an increased need for cleaning services and repairs to the facility.

Some people read this argument and do not immediately see the flaw. Restate the argument in a simpler way to clarify the argument's structure:

> *IF unaccompanied under-16's are allowed in the theater....*

> *THEN the theater will have to pay for cleaning and repairs.*

What's missing in the middle of that argument? What does the arguer need to prove in order to make the argument valid?

Consider a slightly different example:

> Smalltown Cinemas currently prohibits movie attendance by elderly women. If this restriction is lifted, the theater's operating expenses will increase because of an increased need for cleaning services and repairs to the facility.

Isn't the argument now very offensive (and strange)? The speaker seems to think that elderly women make a mess in theaters, and break things. That's crazy!

The speaker has made the assumption that elderly women disproportionately mess up and damage theaters. The reason that the assumption was so easy to spot in this case was that it was *not* something most of us intuitively believe.

However, many people take it for granted that teenagers make messes and are likely to break things. The speaker in the original argument played on our prejudice against teenagers. Although the speaker's argument depends on the idea that "teenagers under 16 are more likely to make theaters dirty and to damage the facilities," the speaker didn't even bother to *write* that—and he or she certainly didn't *prove* it. **Don't take anything for granted**, and don't bring in outside ideas.

Here's another example:

> The Urban Apartment Towers complex has seen a number of police visits to the property recently, resulting in the police breaking up loud parties held by young residents and attended by other young people. These police visits and the reputation for loud parties are hurting Urban Apartment Towers' reputation and ability to attract new residents. To reduce the number of police visits and improve profitability, Urban Apartment Towers plans to advertise its vacant apartments in a local publication for people aged 50 and up.

What is this argument assuming but not proving? That *people aged 50 and up are less likely to have loud parties or attract police visits.* This doesn't sound like a totally unreasonable assumption, but it's an assumption nonetheless. It's the arguer's job to prove such an assumption. It's your job to notice that the arguer hasn't done so.

If you see something like this…

> Spider silk cannot be made in a lab; it can only be harvested directly from live spiders. So it is impractical to produce spider silk on an industrial scale.

…then think something like this:

> *Wait, who says you can't have a spider silk factory with lots and lots of spiders? Maybe they'll all bite each other's heads off, but there's no support for that in the argument.*

9

Write your own argument that incorporates this flaw:

_____

_____

_____

_____

2. Draws Extreme Conclusion

The conclusion uses language so extreme that the premises cannot justify that conclusion:

> People who jog more than 10 miles per week have a lower incidence of heart disease than people who exercise the same amount on stationary bicycles. Therefore, jogging is the best method of exercise for reducing heart disease.

The conclusion is the final sentence: *Jogging is the best method of exercise for reducing heart disease.* The word *best* is quite extreme. Jogging is the best method ever? Better than swimming, tennis, and a million other things? Even if you prove that jogging is better in some respect than stationary bicycling, all you can say is that jogging is better than one other activity, not that it's the best.

Watch out for these extreme words: *only, never, always, cannot, certainly, obviously, inevitably, most, least, best, worst.* Look for dramatic predictions and assertions: *X costs far more than Y, an immediate increase in Z, a sharp decline in W.*

Keep in mind that even a perfectly reasonable argument can be destroyed by too strong a conclusion. A scientifically sound experiment might indicate that studying in a quiet environment leads to greater retention of information than studying in a noisy environment. That seems reasonable. But if you explain the experimental results and follow up with the conclusion, "Studying in *total silence* is the *only* way to succeed," you've just ruined your own argument. The experiment cannot support such an extreme conclusion.

If you see something like this…

> Whenever there is political unrest in the world, the price of oil goes up. So political unrest must be the most important influence on the price of oil.

…then think something like this:

> *Why does it have to be the MOST important influence?*

Write your own argument that incorporates this flaw:

_____

_____

_____

_____

3. Assumes Skill and/or Will

For people to do something, they have to **be able** to do it, and they have to **want** to. Both skill and will are necessary.

Some arguments give you one piece but not the other. A recommendation that *everyone should exercise two hours every day* might give reasons why people should want to do so, but ignore the fact that not everyone *can* exercise that much (e.g., people who are seriously ill). Or consider the following example:

> The school should offer green vegetables at every lunch. Children who eat green vegetables are healthier, and green vegetables are cheaper than processed food, so the budget can accommodate the change.

What's the problem here? Maybe the school can afford to offer vegetables (the skill side). The argument makes a nod toward the will side: maybe the *parents* would want their kids eating vegetables. But what about the will of the children themselves? How many kids eat green vegetables voluntarily?

The *Urban Apartment Towers* argument on the previous page also has a Skill/Will problem. Maybe over-50 people in the local area cannot afford to live in the Towers. And how badly do people over 50 want to live in an apartment complex where the police are always raiding loud parties? It's the responsibility of the arguer to answer.

If you see something like this…

> People don't save enough for retirement. So they must not want to retire.

…then think something like this:

> *Are people ABLE to save enough for retirement? Maybe something's holding them back.*

Write your own argument that incorporates this flaw:

_____

_____

_____

9

4. Uses Vague or Altered Terms

Just as you are on the lookout for extreme language, you're also on the lookout for vague or altered language throughout the argument. Recall the *People who jog* argument:

> People who jog more than 10 miles per week have a lower incidence of heart disease than people who exercise the same amount on stationary bicycles. Therefore, jogging is the best method of exercise for reducing heart disease.

What on earth does it mean to *exercise the same amount* as someone who is jogging 10 miles? Does it mean biking for the same amount of *time* or the same *distance*? The same number of calories burned? It's much faster to ride 10 miles on a stationary bike than to jog 10 miles, so if the arguer means that the distances are the same, then there's another reason (besides the author's conclusion) that the joggers have less heart disease: they are exercising more hours per week. *Exercise the same amount* is overly vague. **Question any term that's insufficiently precise.**

Likewise, **any change in terms** through the course of the argument should make you arch an eyebrow. Whether the terms become more general or more specific, the argument now has a fissure in its logic.

If you see something like this…

> Consumers used their cell phones more this month than last month, but they talked for fewer minutes. So they must have sent more text messages this month than last month.

…then think something like this:

> *What does "used their cell phones more" mean? More frequent occasions, or more total minutes? And if it's more total minutes, then all we can say is that the NON-talk time has increased. That's not the same as texting time, and certainly not the same as the number of text messages.*

Write your own argument that incorporates this flaw:

_____

_____

_____

_____

9

5. Assumes Signs of a Thing = Thing Itself

This version of Vague or Altered Terms is worth calling out on its own. **Don't confuse external signs and reality.** Quite often, the signs can be misleading.

For instance, medical tests often report false positives, while failing to catch everyone who actually has the disease. The number of people who test positive for a disease is not identical to the number of people who have the disease.

A **false reporting** effect is especially acute when people have an incentive (such as money) to over-report, or an incentive (such as fear or laziness) to under-report. For instance, reports of crimes such as littering and jaywalking are infrequent—that doesn't mean people aren't committing those crimes all the time. Reports of whiplash from car accidents, however, tend to be highly inflated (at least in the U.S.), since victims are often in a position to gain money from insurance companies. Reports of workplace harassment or other improper working conditions may be less frequent than actual incidents if workers fear losing their jobs.

Consider this argument:

> Bowbridge University, a prestigious institution with a long history of educating great scholars and national leaders, launched a distance learning program five years ago. Bowbridge students were very happy with the flexibility afforded to them by the program; for instance, they could continue studying with professors on the Bowbridge campus while conducting research, traveling, or volunteering anywhere in the world. A study showed that students' grades did not decrease. Thus, if the tuition-free Local City College implements a distance learning program, student satisfaction will increase without compromising quality of education.

Notice that *students' grades* and *quality of education* are not the same thing. Maybe professors grade online students more leniently or give them easier assignments.

Another common variation on this problem assumes that, because a law exists, people must be following it. A law is not the same as compliance with a law. Consider this argument:

> City Z instituted a policy of water rationing three months ago. Since then, local businesses have seen revenues decline. Therefore, water rationing is hurting businesses.

However, the fact that a regulation exists doesn't mean that it is being followed. As a first step toward establishing causality, the arguer has to show that businesses are even obeying water rationing in the first place. If there's no enforcement, it's entirely likely that at least some businesses would simply ignore rationing.

9

If you see something like this…

> There's a stop sign at this intersection. So it's safe for pedestrians to cross without looking.

…then think something like this:

> *Don't drivers ever break traffic laws?*

Write your own argument that incorporates this flaw:

_____

_____

_____

_____

B. Causation Errors

Causation errors are prevalent on the GMAT. They can be seen as a species of Unjustified Assumption, but they're so important that they deserve their own heading.

Many conclusions assert that something is the cause of something else, usually without the word *cause* itself. If you claim that *sunscreen protects against skin cancer,* you are asserting that the presence of sunscreen at least contributes to the absence of skin cancer. This is at least partial causation. Causation can also be assumed by this sort of conclusion: *To reduce the elk population, wolves should be re-introduced to the park.* This conclusion assumes that the presence of wolves can cause a reduction in the elk population. **Look closely at the verb:** *cause, make, force, lead to, prevent, protect, increase/decrease, reduce.* Also look at infinitives (*to reduce*), which often indicate goals. The achievement of goals requires causation.

Following are different types of causation errors.

6. Mixes Up Correlation and Causation

You've already seen this error. If two things occur together (correlation), you can't automatically conclude that a particular causal model is at work.

To review: If X and Y seem to be correlated, then there are four possibilities:

(1) X causes Y.
(2) Y causes X.
(3) Z (some other phenomenon) causes both X and Y.
(4) It's an accident; you don't have all the data.

These four options are the *only* possibilities. Memorize them! Logically, you cannot pick one of the four without eliminating all of the other three. On the GMAT, you'll never be able to eliminate all three alternatives. But eliminating even one will strengthen your case.

The situation is often scientific or medical. For example:

> Research has shown that very tall people are more likely to have thyroid problems. So being very tall leads you to have thyroid problems.

When an argument **jumps to a causal relationship**, question that relationship. Couldn't it be the other way around? Maybe thyroid problems cause people to be very tall. Or maybe they're both caused by something else (e.g., genetic factors). In this case, possibility (4) is unlikely—remember, you want to take the premises as given. In this case, the premise is stated in a fairly definitive way, so the answer to whatever question is posed is probably not going to be, "The research is incomplete."

Consider this argument:

> According to a recent study, cats that eat Premium Cat Food have healthier coats and shed less hair than those that don't. While Premium Cat Food costs more, the time saved cleaning up pet hair from furniture and rugs makes Premium Cat Food a wise choice for cat owners.

Two things are happening at the same time: cats are eating Premium Cat Food, and they are shedding less. The conclusion is that this brand of cat food is a *wise choice*. This conclusion clearly assumes that Premium Cat Food is able to cause the healthier coats and reduced shedding (otherwise, it would not be a wise choice). But is it necessarily so that the cat food has these beneficial effects?

Well, it's unlikely here that causation runs in reverse (shedding less hair causes cats to eat Premium Cat Food). However, it's very possible that some other factor is causing both the eating of Premium Cat Food and the reduced shedding/healthier coats.

After all, Premium Cat Food costs more. Perhaps people who can afford to purchase Premium Cat Food (and choose to do so) also provide their cats with grooming, top-notch health care, or other amenities that reduce shedding and make coats healthier. Perhaps richer individuals tend to have special breeds of cats that naturally shed less.

Correlation/Causation errors often have to do with changes or events that occur at the same time or in sequence. **Don't assume that simultaneous events are necessarily connected.** Likewise, if X happened shortly after Y, you cannot necessarily conclude that X was caused by Y.

These logical timing errors often take place in the context of business or politics. Leaders love to take credit for improved conditions, but the improvements might not be related to whatever harebrained initiatives the leaders put in place.

9

If you see something like this…

> After the Super Bowl, sales of Bran Blast cereal increased by 20%. So the Bran Blast advertisement during the Super Bowl was worth the expense.

…then think something like this:

> *How do you know it was the ad that made the sales increase? Maybe a problem in the distribution of the cereal was resolved, or a new partnership with a major grocery-store chain was initiated. Or maybe sales of cereal normally fluctuate this way, at random.*

Write your own argument that incorporates this flaw:

_____

_____

_____

_____

7. Assumes the Future = the Past

To comply with consumer protection laws, investment firms have to tell you that "**past performance is no guarantee of future results**." So why do they trumpet the fact that their precious metals mutual fund exceeded its benchmark for the last three quarters?

Because they know that people fall into this logical trap. Of course, in many ways the future *will* be like the past. If you didn't assume so, you would go crazy. But this assumption goes too far. You hear that, yes, the future might be different, but you keep plowing your money into Internet stocks (late 90s) or mortgage-backed securities (mid-00s) or whatever the next inflated asset class will be, believing that the ride won't end. (You also have a selective memory. You say that "this time, it's different" from the last time things blew up.)

Remember that the future does not have to mimic the past. In a sense, every plan and proposal is guilty of this error, since every plan and proposal is forward-looking but uses the past as evidence. But some plans are more guilty than others.

If you see something like this…

> This stock went up eight months in a row, when the market was flat. So I should buy this stock.

…then think something like this:

> *How do you know that it will keep going up? Maybe the stock has already risen too far. Maybe the rise is random: after all, if enough people flip coins, someone will flip heads eight times in a row.*

Write your own argument that incorporates this flaw:

_____

_____

_____

_____

8. Assumes the Best Means Success

This flaw could also be called "Just because a plan didn't work doesn't mean it wasn't our best shot," or "Just because a protection fails doesn't mean it wasn't protecting."

Sometimes, a variety of options are available to solve a problem, but none of those options are very likely to succeed. This does not affect whether an option can be considered the best, whether it had some beneficial effect, or whether it could still be the best solution to a less severe version of the problem.

For instance, if a new CEO is hired to try to rescue a company on the brink of bankruptcy, even the best possible effort simply may not be enough. If someone dies of a terrible disease, that does not mean that he did not receive optimal medical care. **Sometimes even the best thing fails.** For example:

> For over 100 years, the nation of Relmeer has had a mutual defense pact with the neighboring country of Gherfu. Yet, last month, the government of Relmeer fell to an invasion from the United Provinces of Antocia. Thus, Gherfu is at fault for not abiding by the mutual defense pact.

It will help to break it down. Gherfu was supposed to help Relmeer, but Antocia completely defeated Relmeer anyway. Therefore, Gherfu didn't help? You don't know that. Maybe Relmeer and Gherfu are small nations, and the United Provinces of Antocia is a very large and powerful nation. Maybe Gherfu did absolutely everything it could. Maybe soldiers from Gherfu died valiantly in battle, trying to protect Relmeer. Here is another example:

> Amateur boxers wear headgear to protect against brain injuries from boxing. Yet, last year, three amateur boxers suffered serious brain injuries in the ring while wearing the headgear. Therefore, the headgear does not protect against brain injuries.

Well, it certainly seems true that the headgear is not 100% effective (although it would be helpful to confirm that the injured boxers were wearing the headgear correctly). However, there is a huge gap between saying that the headgear is not 100% effective (not much in life is), and saying that it *does not protect*. There are lots of things—automobile airbags, contraception, sunscreen, bulletproof vests—that do not work 100% of the time, but certainly still have a protective effect.

9

Here's one more example, this time with a choice of two multiple-choice answers:

> Pancreatic cancer patients as a group have only a 5% survival rate after 5 years. With a surgical procedure called the Whipple, followed by chemotherapy and radiation, this rate can be increased. Therefore, this course of treatment is the best option for all pancreatic cancer patients strong enough to undergo the surgery.
>
> What does this argument assume?
>
> (A)   People who receive the Whipple operation followed by chemotherapy and radiation are likely to live longer than five years.
>
> (B)   No other treatment has a better or equivalent rate of effectiveness.

Note that this argument has another kind of error as well: Draws Extreme Conclusion. This course of treatment is the "best"? In making that conclusion, the argument assumes that other treatments must be worse. You are to take as fact that this course of treatment increases the survival rate, but what if some other course of treatment increases the rate *even more*? The author has neglected to rule out this possibility. The answer is (B).

What about incorrect choice (A)? An argument that asserts that a particular plan is the "best" one does not have to assert that that plan is likely to work—only that nothing else is *more* likely to work. In the case of a very deadly disease, sadly, even the very best treatment may not be that effective. As it turns out, the course of treatment described above leads to a five-year survival rate around 20%—thus, even with the "best" treatment, patients are not likely to survive five years.

An argument stating that such a course of treatment is the "best" assumes that nothing better is available, but it does *not* assume that the treatment will work, or even is likely to work.

If you see something like this…

> I took this medicine, but I still feel sick. So the medicine must have failed.

…then think something like this:

> *Maybe the medicine worked just fine. Maybe it kept you from dying.*

Write your own argument that incorporates this flaw:

_____

_____

_____

_____

C. Comparison Errors

Many arguments make comparisons between two groups, two cities, two companies, two situations, and so on. These comparisons are often flawed.

Like Causation errors, Comparison errors often represent a form of Unjustified Assumption, the assumption typically being that *the two things are similar enough in the important ways to be compared.* These errors are so important and so tricky, though, that they get their own section.

9. Has Selection Bias

Whenever you compare two groups, you have to make sure that the two groups are legitimately comparable. So the membership of each group has to be selected appropriately. This is particularly tricky when the two groups *seem* comparable—for instance, when they are both drawn from the same population.

There are a few variations of selection bias.

Unrepresentative Sample

Marketers, pollsters, and social scientists of all stripes use **samples**. It's impossible to ask everyone in the entire population for their opinions on single- versus double-ply toilet paper, so instead you ask 100 people. You have to ensure that the sample is representative, though. In particular, you have to be wary of volunteers, as noted above. For example:

> Some customers who filled out a long survey for free said that they love our company. So our customers love our company.

Wouldn't that sample of customers be biased toward people who like you? After all, they filled out a long survey for free. The potential for self-selection bias is strong here.

Survivor Bias

It is not logical to judge an entire group by concentrating only on who or what survived a process or time period, while ignoring the non-survivors. It's easy to fall into this trap, though; after all, it's often hard to find out much about the people or things that didn't make it!

When you say *survive*, you might mean it literally—for instance, the population of living people over 100 years old (those who survived that long) is not representative of all people born 100 or more years ago. Those alive today are very likely different in important ways—better access to nutrition, fewer genetic maladies, etc. For example:

> A survey of living people over 100 showed lower rates of cigarette smoking than were shown in every other age group age 15 and up. Therefore, smoking is on the rise.

9

Here, it is likely that those who lived to be 100 did so in part by not smoking, and that plenty of people born 100 or more years ago did smoke and did not live to be 100.

Survivor bias can also involve nonliving things:

> Most ancient Greek coins made of gold and silver have been found buried in the ground. So the ancient Greeks must have buried most of their gold and silver coins.

What about the ancient Greek coins that *weren't* buried? They were probably dispersed, melted down, or otherwise destroyed. The sample of surviving coins is not representative.

Ever-Changing Pool

Many groups of people have a rotating cast of members. If a civic club voted in favor of something yesterday and against it 20 years ago, you wouldn't automatically conclude that people in the club changed their minds over time; it's pretty likely that the club includes different people than it did back then. For example:

> A petition is circulating in Capital City opposing the building of a new sports center at State University, on land now occupied by abandoned strip malls. Five years ago, many city residents opposed the building of the new State University dormitory complex, yet in a poll this year, 80% of respondents said that building the dormitory complex had been a good idea. If the people who currently oppose the new Sports Center are patient, they will change their minds.

Five years ago, people opposed the new dorm, and now 80% of respondents to a poll like the dorm. Are the poll respondents the same population as the voters? Maybe the poll was conducted on or near campus; a high percentage of students in the poll would certainly skew results.

Even if the poll were representative of the city's current residents, it's not clear that they are the same residents as five years ago. Maybe some residents disliked the college's expansion plans enough to move out of town! Maybe the new dorm allowed the college to admit significantly more students, thus *diluting* the pool of people who disliked and still dislike the dorm.

If you see something like this…

> Students who joined social clubs at Hambone University last year and were elected officers of their clubs had worse grades than average across all students at Hambone over the last decade. Therefore, participation in social clubs at Hambone causes lower grades.

...then think something like this:

> *That may be true, but so what? Self-selection bias: these kids wanted to prioritize socializing by joining social clubs. Survivor bias: these students were elected officers, meaning that they made it even further into socializing. Ever-changing pool: students from last year are being compared with students over the last decade. The composition of the school may have changed, for one.*

Write your own argument that incorporates this flaw (or one variation of it):

_____

_____

_____

_____

10. The Troubled Analogy

There's nothing wrong with a good analogy, but analogies in GMAT arguments are never good. Every time you make an analogy, you're saying that something is like something else—except that it isn't *exactly* like that, or you'd just be talking about the original topic. It's your job to **note the possible dissimilarities**. Remember Bowbridge University?

> Bowbridge University, a prestigious institution with a long history of educating great scholars and national leaders, launched a distance learning program five years ago. Bowbridge students were very happy with the flexibility afforded to them by the program; for instance, they could continue studying with professors on the Bowbridge campus while conducting research, traveling, or volunteering anywhere in the world. A study showed that students' grades did not decrease. Thus, if the tuition-free Local City College implements a distance learning program, student satisfaction will increase without compromising quality of education.

Is Bowbridge University similar enough to Local City College? You're told that Bowbridge is prestigious, and that its students travel, volunteer, and conduct research around the world. They sound like a wealthy bunch! The students at the free Local City College may not have the same material advantages. Do they need distance learning? It's not clear that someone who attends a local college would want—or have the means—to attend that college from halfway around the world.

In the end, you don't know that much about Local City College. It's not your job to prove that distance learning *won't* work there. Rather, it's your job to point out that the arguer has not established enough similarities between the two schools to draw an effective analogy between them.

If you see something like this…

> The Town of Simpletown's new monorail train has reduced traffic congestion in that town. So if the City of Springfield gets a new monorail, traffic congestion will be reduced there as well.

…then think something like this:

> *How do I know that what worked in Simpletown will work in Springfield? They could be very different places.*

Write your own argument that incorporates this flaw:

_____

_____

_____

_____

D. Math Errors

You might not want to hear this, but even on the Verbal section of the GMAT, you can't completely get away from the Quant. A few Critical Reasoning arguments do trade on math issues. Fortunately, these issues almost never require any computation, and even in the worst case, you'll just be comparing one ratio to another.

In real life, one source of logical error in arguments is the lack of numbers altogether. People make claims that *could* be supported by numbers, but aren't. For instance, the argument about Premium Cat Food said that it was a *wise choice for cat owners*, because they would save time cleaning up cat hair.

To validate this claim, even just for one cat owner, you would need to know 1) how much more the cat food costs than the kind that the cat owner currently buys, 2) how much time the cat owner spends cleaning up hair, and 3) the monetary value of the cat owner's time. That's substantial!

However, the GMAT won't make you come up with tables of numbers. Rather, you'll have to find **mathematically provable conclusions**. Here's an example: *Alice worked fewer days last month than Bob, but she earned more dollars last month than Bob.* What can you definitely conclude? *Alice had to have a higher daily wage (dollars per day) than Bob.*

Notice that this conclusion is based only on inequalities and ratios. This is the way that the GMAT can avoid putting real numbers into arguments and yet still have a rigorous, airtight conclusion.

11. Confuses the Quantities

Mathematical flaws in Critical Reasoning arguments usually rely on conceptual confusion.

For instance, you will need to **keep percents and real numbers straight**. If David gets a 10% pay raise and Marie gets an 8% pay raise, who now has a higher salary? Without knowing how much the two people made before, who knows? Don't confuse percents with actual numbers of dollars, people, etc.

Consider this argument:

> Cetadone, a new therapy for the treatment of addiction to the illegal drug taro-caine, has been proven effective in a study centered around Regis Hospital in the western part of the state of New Portsmouth. The study involved local tarocaine addicts who responded to a newspaper ad offering free treatment. Participants who received cetadone and counseling were 40% more likely to recover than were patients assigned to a control group and who received only counseling. Conventional therapies have only a 20% recovery rate. Therefore, the best way to reduce deaths from tarocaine overdose throughout all of New Portsmouth would be to fund cetadone therapy for all tarocaine addicts.

40% certainly looks like a higher number than 20%. And there are no real numbers of people here anywhere, so we're not confusing a percent with a real number.

However, the 20% is an actual *recovery rate for* conventional therapies.

The 40% is a *percent increase on an unknown figure*—the recovery rate of the control group. You have no way to compare this to an actual 20% recovery rate. For instance, what if the control group had a 50% recovery rate? Then the cetadone group would have 70% recovery rate (1.4 × 50). But what if the control group had a 1% recovery rate? Then the cetadone group would have a 1.4% recovery rate, making it much less successful than conventional therapies. Notice that you are mentally plugging in numbers to test a couple of valid cases at the extremes. Be ready to do the same.

In short, if any numbers or numeric relationships are presented in an argument, determine whether they are being cited in a logical way. This is the exact same reasoning about percents and percent change that you will need for the Quantitative part of the exam (and, of course, the math on the actual math section is much harder than anything that would ever occur in Critical Reasoning), so it pays in numerous ways to have a solid knowledge of percents.

A few other standard mathematical relationships show up in Critical Reasoning as well:

Rate × Time = Distance
Profit = Revenue − Costs
(Dollars per Hour) × Hours = Dollars

You have to know these for the Quant section of the test, of course. Ratios in general (such as *dollars per hour, miles per gallon*, etc.) are fair game. Again, you won't have to compute anything; you need to be able to follow a couple of steps to a mathematical conclusion.

If you see something like this…

> **Mike walks faster than Jane. So Mike takes less time to walk to school than Jane.**

…then think something like this:

> *Wait, what if Mike has to walk a lot farther than Jane? I can't assume they live the same distance from school.*

Write your own argument that incorporates this flaw:

_____

_____

_____

_____

E. Communication Errors

A few Critical Reasoning arguments involve more than one point of view. Sometimes there is only one speaker: *Some people say… but they're wrong, because…* At other times, there are two speakers. *Larry: This journal article is flawed, because… Dana: I disagree, because….*

Either way, once you have more than one position, the door is opened for communication errors.

12. Missing the Point

Marilyn vos Savant, listed in the *Guinness Book of World Records* for "highest IQ," has for many years answered reader questions in a magazine column. Most of these questions do not take a genius to answer ("Can watermelon seeds sprout in your stomach?"). However, someone once wrote in with an excellent example of two people arguing at cross-purposes. A man reported that he and his wife were having an argument: one of them said that forks should go in the dishwasher with the pointy parts up because the forks get cleaner that way, and the other said they should go with the pointy parts down so neither person would be stabbed when reaching into the dishwasher. Who was right?

Well, neither—or both—of them. Vos Savant wisely pointed out that both facts were true: "up" gets the forks cleaner and "down" is safer. So which is more important—cleanliness or safety?

When two people argue with one another on the GMAT, one of them often misses the point:

> Ling: The new health insurance plan won't solve the problem of a lack of insurance for those who are above the poverty line, but still can't afford insurance in the private market.
>
> Mark: But health insurance is a human right—without health, other rights don't even matter that much.

Ling points out a practical failing with a particular health insurance plan—there is a segment of people who won't be helped.

Mark completely misses the point by arguing how important health insurance is (it seems that Ling already agrees with that point to some degree, since she refers to a lack of health insurance as a "problem"). If health insurance is so important, maybe Mark should address whether this particular plan is indeed a good one to support.

This type of flaw is very common when people argue over causes they feel deep emotions about. For instance, if you suggest that a Twitter campaign against child abuse is likely to have no effect on actual child abuse, it is very likely that other people will question whether you are really opposed to child abuse. These people are missing the point. Almost everyone is against child abuse, but that has no bearing on whether a particular measure for reducing child abuse is likely to be effective. (Of course, that is difficult to express on Twitter in 140 characters.)

If you see something like this...

> Some people say we should consume less oil to lower our dependence on supplies from politically unstable regions. But no one has yet proven the link between oil consumption and climate change.

...then think something like this:

> *You missed the point. The first group has a particular purpose in mind: consume less oil in order to lower our dependence on unstable countries. You didn't address that purpose at all.*

9

Write your own argument that incorporates this flaw:

_____

_____

_____

_____

Whew—that was a lot of flaws! Here's a list:

A. **Unjustified Assumptions**	**1. Assumes Shared Beliefs**
	2. Draws Extreme Conclusion
	3. Assumes Skill and/or Will
	4. Uses Vague or Altered Terms
	5. Assumes Signs of a Thing = Thing Itself
B. **Causation Errors**	**6. Mixes Up Correlation and Causation**
	7. Assumes the Future = the Past
	8. Assumes the Best Means Success
C. **Comparison Errors**	**9. Has Selection Bias**
	(unrepresentative sample, survivor bias, ever-changing pool)
	10. The Troubled Analogy
D. **Math Errors**	**11. Confuses the Quantities** (percents, rates, ratios)
E. **Communication Errors**	**12. Missing the Point**

Grade Yourself

How did you do in this section?

- ☐ **A** - I totally get this!
- ☐ **B** - I'm okay with this. Maybe review later if there's time.
- ☐ **C** - I'll make a note to review this later.

9

Gaps in Critical Reasoning Arguments

While many Critical Reasoning arguments contain the types of flaws discussed in the last section, other arguments can be hard to categorize. Fortunately, the idea of finding and filling the gap can be very helpful in Critical Reasoning arguments, including both the types that have already been discussed and those that are unique.

A gap is the **argumentative leap** between one premise and another premise, or between a premise and a conclusion.

Gun legalization: The legislature in Eterna is considering legalizing gun ownership for all citizens. If this happened, all of the sudden armed people would be everywhere, and deaths from shootings would skyrocket.

This argument has two pretty big gaps:

Guns might become legal.

People with guns would suddenly be everywhere.

They would shoot each other to death.

The gaps are represented by the arrows. Ask yourself this question: on that arrow's path from one step to the next, **what could logically go wrong?** (not with the guns, but with the logic.) What could cause you *not* to wind up at the next statement?

First arrow: Guns could become legal, but not very many people actually obtain them. There's a logical gap between legalizing guns and having armed people *everywhere*.

Second arrow: There's a logical gap between people having guns and people fatally shooting each other.

(It's also possible that *illegal* guns are already so prevalent that legalizing guns would make little difference.)

Sometimes an argument's gap is pretty small and reasonable:

Surprisingly, the impoverished nation of Beltraja has several hospitals that practice good sanitation and employ well-trained doctors. However, these doctors report that thousands of patients per year die because of a shortage of antibiotics. Therefore, a relief plan to provide regular shipments of antibiotics to Beltraja's hospitals should save lives.

This seems like a pretty decent argument. Note that the conclusion is not too extreme—the argument does not say that *all* of the people will be saved. Consider the two gaps:

People are dying because of a lack of antibiotics.

We could give the hospitals antibiotics.

Some of the people won't die.

9

In either arrowed location, can you insert a problem? In the first gap: what if somehow giving antibiotics is the wrong solution? Maybe the doctors are wrong about the cause of the deaths. This possibility seems pretty remote, though—you are told that the doctors are *well-trained*.

The second gap provides more possibilities. There's a bigger gap between (1) some unknown agency outside of Beltraja sending in antibiotics, and (2) patients actually receiving them. What if the shipments are intercepted by a corrupt government? What if corrupt hospital officials sell them on the black market? What if someone at the hospital administers the antibiotics ineffectively—for instance, stretching the supply by giving each patient less than is needed to fight infection?

Even so, almost anyone would agree that sending antibiotics to Beltrajan hospitals is a good idea (although extra precautions might need to be taken to ensure that the medicines arrive safely and are administered effectively). Even good arguments have little gaps.

Try this one:

> *Consumption of fast food contributes to obesity. If a fast food restaurant is permitted to open right next door to our school and to sell to students during lunchtime, the students will become obese and our school's scores on a national fitness test will decline.*

List the steps leading to the conclusion (it's okay if you use a different number of "steps" than the lines given):

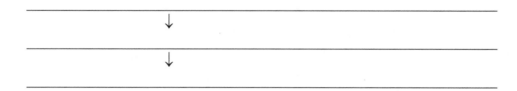

Here's one possible response:

fast food place sells to students
↓
students become obese
↓
students do worse on fitness test

There are some huge gaps in this argument, especially between the last premise and the conclusion.

First arrow: Maybe the students won't buy the food or won't buy it that often. Maybe the students can eat fast food without becoming obese (young people have fast metabolisms, are physically active, etc.). Obviously, not everyone who eats fast food becomes obese, even if consumption of fast food contributes to obesity.

Second arrow: Maybe the fitness test is very easy. Maybe obese people succeed at the test at the same rate as non-obese people. Even if every student in the school ate the fast food and became obese (a pretty unlikely outcome), the conclusion still rests upon the unproven assumption that obese people will do worse on a particular test of fitness.

This *national fitness test* practically comes out of nowhere. That's a real weakness of this argument.

> ### Grade Yourself
>
> How did you do in this section?
>
> - ☐ **A** - I totally get this!
> - ☐ **B** - I'm okay with this. Maybe review later if there's time.
> - ☐ **C** - I'll make a note to review this later.

Gaps Related to Conclusions

Sometimes, very large gaps are created in arguments when the conclusion gets too ambitious. Earlier on, the flaw of Draws Extreme Conclusion was discussed. This topic is so important that it deserves further analysis here.

In the last section, the argument about sending antibiotics to Beltraja was praised because its conclusion (*a relief plan to provide regular shipments of antibiotics to Beltraja's hospitals should save lives*) was modest—that is, not too ambitious.

Here is the argument again, with a few changes (in bold):

> Surprisingly, the impoverished nation of Beltraja has several hospitals that practice good sanitation and employ well-trained doctors. However, these doctors report that **approximately 3,000** patients per year die regularly because of a shortage of antibiotics. Therefore, a relief plan to provide regular shipments of antibiotics to Beltraja's hospitals **will save thousands of patients per year**.

The original conclusion seemed extremely reasonable—if people are dying because of a lack of antibiotics, sending some antibiotics ought to save some indeterminate number of people (technically, if you save just two people, you've "saved lives").

But, in this new version of the argument, the original problem has been quantified—about 3,000 people are dying. The new conclusion is that you'll save *thousands*, which seems to imply more than 2,000. Can the plan save approximately two-thirds of the people who are dying? That is a much more ambitious goal, and more evidence would help support such a big conclusion. For instance, you would want to know whether a lack of antibiotics is merely masking other, potentially fatal conditions.

Here's another example:

> Studies have shown that students who go without lunch do poorly in school. Many students are hungry in school because they cannot afford to pack or buy lunch. Therefore, a program of free school lunches should help these students perform at grade level.

You might summarize the argument this way:

students can't afford lunch
↓
go without lunch → do poorly in school
↓
free lunch → help students perform at grade level

Note that the order of the premises has been slightly rearranged to put them in time order. Start at the beginning. Students can't afford lunch, so they don't eat lunch, so they do poorly in school. Is there a gap?

While it certainly does seem reasonable that a lack of food would contribute to poor academic performance, the gap here is related to Causation. Yes, the students are hungry and they are doing poorly, but is the hunger really causing the poor performance? How much of the poor performance is it causing? Could there be some other factor contributing to the poor performance?

The second gap is much larger, though. Free lunch will help students *perform at grade level?* That's quite ambitious. Unfortunately, there are entire schools in which the majority of children perform far below grade level, and it is doubtful that lunch alone would fix the entire problem.

This argument is weak because its premise (*lack of lunch causes poor performance*) is too weak to support a conclusion about raising performance *to grade level*. Here's a modified version of the argument, with changes in bold:

> Studies have shown that students who go without lunch do poorly in school, **and that when provided with lunches, those same students do much better**. Many students are hungry in school because they cannot afford to pack or buy lunch. Therefore, a program of free school lunches should help these students **do better in school**.

The first bold portion makes a strong case for causal relationships (between lack of lunch and poor performance, and between actual lunch and better performance). This fills the first gap that was discussed above. While other factors, such as socioeconomic conditions, may be a common cause of both lack of lunch and poor performance, you still can break the cycle to some extent by providing lunch.

The second gap that was discussed above (lunch alone is unlikely to bring students up to grade level) is greatly reduced by substituting a more modest conclusion: if evidence shows that hungry students who are given lunches do better, and you give hungry students some lunches… well, yes, you certainly would expect that the students would do at least a little bit better.

The more modest the conclusion, the easier it is for the premises to support that conclusion—and thus, the stronger the argument.

In conclusion, watch out for extreme wording or new ideas! Altered terms or standards (such as *fitness testing* or *at grade level*) can seriously weaken an argument.

In analyzing gaps, you've started laying out arguments visually, using abbreviated premises and arrows. The next chapter is about argument diagramming—what you want to write on your paper when you see a Critical Reasoning argument on the real exam.

Grade Yourself

How did you do in this section?

- ☐ **A** - I totally get this!
- ☐ **B** - I'm okay with this. Maybe review later if there's time.
- ☐ **C** - I'll make a note to review this later.

9

Chapter 10
of
Foundations of GMAT Verbal

Diagrams

In This Chapter...

Introduction to Argument Diagramming

Decoding the Question Stem

Chapter 10:
Diagrams

An Introduction to Argument Diagramming

Remember this argument from Drill 8.1?

> Quoting sources in your papers without attributing the quotes to those sources is forbidden on this campus. Plagiarism is strictly forbidden by our code of conduct, and quoting without attribution is a form of plagiarism.

The argument below follows the same pattern. You can use Q for *quoting without attribution*, P for *plagiarism*, and F for *forbidden*. The equals sign represents the word *is*.

$$Q = P$$
$$P = F$$
Therefore, $Q = F$

This argument is plainly valid! If the premises are true, the conclusion is as well.

While most arguments cannot be converted as cleanly into math-problem format as the one above, you can still make the structure of arguments much more clear with some clever notetaking.

The first principle will be to assign variables or abbreviations to important premises or ideas in the argument. Whether you use variables or abbreviations to refer to entire premises (*B = the company will go bankrupt*) or merely words (*FF = fireflies*) will depend on the complexity of the argument. Your preferences will play a large role here.

Do *not* write down what the variables mean—you won't need to read your notes later. The purpose of taking notes is to create meaning *in the moment*. What you write just has to make sense to you for about two minutes.

Here are some symbols you may find helpful. Feel free to use whatever makes sense to you (these symbols are to be used in the following examples, though). These diagrams are deliberately being hand-draw, so that you try them yourself:

$$\sim \qquad \text{happening at the same time}$$

$$\rightarrow \qquad \text{causes}$$

$$\therefore \qquad \text{therefore}$$

The next principle is simply to arrange the pieces of the argument in a logical order, with the conclusion last. Some perfectly valid diagramming schemes involve the conclusion at the top, but in this book, only one suggestion for notetaking in Critical Reasoning is being discussed.

Try this argument:

> A study of 120 elderly, hospital-bound patients in the United Kingdom showed that daily consumption of Nutree, a nutritional supplement containing vitamins, fiber, and sugar, increased by an average of four months the typical life expectancy for patients of the same age and physical condition. Thus, anyone who wants to live longer should drink Nutree every day.

Using N for *Nutree*, here is one possible diagram:

$$\text{daily N} \rightarrow \text{+4 mos. for elderly}$$
$$\therefore$$
$$\text{daily N} \rightarrow \text{"live longer" for anyone}$$

This diagram makes the argument structure so clear because you thought ahead for a moment before writing. You could have written *elderly have daily N, live 4+ mos.*, but arranging the premise and conclusion in the same order (beginning with drinking the Nutree and then leading into the results) made the structure of the argument easier to see. It's generally a good idea to rearrange the content slightly to clarify relationships or fit a pattern you're used to. For instance, always putting causes on the left and effects on the right is a fine habit to adopt.

Do you see the problem with the original argument? This is a Troubled Analogy. Certainly what works for the elderly may not work for everyone (and here, the word *elderly* is actually standing in for *120 elderly, hospital-bound patients in the United Kingdom,* so the analogy is actually even more troubled).

Drill 10.1 — Diagramming Arguments

Try diagramming these arguments in the space below each one. You've seen four of the five before.

1. People who eat diets rich in tropical fruits rate higher in surveys of happiness. Therefore, a diet rich in tropical fruit is a cause of happiness.

2. The difference between a weed and a garden plant depends entirely on the opinion of the person who owns the land. Thus, it is impossible to develop a flawless garden "weed-killer" that kills all types of weeds and leaves all types of garden plants unharmed. The Vytex Company's attempt to develop a perfect garden weed-killer will fail.

3. The city parks are overcrowded, leading to long wait times for athletic fields and courts and lessening citizens' enjoyment of the parks. A new park should be built at the southern tip of the city, which does not have its own park. Because the heavily populated south of the city lacks a park, residents regularly travel to other parts of the city to use those parks, thus leading to overcrowding.

4. Bowbridge University, a prestigious institution with a long history of educating great scholars and national leaders, launched a distance learning program five years ago. Bowbridge students were very happy with the flexibility afforded to them by the program; for instance, they could continue studying with professors on the Bowbridge campus while conducting research, traveling, or volunteering anywhere in the world. A study showed that students' grades did not decrease. Thus, if the tuition-free Local City College implements a distance learning program, student satisfaction will increase without compromising quality of education.

5. The SML-1 is a test of computer programming abilities used by Human Resources departments in hiring and employee assessment. The Cyvox Corporation reported an average score of 65 out of 100 for its job applicants. At Vectorcom Company, employees achieved an average score of 83—nearly twenty points higher than Cyvox. Therefore, Vectorcom's employees are better computer programmers than Cyvox's.

Answers can be found on page 235.

10

> *Grade Yourself*
>
> How did you do in this section?
>
> ☐   **A** - I totally get this!
> ☐   **B** - I'm okay with this. Maybe review later if there's time.
> ☐   **C** - I'll make a note to review this later.

Decoding the Question Stem

You have spent all of the Critical Reasoning portion of this book so far discussing *Arguments*. Of course, it is also crucially important to **understand the question** being asked about that argument.

People make a lot of mistakes when they don't pay enough attention to the question. Many times, a careless student will read an argument and pick an answer that seems to "go along" with the argument, but that does not do what the question specifically asks!

GMAT Question stems fall into a few broad categories:

Questions About Assumptions — These include questions that ask directly about assumptions, as well as questions that ask us to strengthen and weaken arguments.

Questions About Evidence — These questions might ask us what other information would be most helpful in evaluating a conclusion. Or they might ask us to resolve a discrepancy or a paradox (an apparent contradiction that may not really be self-contradictory), or draw an inference or conclusion.

Questions About Structure — These questions will sometimes have two bold statements within the argument and ask you to pick the answer that tells the role of those two statements. An answer might read, "The first bold statement is the main conclusion of the argument and the second bold statement is a claim the author opposes."

Consider some question stems in GMAT problems from the *The Official Guide for GMAT Review, 13th Ed.*

1. Which of the following most logically completes the argument below?

2. The consultant responds to the lawmaker's argument by _____.

3. This argument is most vulnerable to the objection that it fails to _____.

4.   Which of the following would be most useful to determine in order to evaluate the argument?

5.   The argument depends on which of the following assumptions?

6.   Which of the following, if true, most strengthens the argument above?

7.   Which of the following, if true, would most weaken the criticism made above of the anthropologists' strategy?

8.   Which of the following, if true, most helps to resolve the paradox outlined above?

9.   Any of the following statements, if true about last year, helps to explain the rise in profits EXCEPT:

A few of the stems aren't technically questions (e.g., *The consultant responds to the lawmaker's argument by*), but rather are statements that you are asked to complete. These can easily be rephrased as questions (*How does the consultant respond…?*).

It can be helpful to categorize each question as involving Assumptions, Evidence, or Structure. The most important thing is that you understand what the question *specifically* wants you to do. It is also recommended that you write down a brief note about the question as a reminder.

Looking again at each of the stems above, determine what the question is asking:

1. Which of the following most logically completes the argument below?

> This question stem would follow an argument with the last line ending in a blank. For instance, "Therefore, the decrease in profits will be minimal, because _____." The question is asking for the conclusion, or for the final part of the conclusion.

> On your paper, you could simply write *Conclusion* (you can just abbreviate "C").

2. The consultant responds to the lawmaker's argument by....

> The question is NOT asking you to rephrase what the consultant said—that would be too easy. The question is about the *role* that the consultant's comments play in the argument. Possible answers might be things like, "Denying the truth of the evidence on which the lawmaker has based his reasoning" or "Suggesting that the evidence provided by the lawmaker does not support the lawmaker's conclusion."

> On your paper: *Role of lawmaker's argument* (or, abbreviated, something like "role of L's arg").

10

3. This argument is most vulnerable to the objection that it fails to....

This question is about argument flaws, and probably about assumptions.

On your paper: *Flaw?*

4. Which of the following would be most useful to determine in order to evaluate the argument?

Here, you will need to identify the argument's assumptions or gaps, so you can pick an answer that describes the information that would fill the gap. For instance, in an argument that assumed that teenagers were more likely to mess up and damage movie theaters, an answer might read, "Whether evidence exists that teenagers under age 16 are, as a group, more likely to leave theaters dirty or damage facilities than are other age groups."

On your paper: *Info needed to evaluate?*

5. The argument depends on which of the following assumptions?

This question asks directly about assumptions. It is important to process the argument on your own by thinking of assumptions, as you have been doing in this book, before reading the answer choices. Otherwise, it is very likely that more than one answer will sound good, and you will have a hard time going back and analyzing once you have already seen the choices. Avoid going to the choices too early; after all, four of them are wrong. They are there to distract you and pollute your mind. Become sure of the argument as given, and come up with a hypothesis as best you can for the missing assumption before looking at the answers.

On your paper: *Assumption?* (Or, "A?")

6. Which of the following, if true, most strengthens the argument above?

This question asks you to strengthen the argument. To do so, you must know what the argument's assumptions are. The correct answer may well *contain* the assumption, but be presented as a fact. For instance, "A study from the Theater Owners Association of America shows that teenagers under age 16 are disproportionately likely compared to other age groups to leave theaters dirty and to damage facilities." Note that the question stem says "if true." The correct answer could be pretty extreme—after all, if something extreme were true, it might strengthen the argument *extremely* well!

On your paper: *Strengthen* (Or, "S")

10

7. Which of the following, if true, would most weaken the criticism made above of the anthropologists' strategy?

> This question asks you to weaken the argument. To do so, you must know what the argument's assumptions are. The correct answer could resemble the assumption with a word such as "not" inserted somewhere. For instance, for the movie theater argument, a *weaken* answer choice might read, "Teenagers under age 16 are *not* more likely than other patrons to leave theaters dirty or damage facilities." Note that this question actually uses the word *weaken*, but other questions might use the synonym *undermine* or an expression such as *cast doubt on*.
>
> On your paper: *Weaken* (Or, "W")

8. Which of the following, if true, most helps to resolve the paradox outlined above?

> A paradox is a seeming contradiction. For instance, "Cash expenses went down and revenues went up, but reported profits have declined." That might seem, on the face of it, impossible. However, a real-life resolution to the paradox might be that the reported profits are measured by a non-cash accounting system. (Don't worry, you'll get to that in business school. The GMAT doesn't require you to know anything about cash vs. accrual accounting!)
>
> In a paradox question (or a question that mentions a *contradiction* or *discrepancy*), there is always a perfectly reasonable explanation for something that looks like a contradiction or impossibility. Pay attention to the exact wording (e.g., *cash expenses* vs. *reported profits*); the subtle differences are often what crack the problem open.
>
> On your paper: *Paradox* (this is short, of course, for *Pick the answer that resolves the paradox*)

9. Any of the following statements, if true about last year, helps to explain the rise in profits EXCEPT:

> Questions that contain NOT or EXCEPT in the stem can be tricky. Fortunately, the GMAT is nice enough to capitalize those words to help you out. Read the stem without the EXCEPT part: *Any of the following statements, if true about last year, helps to explain the rise in profits.* Four of the answer choices do just that. You want the one that *doesn't*.
>
> On your paper: *Which DOESN'T explain rise in profits?*

10

Drill 10.2 — Decoding the Question Stem

For each example, note what you would write on your paper about the question stem. It can be as simple as "S" for *Strengthen*, or, occasionally, as specific as *Which DOESN'T explain rise in profits?*

1.   Which of the following, if true, most seriously undermines the politician's argument?

2.   In the passage, the author develops the argument by....

3.   Which of the following, if true, most helps to explain the apparent discrepancy between increasing incidence of fatal illness and the increased life expectancy among the same population?

4.   Which of the following most logically completes the argument?

5.   Any of the following, if true, is a valid reason for hiring based in part on results of the personality test described EXCEPT:

Answers can be found on page 237.

Grade Yourself

How did you do in this section?

- ☐   **A** - I totally get this!
- ☐   **B** - I'm okay with this. Maybe review later if there's time.
- ☐   **C** - I'll make a note to review this later.

Chapter *of* 11

Foundations of GMAT Verbal

Putting It All Together

In This Chapter...

Chapter 11:

Putting It All Together

Consider a new example. One step in your strategy is always going to be to **read the question stem first,** so you've got it in the back of your mind what you will ultimately be doing with the argument. For example:

> While many people think of the lottery as a harmless way to have fun and possibly win some money, buying lottery tickets is a form of gambling. Therefore, public officials shouldn't buy lottery tickets.
>
> Which of the following, if true, would most strengthen the conclusion?

The question is asking you to *strengthen*. Okay, great, you need to find the assumption in the argument so you can beef up the conclusion or show it to be actually true.

Now read and diagram the argument. Take a moment to do this on separate paper.

The conclusion is clearly *Therefore, public officials shouldn't buy lottery tickets.* But the first part—*While many people think of the lottery as a harmless way to have fun and possibly win some money*—doesn't seem like part of the argument. The author mentions what *many people* think only to create a contrast with his or her own opinion. These other people are not really part of the argument. You can mentally dismiss that part and think of the argument this way:

> *Buying lottery tickets is a form of gambling. Therefore, public officials shouldn't buy lottery tickets.*

Use L for *buying lottery tickets*, G for *gambling*, and PO for *public official.*

$$L = G$$
$$\therefore$$
PO's shouldn't L

This diagram should make the missing assumption or gap in the argument easier to see. L and G are the same thing, and PO's shouldn't L? Well, why not?! What should the arguer have said after *Buying lottery tickets is a form of gambling* and before *public officials shouldn't buy lottery tickets?*

Express the missing assumption yourself before proceeding. In general, **identify assumptions *before* reading the answer choices**, so you don't get tricked by evil wrong answers that are there to distract you.

Now that you have the assumption in your mind, proceed to the full question. In order to do process of elimination, you're going to add this to your paper:

A

B

C

D

E

Here is the full problem:

> While many people think of the lottery as a harmless way to have fun and possibly win some money, buying lottery tickets is a form of gambling. Therefore, public officials shouldn't buy lottery tickets.
>
> Which of the following, if true, would most strengthen the conclusion?
>
> (A) Individuals who play the lottery are less likely to win a big payout than they are to be killed in a car crash.
> (B) Some public officials are guilty of much more serious offenses than gambling.
> (C) Public officials shouldn't gamble.
> (D) Many public officials are easily tempted to violate rules governing their positions.
> (E) Most lottery winners are not made as happy by their winnings as they expected.

Some students' initial reaction to the question is, "They all strengthen the conclusion!" Some of the choices, for instance, provide reasons why *no one* should buy lottery tickets—you're not likely to win (choice (A)), and even if you do, it won't make you happy (choice (E)).

However, keep in mind that you're not just looking for a choice that supports the statement *public officials shouldn't buy lottery tickets*. You are looking specifically for a choice that supports this conclusion *in the context of this argument*. You need an answer that **links the premise to the conclusion**.

Adding "more evidence" to an argument won't help if it's the wrong kind of evidence. To strengthen an argument, link the premise(s) to the conclusion—that is, fill the gap.

In order to pick the right answer, you should identify the gap—in this case, a missing assumption. Did you state the missing assumption in your head a couple of minutes ago? Look at the diagram again.

$$L = G$$
$$\therefore$$
$$PO's \; shouldn't \; L$$

If you're still not sure, consider this argument, which follows the exact same format:

> *Weight lifting is a form of exercise. Therefore, public officials shouldn't lift weights.*

Wait, what? That's crazy. Just because weight lifting is a form of exercise doesn't mean public officials shouldn't do it. That's like saying they should never exercise!

And there's your assumption. This argument sounded so crazy because the assumption *Public officials shouldn't exercise* is something no one believes. It was easy to figure out. If you're having trouble with your original argument, **translate it to a simpler, crazier version**.

Back to the argument:

> *Buying lottery tickets is a form of gambling. Therefore, public officials shouldn't buy lottery tickets.*

The assumption here is *Public officials shouldn't gamble.* In your diagram, you would see it as *PO's shouldn't G.*

Either way, answer choice (C) is a word-for-word match with this idea. If you didn't see a match right away, you would cross off any answers that did *not* fill this gap in order to move towards a match.

An assumption is something that, if it were true, would strengthen the argument. After all, it's something the speaker should have said (and provided evidence for) in the first place. If it turns out that there is a law against gambling by public officials, and it's also true that buying lottery tickets is a form

11

of gambling, then the conclusion that public officials shouldn't buy lottery tickets would be pretty undeniable!

Not everything that strengthens an argument is an assumption, but arguments certainly depend on assumptions. In fact, if you are able to deny an assumption of an argument, the argument falls apart.

On the other hand, a good way to *strengthen* an argument is to turn an assumption into a fact. Answer choice (C) does exactly that. (C) is our answer.

By the way, a correct GMAT assumption is not a statement completely out of the blue, such as *The moon is made of green cheese*. It's usually something that you already might think, or are at least familiar with as an idea. Be careful, because the most common flaws in arguments have to do with Unjustified Assumptions and Assumes Shared Beliefs. That said, a GMAT argument is usually straightforward at the end of the day. You have to pay attention to the specific wording, but together with the missing assumption, **the argument should make sense**.

Grade Yourself

How did you do in this section?

☐   **A** - I totally get this!
☐   **B** - I'm okay with this. Maybe review later if there's time.
☐   **C** - I'll make a note to review this later.

Critical Reasoning "Hints" Drill

The following drill contains ten Critical Reasoning questions, representing a variety of question types.

For every question, you're going to get some "help"! First, you will see just the argument and question stem (no answer choices) and a reminder of the strategy you should follow.

Then, once you've done your analysis, you will see the full question with answer choices. (You may wish to cover part of the page so you don't skip ahead.)

Answers begin on page 225.

Question #1 Instructions

> President of Teachers' Union: **Many people are convinced that declining test scores in our district are the fault of teachers**. Yet, our school district has recently seen a large influx in the rise of enrolling students who do not speak any English at all. Nearby districts that have seen a similar influx of students who do not speak English have all experienced much larger drops in test scores. It is a testament to the skill and dedication of our teachers that test scores in our district have dropped so little.
>
> The bold statement in the argument plays which of the following roles?

HINT: You definitely want to answer this question in your own words before you read the answer choices. In order to do so, it will help to diagram.

A good first step in diagramming is to rephrase each fact or premise in your head in simpler language (but without losing information). Like this:

> Some people think bad test scores are the fault of teachers.
> But many of our new students don't speak English.
> Other schools with many new students who don't speak English have had even worse test scores.
> Our teachers are doing a good job in keeping scores from dropping too much.

The argument has exactly four statements. Three of them represent one point of view, and one of them represents another point of view. Of the three statements that represent the speaker's point of view, the "biggest" and most important claim is the conclusion. Which statement is the conclusion? What role does the bold statement (#1) play in the argument?

Decide for yourself before proceeding. DO NOT EVER read Critical Reasoning answer choices without first intellectually processing the argument and anticipating the answer.

11

Upcoming Vocabulary:

"Corroborate" means "support with evidence"
"Refute" means "disprove."
A "finding" is simply any information that has been discovered.

Go ahead and try it!

Question #1

President of Teachers' Union: **Many people are convinced that declining test scores in our district are the fault of teachers.** Yet, our school district has recently seen a large influx in the rise of enrolling students who do not speak any English at all. Nearby districts that have seen a similar influx of students who do not speak English have all experienced much larger drops in test scores. It is a testament to the skill and dedication of our teachers that test scores in our district have dropped so little.

The bold statement in the argument plays which of the following roles?

(A)   It is the main conclusion of the argument.
(B)   It is a finding that the argument seeks to explain.
(C)   It introduces an explanation that the argument seeks to refute.
(D)   It provides support for the main conclusion of the argument.
(E)   It is a judgment that the argument corroborates.

Record your answer: _____

Question #2 Instructions

The drug Nephoprene has been proven to help certain harmful medical conditions, but it also has serious side effects. Doctors are responsible for weighing the benefits of a drug against the possible harm to the patient from side effects, and most doctors have chosen not to prescribe Nephoprene even to patients who would experience benefits.

Which of the following follows most logically from the argument?

HINT: "Which of the following follows most logically from the argument?" is a way of asking you to draw a conclusion. Once again, it is very important that you answer this for yourself before viewing the answer choices. It will help to diagram.

This argument has three statements (call Nephoprene "N" to make things easier):

N has benefits and side effects.

Doctors are responsible for weighing the benefits and side effects.
Most doctors have chosen not to give N.
Therefore... ?

Using only the facts presented, what logically comes next? Answer for yourself, in your own words, before proceeding.

Question #2

The drug Nephoprene has been proven to help certain harmful medical conditions, but it also has serious side effects. Doctors are responsible for weighing the benefits of a drug against the possible harm to the patient from side effects, and most doctors have chosen not to prescribe Nephoprene even to patients who would experience benefits.

Which of the following follows most logically from the argument?

(A) Nephoprene will not cure patients.
(B) Most doctors have determined that the side effects of Nephoprene outweigh the benefits.
(C) Patients who want to take Nephoprene are not able to obtain prescriptions for it.
(D) Not all patients with medical conditions that can be helped by Nephoprene will actually experience benefits when taking it.
(E) The doctors who decline to prescribe Nephoprene are not fulfilling their duties as doctors.

Record your answer: _____

Question #3 Instructions

A candidate for governor has suggested lifting the state law requiring cigarette advertisers to print a warning label about the dangers of smoking on every cigarette pack, and instead requiring cigarette manufacturers to publish recent data and studies about the dangers of smoking on websites that the manufacturers will create for this purpose. The candidate argues that the plan will provide consumers with more detailed information so that they may make wise decisions about smoking.

The argument assumes that:

HINT: The question stem is asking you for an assumption inherent in the argument. Once again, it is very important that you answer this for yourself before viewing the answer choices. It will help to diagram.

Here is a paraphrase of the statements in the argument:

> Candidate wants to replace warning labels with website of "recent data."
> Candidate says this more detailed info will ➔ better smoking decisions.

When looking for an assumption, you are asking yourself "What would have to be true for this argument to be really solid?" For instance, the argument assumes that people make decisions about smoking in a rational way (by reading studies and data).

You should be able to think of one or two more assumptions. Don't ignore the really obvious stuff—can you imagine smokers you know behaving in the way the candidate suggests?

In many GMAT Critical Reasoning problems, there is just one big assumption, but here there is definitely more than one, so you should jot down a couple of things—one of them ought to appear in the answer choices.

Question #3

A candidate for governor has suggested lifting the state law requiring cigarette advertisers to print a warning label about the dangers of smoking on every cigarette pack, and instead requiring cigarette manufacturers to publish recent data and studies about the dangers of smoking on websites that the manufacturers will create for this purpose. The candidate argues that the plan will provide consumers with more detailed information so that they may make wise decisions about smoking.

The argument assumes that:

(A) Smoking leads to higher mortality rates.
(B) Consumers are willing and able to visit the websites and evaluate the data and studies presented.
(C) Competing candidates for governor have not introduced the same or a superior plan relating to cigarette warnings.
(D) Most people are not able to break their addictions to cigarettes.
(E) Smoking will become more popular if this plan is not enacted.

Record your answer: _____

Question #4 Instructions

Researchers have noted that panda bears that have given birth to live young live longer in the wild. Therefore, these researchers have concluded that giving birth to live young increases a panda's lifespan.

The argument makes which of the following assumptions?

HINT: The question stem is asking for an assumption inherent in the argument. Once again, it is very important that you answer this for yourself before viewing the answer choices. It will help to diagram.

Here is a paraphrase of the statements in the argument (let's use P for pandas, B for "giving birth to live young", and L for "increased lifespan").

> P that B have L
> Therefore, B causes L

Whoa! That is a classic causality mistake. What is the author assuming?

Answer in your own words before proceeding.

Question #4

> Researchers have noted that panda bears that have given birth to live young live longer in the wild. Therefore, these researchers have concluded that giving birth to live young increases a panda's lifespan.
>
> The argument makes which of the following assumptions?
>
> (A) Pandas that have given birth to live young will not be killed by predators.
> (B) Since male pandas cannot give birth, female pandas live longer than male pandas.
> (C) Pandas that are already likely to live longer are also more likely to give birth to live young.
> (D) Female pandas are not likely to die while giving birth.
> (E) Pandas that have given birth to multiple live young are likely to live even longer than pandas that have given birth to only a single live offspring.

Record your answer: _____

Question #5 Instructions

> The following appeared in a newspaper editorial:
>
> It is important that penalties for drug dealing on school grounds remain extremely severe. If the penalties became less severe, more of our students would become addicted to drugs.
>
> The argument assumes which of the following:

HINT: This is another assumptions question. Once again, it is very important that you answer this for yourself before viewing the answer choices. It will help to diagram.

Note that the first sentence of the argument doesn't say much—it says that penalties should remain severe, but doesn't say why. Then, the arguer goes on to give a single reason. Put it all in order:

> IF penalties for drug dealing on school grounds are lessened
> THEN more students become addicted to drugs
> Therefore, penalties should remain severe

This argument contains MANY assumptions. To find them, ask yourself, "Even IF penalties were lessened, what would ALSO have to be true for more students to become addicted to drugs?" (For instance, the students would have to actually take the drugs.)

You should be able to think of several assumptions before you proceed!

Question #5

The following appeared in a newspaper editorial:

It is important that penalties for drug dealing on school grounds remain extremely severe. If the penalties became less severe, more of our students would become addicted to drugs.

The argument assumes which of the following:

(A) Drug dealers are currently being deterred from drug dealing on school grounds due to the penalties at issue.

(B) Drug use is harmful to the academic careers of students.

(C) Drug dealing on school grounds is punished more harshly than drug dealing off school grounds.

(D) Those who deal drugs on school grounds are not students at those schools.

(E) There is a significant chance that some of those addicted to drugs will ultimately die from drug-related causes.

Record your answer: _____

Question #6 Instructions

In the last ten years, usage of pay phones in Bridgeport has dropped by 90%. Since cell phone usage is much higher among middle- and upper-income residents of Bridgeport than among lower-income residents, the Bridgeport City Council has decided to remove pay phones from middle- and upper-income neighborhoods, while retaining those in lower-income neighborhoods, reasoning that this plan will respond appropriately to demand for pay phones and thereby inconvenience very few people.

11

Which of the following would be most helpful to know in order to evaluate the reasoning of the City Council?

HINT: A question that asks you what information it would be most helpful to know is asking you about the assumptions in the argument. While the argument contains only two sentences, it could reasonably be broken into five or so smaller statements:

> pay phone usage down 90%
> upper/middle residents use more cell phones than lower-income residents
> remove payphones from upper/middle neighborhoods
> keep payphones in lower-income neighborhoods
> plan will "inconvenience very few people"

Think about the "gaps" between each statement and the next. This argument contains many assumptions. (Since this is a very real-world situation, imagine yourself as one of these low-income residents who uses pay phones. Would you be happy with this plan? Why not?)

Make sure to diagram the argument and answer for yourself before moving forward.

Question #6

In the last ten years, usage of pay phones in Bridgeport has dropped by 90%. Since cell phone usage is much higher among middle- and upper-income residents of Bridgeport than among lower-income residents, the Bridgeport City Council has decided to remove pay phones from middle- and upper-income neighborhoods, while retaining those in lower-income neighborhoods, reasoning that this plan will respond appropriately to demand for pay phones and thereby inconvenience very few people.

Which of the following would be most helpful to know in order to evaluate the reasoning of the City Council?

(A) Whether pay phones are used by criminals conducting drug deals
(B) A comparison of pay phone usage between middle income and high income residents
(C) How many low-income residents use cell phones
(D) Whether low-income residents typically use pay phones close to home
(E) Whether eliminating pay phones would lose revenue for the city

Record your answer: _____

11

Question #7 Instructions

The Orange Corporation is conducting market research in preparation for the launch of its new device, the 3-D eSlate. Thus far, in Orange's market research, two groups have emerged as likely buyers of the eSlate: medical professionals and people making more than $250,000 a year. Since the number of medical professionals in the target market plus the number of people making more than $250,000 a year in the target market is over 20 million people, Orange projects that if one-fourth of people in these target markets buy the eSlate, Orange will sell over 5 million units of the eSlate.

Which of the following, if true, would most weaken the author's conclusion?

HINT: An argument asking you to weaken a conclusion is generally asking you to identify the assumptions and then select an answer that says that one of those assumptions is not true.

In order to do this, you must diagram the argument, and be able to identify the conclusion you are trying to weaken.

The first sentence of the argument is just giving background information and doesn't seem to really be part of the argument. The premises in the argument seem to go as follows (use "MPs" for "medical professionals" and "250Ks" for "people making more than $250,000 a year"):

> eSlate likely buyers: MPs and 250Ks
> MPs + 250Ks = over 20 million
> **IF** 1/4 of those buy the eSlate, **THEN** over 5 million will buy

Is there a problem with this logic?

Keep in mind that the argument DOES NOT say that one-fourth of the target market WILL buy the eSlate. It only says that IF they did buy it, more than 5 million sales will result.

Therfore, some of the WRONG answers are likely to try to prove that one-fourth of the target market will not buy the eSlate. You don't care! The argument will NOT be weakened by that assertion. The "if" in the argument is very important! (For instance, the argument, "IF America became a monarchy, it would be likely to allow female monarchs" is not weakened by the assertion that America is very unlikely to become a monarchy.)

Examine the premises of this argument as a little math problem. Two groups add up to over 20 million people. If one-fourth of the people in those groups buy a product, over 5 million products will be sold. What's wrong with that?

Answer for yourself before you move forward.

Question #7

The Orange Corporation is conducting market research in preparation for the launch of its new device, the 3-D eSlate. Thus far, in Orange's market research, two groups have emerged as likely buyers of the eSlate: medical professionals and people making more than $250,000 a year. Since the number of medical professionals in the target market plus the number of people making more than $250,000 a year in the target market is over 20 million people, Orange projects that if one-fourth of people in these target markets buy the eSlate, Orange will sell over 5 million units of the eSlate.

Which of the following, if true, would most weaken the author's conclusion?

(A) In surveys, less than 5% of medical professionals in the target market said they would buy the eSlate.

(B) The eSlate has many more uses for education professionals than for medical professionals.

(C) Previous projections from the Orange Corporation have generally been too optimistic.

(D) Many medical professionals make more than $250,000 a year.

(E) People who make more than $250,000 a year buy more electronic devices than people who make less than $250,000 a year.

Record your answer: _____

Question #8 Instructions

A study of full-time employees in Britain revealed that female workers take more days off from work due to illness than do male workers. The same study also revealed that female workers are more likely than male workers to go into work when they are sick.

Which of the following most logically proceeds from the argument?

HINT: This question is asking you to draw a conclusion. Make sure to stick closely to the facts presented. Do not introduce any additional assumptions.

Conclusions in "draw a conclusion" questions should be "small." They should be un-ambitious, uninteresting, and un-insightful. They should be obvious and boring. They may even seem trivial. Stick to the facts. For instance:

Women take more sick days.
AND, they also come into work more often when sick.
Therefore… ?

11

What is the implied conclusion?

If you're still having trouble, plug in some numbers. Imagine a 30-day month. The men take 2 sick days and the women take 3 sick days (for example). And, the men come into work sick on 1 day per month, while the women come into work sick on 2 days per month. (You're just making up numbers here that match the facts presented). What can you conclude without adding any new assumptions?

Answer in your own words before proceeding.

Question #8

A study of full-time employees in Britain revealed that female workers take more days off from work due to illness than do male workers. The same study also revealed that female workers are more likely than male workers to go into work when they are sick.

Which of the following most logically proceeds from the argument?

(A)   Many illnesses are more common in women than in men.
(B)   Female workers are absent from work more often due to childbearing and related medical conditions.
(C)   Both male and female workers sometimes call in sick when they are actually healthy.
(D)   Female workers in Britain are sick on more days of the year than are male workers in Britain.
(E)   Having sick people in the workplace spreads illness.

Record your answer: _____

Question #9 Instructions

This year, the Rocktown school district offered a free summer enrichment program called "History Rocks" to its rising fourth-grade students. Therefore, fourth graders in the Rocktown school district will score better this year on American history tests.

Which of the following, if true, would NOT strengthen the author's conclusion?

HINT: This question stem tells you that the answer choices will have four "strengtheners" and one answer that doesn't strengthen (that answer — the correct answer — may weaken, but it also might simply be neutral or even irrelevant).

In order to anticipate what might strengthen the argument, you need to diagram the argument and find its flaws. Fortunately, diagramming is pretty easy — there is only one premise:

11

"History Rocks" was offered to rising 4th graders.
THEREFORE
4th graders will score better on American history tests.

Hmmn, interesting. What could go wrong in between making a summer program available, and test scores going up during the upcoming school year? *Think of several problems before you move on.*

(By the way, "rising fourth graders" are students who have finished third grade and will soon begin fourth grade, so at least the program was *offered* to the right kids.)

Question #9

This year, the Rocktown school district offered a free summer enrichment program called "History Rocks" to its rising fourth-grade students. Therefore, fourth graders in the Rocktown school district will score better this year on American history tests.

Which of the following, if true, would NOT strengthen the author's conclusion?

(A) "History Rocks" focuses entirely on American history.
(B) The majority of the district's rising fourth graders attended the program.
(C) The district decided to make the program free because many students in the area come from low-income families.
(D) The material on fourth-grade history tests in Rocktown is substantially similar to the material being covered in the enrichment program.
(E) It has been proven that students retain knowledge better when learning one subject at a time, as is the case in the "History Rocks" program.

Record your answer: _____

Question #10 Instructions

Over the past three decades, the number of hospital beds available for inpatient psychiatric treatment in the United States has declined from 4 per 1,000 population to 1.3 per 1,000 population. Over the same period in Japan, beds increased from 1 per 1,000 population to 2.9 per 1,000 population. Also during this period, annual mortality rates for persons with mental disorders have risen substantially in the United States, while declining in Japan.

To support a conclusion that the reduction in hospital beds is principally responsible for the increase in mortality in the United States, it would be important to establish which of the following?

HINT: This is a CAUSALITY question. Just because two things happen at the same time (fewer beds, more deaths) doesn't mean that one causes the other. A lot of other things could be going on!

11

The argument tells you that over the last 30 years:

> In the U.S.: beds for mental patients went down and deaths went up.
> In Japan: beds for mental patients went up and deaths went down.

The conclusion is located in the question stem:

> The reduction in hospital beds is principally responsible for the increase in mortality in the United States.

("Principally" means "mainly" or "primarily".)

It's your job to ask, "What could go wrong in between 'fewer beds, more deaths' and the conclusion that having fewer beds caused those deaths?"

Anticipate what kind of information would close this gap. One of the answer choices should provide this information.

Question #10

Over the past three decades, the number of hospital beds available for inpatient psychiatric treatment in the United States has declined from 4 per 1,000 population to 1.3 per 1,000 population. Over the same period in Japan, beds increased from 1 per 1,000 population to 2.9 per 1,000 population. Also during this period, annual mortality rates for persons with mental disorders have risen substantially in the United States, while declining in Japan.

To support a conclusion that the reduction in hospital beds is principally responsible for the increase in mortality in the United States, it would be important to establish which of the following?

(A)   Whether the number hospital beds available for inpatient psychiatric treatment has risen or declined in countries demographically similar to the United States.

(B)   The number of hospital beds available for inpatient psychiatric treatment in the United States prior to the three-decade period under discussion.

(C)   Whether other factors, such as a decreased occurrence of mental disorders, may have led to the decline in mortality in Japan.

(D)   Whether mental health care is more comprehensive in the United States or in Japan.

(E)   Whether other factors in the United States may have led to increased mortality for persons with mental disorders.

Record your answer: _____

Solutions

Question #1 Answer

Answer: **(C)**

In this argument, the teacher's point of view is:

> Many of our new students don't speak English.
> Other schools with many new students who don't speak English have had even worse
> test scores.
> THEREFORE, our teachers are doing a good job in keeping scores from dropping too
> much.

The conclusion is, "It is a testament to the skill and dedication of our teachers that test scores in our district have dropped so little."

The purpose of the speaker's argument is to refute the bold statement (the idea that declining test scores are the fault of teachers).

Question #2 Answer

Answer: **(B)**

To paraphrase the argument:

> N has benefits and side effects.
> Doctors are responsible for weighing the benefits and side effects.
> Most doctors have chosen not to give N.

If doctors are responsible for weighing the benefits and side effects and they decide not to give Nepho-prene, these doctors must have decided that the side effects outweighted the benefits. (B) is a direct match.

Choice (A) seems like it's probably true, but not the conclusion to the argument presented.

(C) might be true (who knows?), but is not the conclusion to this argument, which is about doctors' decision making.

(D) might be true (most drugs don't work on absolutely everybody), but is not the conclusion to this argument.

(E) is an extremely unlikely answer, as a correct GMAT answer will not generally insult anyone.

11

Question #3 Answer

Answer: **(B)**

The argument says that replacing warning labels with a website of data and studies will lead to consumers making better decisions about smoking.

This argument makes many assumptions:

> That people make smoking decisions rationally (not based on addiction or other personal preferences).
> That people will visit the website.
> That people will be able to understand the website.

(B) is an excellent match with the second and third assumptions listed above. Note that choices (A) and (D) are undoubtedly true, but are not assumed by the argument. (The exact OPPOSITE of (D) might actually be a pretty good answer—the argument does assume that people can make decisions about smoking independently of their physical addictions.)

(C) is irrelevant to whether the plan would cause people to behave in the way the candidate suggests. (E) is not indicated at all by the argument.

Question #4 Answer

Answer: **(C)**

The argument says that:

> Pandas that give birth to live young live longer.
> THEREFORE, giving birth causes pandas to live longer.

As you know, of course, just because two things happen at the same time doesn't mean you know which one causes the other! Correlation does *not* equal causation.

The author assumes that the causality does not run the other way—that having the qualities leading to a long lifespan (health, or maybe ability to avoid predators) doesn't cause pandas to be more likely to give birth to live young.

And now that you think about it, it actually makes a lot more sense that healthier pandas would have more babies than that having babies makes pandas healthier!

(C) is a very good match with this assumption.

The other answers, whether true or not, are not necessary to complete and validate the argument as written. (A) and (D) seem to be trying to argue against these female pandas living longer, but since we already know for a fact that pandas that have given birth to live young live longer, (A) and (D) don't really have an impact on the argument—surely, some pandas do die, but that must have already been taken into account. On average, pandas that give birth still live longer.

If giving birth to live young really did cause pandas to live longer, perhaps (B) would be true. But choice (B) still doesn't fix the "hole" in the argument, which is that you need to know which way the causality runs.

(E) also does not fix this "hole." It merely adds more information to the premise that giving birth and living longer seem to be linked. It doesn't fix the problem that you don't know which way the causality runs.

Note that if you pinpoint the problem in your initial diagramming and processing of the argument, you don't have to think too hard about the wrong answers, since (C) would be a perfect match for what you would be anticipating.

Question #5 Answer

Answer: **(A)**

The argument says that if penalties for drug dealing on school grounds were lessened, more students would become addicted to drugs. There are many assumptions in this argument. There are some assumptions related to student behavior:

> That the students will take the drugs.
> That the students have money to buy the drugs.
> That students who take the drugs will become addicted.

There are also assumptions related to the behavior of the drug dealers:

> That drug dealers are aware of and deterred by different levels of penalties in different situations.

Answer choice (A) is a very close match with this idea. The argument certainly does assume that drug dealers care about what the penalties are—it assumes that the current high penalties are keeping drug dealers away, and that lower penalties would attract them.

Note that (B) and (E) are probably true, but are not required for the argument to work. The argument does assume that students becoming addicted to drugs is bad (since the conclusion seems to be that penalties should be kept high to prevent this from happening), but not necessarily for the reasons in (B) and (E). Another way to look at it is that, while (B) and (E) are *consistent* with the thrust of the argument, they do not fix the main hole in the argument.

This is also the main problem with (C). Most people would probably assume that drug dealing on school grounds is punished more harshly than drug dealing in general, but that assumption doesn't really help this particular argument—the argument compares current, high penalties for dealing on school grounds with new, lower (theoretical) penalties for dealing on school grounds. Penalties for dealing off school grounds are not relevant.

(D) has no impact on the argument. (The argument doesn't assume that the dealers aren't students—whoever they are, the speaker wants high penalties to deter them.)

Question #6 Answer

Answer: **(D)**

The argument tells us that low-income residents use pay phones more, and therefore, to accommodate these residents, the city will retain pay phones in their neighborhoods only. Hmm, that's kind of weird. Wouldn't you think that people who depend on pay phones would need to use them even when they're away from home? (Perhaps they use them to call home?) (D) is a very good match for a major assumption in the argument.

The argument also makes some weird assumptions about cell phone usage (it seems to assume that people who use cell phones more would use pay phones less and vice versa). However, just because upper- and middle-income residents have higher cell phone usage doesn't actually tell us that lower-income residents are the ones still using pay phones.

For instance, maybe lower-income residents have cell phones, but keep their costs down by making fewer calls. Or maybe they just use home or office phones and don't use cell OR pay phones. Maybe the few people still using pay phones are high-income criminals trying to conceal their identities. You just don't know.

So, an answer choice that said something to the effect of "Whether low-income residents are the primary users of the city's pay phones" or "Whether residents with low cell phone usage are the primary users of the city's pay phones" would be a good choice, but none of the answer choices available match up with these ideas.

Note that (A) might seem attractive, but without knowing whether these criminals are high-/middle-income residents or low-income residents, this actually wouldn't help you evaluate the plan (keep in mind that the conclusion simply says that the plan "would inconvenience very few people," so for the purposes of evaluating this argument, you don't really care about the real-world consideration that some of these people might be doing something wrong).

(B) is irrelevant—in order to evaluate this argument, you don't need any data splitting the upper- and middle-income groups from each other.

Note that (C) wouldn't help the argument at all, since you don't know what the relationship is between cell phone usage and pay phone usage. You can't FIX an assumption by making additional assumptions (such as that more cell usage means less pay phone usage).

(E) is an excellent example of a common GMAT trap regarding real-world considerations. In the real world, anyone proposing this plan would be concerned about the financial impact of the plan. However, the conclusion of this argument is about inconveniencing people. You are merely evaluating what information you would need to better judge whether the premises of THIS ARGUMENT lead up to THIS ARGUMENT'S CONCLUSION. (E) is irrelevant.

Question #7 Answer

Answer: **(D)**

The argument says that medical professionals and people making more than $250K are likely to buy the eSlate.

> If you add up the people in both groups, you get over 20 million people.
> So if 1/4 of the people in both groups buy the eSlate, over 5 million eSlates will be sold.

What's the problem here? It certainly is true that one-fourth of "over 20 million" = "over 5 million."

One problem might be that many people who make more than $250,000 are married or coupled with other people who make more than $250,000 (and perhaps the same is true for medical professionals). So maybe they'll only buy one per couple. This is an interesting "real-world" concern, but here, you don't care—since the argument is only saying that **IF** one-fourth of the individual people in these two groups bought the eSlate, over 5 million eSlates would be sold. So, anything telling you that fewer than one-fourth of the people will buy is not relevant. This knocks out (A) and (C).

(B) is completely irrelevant. Maybe that means that medical professionals will buy a lot of eSlates, and education professionals will buy even more (or maybe medical professionals will buy hardly any eSlates, and education professionals will buy a few more than that). Even so, it would be introducing a new assumption to say that usefulness translates to sales.

(E) is actually seeming to support the conclusion a tiny bit, or at least support the idea that people making more than $250,000 a year are likely to buy an eSlate (although it would be introducing many new assumptions to say that just because one group buys more devices than another group, that that group will buy any particular device).

Choice (D) addresses the real mathematical problem—the argument never says that there are actually over 20 million people in its target market!

It actually says that if you add up two different target markets, you get over 20 million. But what if there's an overlap?

For instance, what if a university reported that it had 5,000 female students and 4,000 English majors, so therefore the number of female students and English majors combined was 9,000? Pretty ridiculous, right? It is very likely that some of the English majors are female, and those people have been double-counted. Same here—if there is an overlap between medical professionals and people making more

11

than $250,000 (seems pretty likely), then the 20 million number (and thus the 5 million number) is no longer supported.

Question #8 Answer

Answer: **(D)**

Given only the facts that (among full-time workers in Britain):

> Women take more sick days
> AND, they also come into work more often when sick

The only thing you can conclude is that women are sick on more days. (D) is a perfect match.

You cannot conclude (A), that more types of illnesses strike women (a person doesn't have to have lots of different illnesses to be sick for many days). For all you know, every single sick person in Britain has exactly the same illness.

(B) might be true, but who cares? You already know that women are out sick more often, so the REASON behind that premise certainly isn't going to be the conclusion to the whole argument.

(C) is almost certainly true, but has no impact on anything—you already know that women take more days off due to actual illness, so any days that people take off for other reasons aren't part of this argument.

(E) is undoubtedly true in real life, but not at all indicated by the information presented in the argument.

Question #9 Answer

Answer: **(C)**

The argument tells us that:

> "History Rocks" was offered to rising 4th graders.
> THEREFORE
> 4th graders will score better on American history tests.

There are a great many assumptions in this argument. The argument assumes that students will actually sign up for and attend the free class. It assumes that the material in "History Rocks" is the same kind of material tested on American history tests (maybe "History Rocks" teaches the history of Ancient Greece, for instance), and that the students will remember what they learned long enough to score well on tests during the upcoming school year.

Choices (A) and (D) strengthen by filling the gap related to whether "History Rocks" teaches the same kind of material tested on American history tests.

Choice (B) strengthens by filling the gap related to whether students will actually sign up for and attend the free class.

Choice (E) strengthens by filling the gap related to whether students will remember what they learned long enough to score well on tests during the upcoming school year.

Choice (C) simply gives you a *reason* for something you already know—the program is free. Since the original argument identified "History Rocks" as "a free summer enrichment program," knowing that the program is free, or why it is free, doesn't help solve any of the problems with the argument.

(C) is a good example of "piling on"—this choice is consistent with the argument, but it isn't really strengthening, because it is just repeating something you already know. To really strengthen an argument, a choice has to fix a problem.

Question #10 Answer

Answer: **(E)**

This is a CAUSALITY question. Just because two things occur over the same time period (fewer beds, more deaths) doesn't mean that you know what's causing what.

Most obviously, there could be a lot of other explanations for the increased deaths in the U.S.: health care could've gotten worse overall, changing policies or attitudes about mental health care might be bad for patients, access to health care may have gone down, drug addiction or poverty might have gone up in the population of people with mental illnesses, etc.

Note that the information about Japan doesn't really solve any of these problems. Certainly having the information about both the U.S. and Japan *suggests* an inverse variation, but much, much more information would be needed to establish causality (for instance, maybe other factors in Japanese society led to improved outcomes for mental health patients, or perhaps to less mental illness in the first place).

Choices (A), (C), and (D) deal with information relating to other countries. These choices will not help to establish causality between two phenomena occurring in the United States. For a "strengthen an argument" question, do NOT pick any answer choices that require additional assumptions. That means don't pick any choices that introduce new analogies or require the assumption that two countries share important similarities.

Choice (B) relates to a time period irrelevant to the argument. You want to know if the decrease in beds during the past 30 years led to the increase in deaths during the past 30 years.

(E) is the answer. In order to establish that the decrease in beds caused the increase in deaths (in the U.S. in the past 30 years), it would be most helpful to establish whether anything else is responsible for the increase in deaths (in the U.S. in the past 30 years).

11

> ### Grade Yourself
>
> How did you do in this section?
>
> ☐ **A** - I totally get this!
> ☐ **B** - I'm okay with this. Maybe review later if there's time.
> ☐ **C** - I'll make a note to review this later.

Critical Reasoning Wrap-Up

Congratulations! You have made it all the way through the Critical Reasoning portion of this book, plus five questions through *The Official Guide, 13th Edition!*

You are now ready to continue working on *Official Guide* problems on your own. Just remember to maintain good strategy: read the question stem first, diagram the argument, anticipate the answer, and use process of elimination.

In addition, go online and access the Question Banks associated with this book. You'll gain additional practice with GMAT-style Critical Reasoning problems that were designed to help you improve your performance.

Our *Critical Reasoning GMAT Strategy Guide* is highly recommended for continued study. This guide has much, much more to say about particular question types in Critical Reasoning, more specific methods of argument diagramming, and eliminating tricky wrong answers. *Critical Reasoning* will also, throughout the book, refer you to particular problems in the *Official Guide,* so you can practice your growing skills on official GMAT problems related to the topics you are studying.

Now, you can proceed to the third and final topic area of this book: *Reading Comprehension.*

11

Answers to Critical Reasoning Drill Sets

Answers to Drill 8.1 — Find the Conclusion

1. **Quoting sources in your papers without attributing the quotes to those sources is forbidden on this campus.** In order, the chain of logic could be summarized: plagiarism is forbidden, quoting without attribution is plagiarism, so quoting without attribution is forbidden.

2. **The Vytex Company's attempt to develop a perfect garden weed-killer will fail.** Based on the first premise, the statement "It is impossible to develop a flawless garden 'weed-killer'" seemed to follow nicely and might have seemed like the conclusion. But this was only a sub-conclusion leading up to a judgment about Vytex's attempt to develop a perfect weed-killer.

3. **An anti-smoking policy would cause a loss of revenue to our town's bars.** The other information provides a scenario laying out the behavior that would cause the loss of revenue.

4. **A new park should be built at the southern tip of the city.** The first and last sentences detail a problem; the new park is the proposed solution.

5. **It is not true that Saddlebrook College provides the best value in our state.** Careful! The conclusion isn't that *Tunbridge College provides the best value in the state*—the speaker has simply pointed out that Saddlebrook can't be the best value, since another college is a better value. It could be that Saddlebrook and Tunbridge are actually the 10th and 7th best values in the state, for instance.

If you have to rephrase a conclusion, **stick to the text**. The speaker's statement of the conclusion is "this simply isn't true." You just have to go back to the previous sentence and substitute in what the speaker means by "this." Don't go beyond what is explicitly stated somewhere.

Be literal. Think about when you say things such as *Uncle Jay thinks he's the smartest person in our family? Even my eight-year-old is better at math than he is!* You're not arguing that your eight-year-old is the smartest person in the family—you're just pointing out that Uncle Jay can't be the best, since at least one other person is above him.

Answers to Drill 8.2 — State the Implied Conclusion

1. **Van Hoyt College is a good college.** The argument gives one requirement for good colleges: ten Rhodes Scholars. Since Van Hoyt has produced at least one Rhodes Scholar per year for the past decade (which is ten years long), it has produced at least ten Rhodes Scholars. Therefore, Van Hoyt is a good college. (While you might think that there are other requirements for a college's being good, keep in mind that this is the speaker's argument, not yours!)

2. **The female arkbird will not lay eggs this winter.** The argument gives two requirements for egg laying: there must be nesting material, and the climate must be moderate. While *moderate* hasn't been specifically defined, it's completely safe to say that "the coldest winter on record" is not *moderate*.

11

Therefore, the bird will not lay eggs. The fact that the nesting material requirement has been filled—even above and beyond what is required—doesn't fix the problem.

3. **John Doe will not be punished by the death penalty for his crime.** The fact that Doe pled not guilty but was convicted on the basis of videotape isn't really important—what's important is that he was convicted of second-degree murder, not first-degree murder. He does not meet the requirements for being subject to the death penalty (at least for this crime).

4. **Doctors should not perform extreme body modification procedures.** The speaker explains extreme body modifications, then tells you that doctors have sworn to uphold the Hippocratic Oath, which forbids doctors from harming a healthy body part. This argument does introduce an assumption: that extreme body modifications really are harming a healthy body part. (Does changing something necessarily qualify as harming? Is it really harm if it is what the patient wants?) However, the speaker clearly meant for "harming a healthy body part" to refer to extreme body modifications, so the implied conclusion is clear, even if it rests on somewhat shaky ground.

5. **The school board is not following the new school lunch guidelines.** The guidelines call for including vegetables in every meal. The school board has replaced French fries with fruit. While this does sound like an improvement, it is still true that the guidelines are simply not being met. (Whether the guidelines are good, or whether fruits are just as good as vegetables, is irrelevant.)

Answers to Drill 9.1 — Match Analogous Arguments

#1 "Running Study" and #6 "Diversity Training"

Pattern: One group chose to do X and got a better result than a group that didn't do X. Therefore, X worked.

Both cases have a specific type of problem related to **causality**. It seems very likely that a separate, outside cause caused both the runners' health and the training participants' high scores—the fact that both groups were **self-selecting** (that is, people were not randomly assigned to run or not, or to take the training or not take the training). Of course, people who volunteer for a study that involves running 30 miles a week would be much healthier than average people before the study even started! Similarly, people who volunteer to attend a four-week diversity training may already be very interested in diversity and might have scored higher on the test even without the training. Or maybe those who signed up for the training wanted to make themselves look good, and therefore were more motivated to lie or cheat on the test.

In any case, if people who volunteer to do X have result Y, it does NOT prove that X caused Y to happen. Maybe it was the quality that made people volunteer in the first place that caused Y.

#2 "Freight Trains" and #4 "Heart Murmurs"

Pattern: Right now, some things towards the end of their life cycle are better than some things towards the beginning of their life cycle. So the older things must have been better to start with.

The problem in both cases is **survivor bias**. In the case of the freight train engines, it is very likely that the poorly built engines from before 1960 have long since fallen apart—only the best ones are left running! So you are illogically comparing the *best* old engines with *all* newer engines. New engines that were badly built haven't yet had much of a chance to fall apart. In the case of the dogs, the 15-year-old dogs are probably mostly the ones who never had heart murmurs in the first place, since their litter-mates who did have potentially fatal heart murmurs did not live to be 15 years old, sadly.

Just as it would be unfair to compare one university's *best* graduates with *all* of another university's graduates, it is illogical to compare a group that has been weeded out (in this case, by long periods of time) with another group that hasn't.

#3 "New Product" and #5 "Peacekeeping Force"

Pattern: In order to solve a problem, two things must happen. If one thing happens, the other one can't. (Therefore, the solution cannot take place.)

The first argument presents as fact that "to make a profit this quarter, we must increase sales of our old product while also introducing a new product that is as profitable as the old one." If this is true—that this is the only way to make a profit this quarter—then the next premise makes it impossible to make a profit, since "Whenever our company introduces a new product, sales of the old product drop sharply." The conclusion, which was not stated in the original argument, is, "We cannot make a profit this quarter." This is not a paradox, nor is the argument flawed. It's just that the plan won't work. This situation might be called the **self-defeating plan**.

The peacekeeping plan is similarly doomed. For the violence to stop, two things must happen: surrounding nations must vote to send in forces, and Nandia must give money. But if Nandia gives money, the other nations won't vote to send in forces. The conclusion (again, not stated in the original argument) is, "The violence will not stop in Kirkenberg." In other words, the plan will fail.

As you have just seen, even very different-seeming arguments can have the same underlying structure. Remember, most of the mistakes in logic have been made many, many times before.

Answers to Drill 10.1 — Diagramming Arguments

Below are sample diagrams; of course, yours may look really different. Determine whether you have the conclusion in the right place (at the end, according to the discussed method). If you find that the sample diagrams make it easier to see the argument's flaws, then consider ways to modify your own diagramming.

Note: On the real test, because of time constraints, test-takers' diagrams would be messier, and would have abbreviated more (for instance, *imp* for *impossible*).

1. This argument was summarized as *Tropical fruit eating is occurring at the same time as happiness. Therefore, tropical fruit causes happiness.* This argument has a Causation error.

$$TF \approx \smile$$
$$\therefore$$
$$TF \rightarrow \smile$$

2. This was summarized as *Weeds vs. Plants is a matter of opinion. So, a perfect weed-killer is impossible. Therefore, Vytex will fail.* This argument is a Self-Destroying Plan. It doesn't seem to have one of the specific flaws that has been discussed, but there is always a gap. In this case, perhaps a perfect weed-killer really isn't impossible—maybe the second premise is just wrong. People often say *impossible* when they really mean *very difficult.*

W or GP = matter of opinion
↓
perfect w killer impossible
∴
Vytex w killer will fail

3. This was summarized as *South residents have no park, so they go to other parks. This causes waiting and lack of enjoyment. Therefore, a park should be built in the south.* This argument doesn't seem to fall into any recognizable categories of flaws, but there is always a gap. In this case, an extra part of the conclusion is implied: *A park should be built in the south … because it will help with overcrowding in the existing parks.* In between the premises and the conclusion, though, plenty could go wrong. Maybe the new park won't be considered as desirable and nothing much will change. Maybe the southern residents are visiting other parks to participate in organized sports leagues with people from other parts of town, so a park near home wouldn't change their behavior.

S. residents ≠ have P so
travel to other P's
↓
O → waits, ∴
∴ build park in S

Putting It All Together

4. This was summarized as *BU has had DL for five years with students happy about flexibility + no drop in grades (edu qual?). Therefore, if CC gets DL, they will get the same results.* This problem has a Troubled Analogy.

BU - DL 5 yrs
  • students ☺ w/flex
  • no ↓ in grades
∴ CC DL —will→ ☺, no ↓ in edu qual

5. This was summarized as *C applicants got a 65 & V employees got 83, so V employees are better than C employees.* That rephrasing and the diagram make it apparent that you have a case of Survivor Bias. You could also categorize this flaw as a Troubled Analogy. Notice that, in the diagram, the word *applicants* really sticks out—it is clear that a premise about the applicants doesn't tell us anything about the employees.

C applicants 65/100
V employees 83/100
∴
V employees > C employees

Answers to Drill 10.2 — Decoding the Question Stem

1. *Weaken* (*undermine* is a synonym for weaken).

2. *Structure of argument?* The answer might be something like "Pointing out that the mayor has neglected to take into account factors that will limit the plan's success" or "Denying that the consultant's evidence supports the given recommendation."

3. *Paradox.* Pick the answer that resolves the paradox by providing a reasonable explanation for what looked, at first, like a contradiction.

4. *Conclusion.* Draw an appropriate conclusion based on the premises.

5. *Which is NOT a good reason to hire based on the test?* On your actual paper, you might abbreviate this greatly—for instance, "NOT reason to use test." Keep in mind that the correct answer might not be a reason that the test is *bad*—the correct answer could be fairly neutral, or even irrelevant. But the four

incorrect answers will be *in favor* of using the test in hiring. You want the answer that does NOT support using the test, whether that answer is against the test, whether it suggests that more study of the test is needed, or whether the answer choice goes totally off topic and talks about something random. An off-topic answer choice, after all, couldn't really support anything, could it? Note that in this case, an off-topic answer choice could be the right answer!

Chapter 12

of

Foundations of GMAT Verbal
Part 3: *Reading Comprehension*

Phases of Reading Comprehension

In This Chapter...

Chapter 12:
Phases of Reading Comprehension

Reading Comprehension

Reading Comprehension passages on the GMAT are typically 2–5 paragraphs in length and appear on the left-hand side of the screen, while one question at a time appears on the right-hand side.

If the passage is long, you will be able to scroll up and down the left-hand side of the screen while the right-hand side remains static. A typical passage is accompanied by three or four questions. Since you can only see one question at a time, you won't know until you answer the third question whether a fourth one will appear. This is how the screen will be laid out:

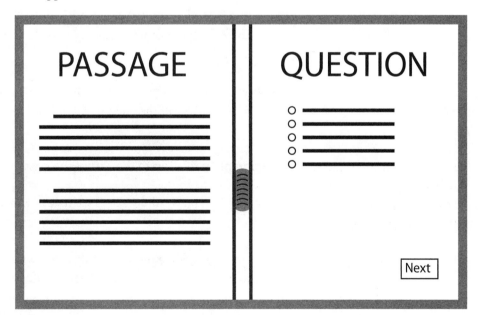

The passages are excerpts from longer works, generally in the fields of business, history, science, and social science. Since the passages have been greatly shortened and adapted, they sometimes seem to begin abruptly; the passages lack the background information or interesting introduction you are accustomed to in much of your reading.

Some of the questions ask about specific details in the passage, while others ask about the main idea, the structure of the passage, or the author's purpose in including certain information. Still other questions ask you to make inferences—this is an area where, as you will see, the hard work you've already done on Critical Reasoning will pay off in Reading Comp as well.

Some people think that you can't improve on Reading Comp—after all, you've known how to read for 20 or more years at this point, right?

These people are completely wrong! It is absolutely possible to improve a great deal on Reading Comp, if you are willing to do the work.

Time to get started!

Why GMAT Reading Comprehension Is Hard (Don't Skip This Intro!)

Why is it hard to read a passage and answer questions about it? After all, you're reading this book right now, right? Obviously, you can read just fine. And, on the GMAT, you're allowed to look back at the passage anytime you want. So why does anyone get *anything* wrong?

There are several answers to that question. One is that GMAT reading passages are a lot harder to read than this book. You also have limited time on the GMAT. You must work quickly, without sacrificing accuracy.

Another reason is that the questions are very specific, and even people who read the passage with a high level of comprehension sometimes get lazy when they actually read the questions. For instance, consider this question:

What is the function of the second paragraph in relation to the rest of the passage?

That's a pretty specific question, but many poor performers on Reading Comp seem to interpret every question as simply asking, "What's going on here?"

If you interpret the question as, "What's going on here?", you will almost certainly pick a wrong answer, because it is very likely that many of the wrong answers are, in fact, *true*. To be clear: *some of the wrong answers in GMAT Reading Comp are 100% true facts*. But they are facts that, for instance, do not explain the role of the second paragraph in relation to the rest of the passage. *Something can be true, but that doesn't make it the answer to a particular question.*

One of the main reasons that many people do poorly is that reading comprehension has declined very seriously since the Internet came into existence, allowing for the development of some really bad habits.

Don't misunderstand: it's difficult not love the Internet. But for purposes of the GMAT, it becomes necessary to turn off your Internet-reading habits and return to your academic-reading habits.

When you read a book or study from a textbook, if you "zone out" and don't remember a thing about the page you just read, you might get frustrated. But you're pretty likely to *realize* what has just happened, and to go back and start again (or go get some coffee!). When you read a page in a book and get nothing from it, you *notice*.

But when people scroll through text on a computer, they do not behave in the same way. When you scroll past eight inches of text and get nothing out of it, what do you do? Do you go back? Probably not. You just keep scrolling… or get distracted and move on to something else (cats on YouTube?).

In order to function in the deluge of information brought by the Internet, many have sacrificed a skill they used to have—careful (but efficient) reading.

Think back to the college-level reading you used to do out of textbooks—certainly you have highlighted and underlined, or typed up your own outlines of the material.

If you have now been in the working world for a few years, have you been reading with the same level of attention and rigor? Probably not—much of the reading you do on the job is straightforward, repetitive, filled with unnecessary junk, and on topics that are already familiar. And you just don't have the time; you have to speed through information in order to get anything done. You read quickly and shallowly because you have to.

Of course, you also have to be quick on the GMAT. But it is crucial that you process and organize information in a rigorous (but efficient) way.

Kill the "Gist"

A student who had done very poorly on the GRE (which tests vocabulary directly) decided to switch to the GMAT and was still having trouble with verbal. "I don't know why anyone would need to know all those words," he said about his former vocabulary studies. "I read the *New York Times* every day and I understand everything."

Right. In reality, you definitely don't. It's this idea that causes people to fail at the GMAT.

What this student meant was that he was getting "the gist." When people give you "the gist" of an article, they often say something like, "It was about the genome and using it for cures and stuff."

The actual main idea of the article was actually something more like, "The previously made observation that the most rare variants in the human genome are the most responsible for disease has been lent support by a new study that shows that more common variants are less likely to be found in functional regions of the genome, and the functional regions are those that actually express themselves, such as in the form of disease."

Big difference.

A student who follows the instructions in this book would have a good grasp of the main idea, because he or she would've written something like this for the first paragraph:

prev. thought: rare Genome variants → most disease
Now — new study agrees

more common → less likely to be in functional region
functional → expression / disease

That doesn't look too hard to do, does it? In fact, despite the handwriting, isn't that even a little easier to understand than a fully written-out version of the main idea?

You have to go much deeper than the "gist." Although the *Reading Comprehension GMAT Strategy Guide* talks about finding the "simple story," some students take this idea of simplification way too far.

Learn to hate the very idea of the gist. The gist is like describing Michelangelo's David as "a guy" or the Taj Mahal as "a building." More on-point, though:

The "gist" is not enough for any GMAT Reading Comprehension question. Not a single one.

You might protest that some questions on the GMAT ask about the main idea of a passage. Can't you answer those, at least, with just the gist?

Not really. You're still going to need to apply a rigorous, word-for-word reading to the answer choices.

From now on, you will do better than people who only have the gist. You will not stop at the gist. You will not be mentally lazy in your reading. You will not rest until you know a passage's **main idea** and **structure**.

Here's what is being referred to by "structure":

- What is the main point of each paragraph?
- Why is each paragraph included and what does it have to do with the main idea?
- Do the main points of the paragraphs form a logical progression, or some other system of relationships?

Consider the following anecdote. Oprah Winfrey once had Nobel and Pulitzer prize winning novelist Toni Morrison (*Beloved, The Bluest Eye*) on her show, and was showering her with praise. And then

12

Oprah said something she meant as a compliment: "Do people tell you they have to keep going over the words sometimes?"

Morrison replied, "That, my dear, is called reading."

Oh, snap!

The Phases of Reading Comprehension

A successful approach to Reading Comprehension can be thought of as a four-phase process:

1. Do a "first read" of the passage, diagramming while you read.

2. Reflect: state the main idea in your head.

3. For each question, rephrase if needed, then anticipate what the answer will say.

4. Use process of elimination to select a final answer. Check your answer word-for-word before hitting "Submit."

Since you get about two minutes per question on the GMAT, all four of the above phases need to occur in 6–8 minutes, from reading the passage to answering all three or four questions.

Here is how to effectively execute each of the four phases.

Phase 1: Do a First Read

A "first read" of a GMAT passage is different from how you might normally read something. In most types of reading, you just start at the beginning, reading everything and seeing what happens.

On the GMAT, your time is very limited, and you are reading with a few distinct goals in mind.

A good amount of time to spend reading a passage is 3 minutes for a short passage and 3.5 to 4 minutes for a longer one. That leaves you about one minute per question.

> Short passages typically have three questions and longer passages typically have four questions. A "longer" passage is any passage that cannot display entirely on the screen at once (that is, you must scroll in order to finish reading).

During this 3–4 minute first read, you will also be diagramming.

12

Depending on how fast you read, you may or may not end up reading every word. If you are not a fast reader, you will focus most of your attention on the beginning of the passage, where the main idea is generally located.

It is very common in GMAT passages that the first paragraph presents a situation or idea, and then the second paragraph gives a **twist**, a **change**, or a **judgment call** on whatever the first paragraph is about. That twist, change, or judgment call is the main idea. Thus, the main idea is sometimes located in the first paragraph, but often "spills over" into the second.

The main time-saving technique in this phase is this: once you've got the main idea, **speed way up**. A guideline that is taught at Manhattan GMAT is that you are aiming for about 90% comprehension of the early part of the passage and 40% comprehension of the later parts of the passage.

How Much of the Passage Should You Read?

Until you figure out the main idea, *read everything*.

Once you know what the main idea is, if you are a fast reader, speed up a bit and write less on your paper. If you are a slow reader, just read the first sentence of each remaining paragraph and add something short to your diagram for each.

There will be some sample diagrams in this chapter. Later on in the *Reading Comprehension GMAT Strategy Guide*, which is recommended for further study, you will learn about making a "headline list" or a "skeletal sketch." These are all just different methods of getting the information down on paper. There are many valid ways to diagram, and everyone's diagram will look a little different.

The important thing in diagramming is to remember that you're not taking notes as though you're going to need to remember the material two weeks later. That means, on the simplest level, *assign variables* to things. *Oligosaccharins* can be "O," and Thomas Jefferson can be "TJ." You're not going to forget your own abbreviations during something that only takes 6–8 minutes!

More importantly, though, the purpose of diagramming is to make your diagram simple and clear, thus exposing the passage's underlying structure. A good diagram is—obviously—a *useful* one. So, if you just blindly write down everything, you're definitely wasting your time. The point is not to take notes about facts; the process of diagramming is supposed to help your thinking.

Think of a diagram as a "reverse engineered" reading passage—you're working backwards to get what the author's outline would have looked like before he or she began writing (assuming, of course, that this author was a very organized and logical person).

Also, your diagram is just for you. It doesn't have to be anywhere close to grammatically correct. As long as you can read your own writing, it can be very messy. Don't practice making beautiful diagrams for your GMAT notes—only practice making the kind of quick and efficient diagrams you will make on the real exam. This isn't college—you won't have to read your diagram the next day or study from it for a big exam next month. Your diagram doesn't even have to be in English! (For most people, mentally translating in and out of a native language slows down the process, but some people end up jotting a few words here and there in whatever lexicon is easiest at the moment.)

Once you have read and diagrammed the passage, move on to Phase 2.

Phase 2: State the Main Idea

The main idea may already be quite obvious from your diagram, since you were reading for the purpose of finding the main idea and structure. But sometimes, the passage's overall main idea seems to be a combination of two or more things you wrote down.

When you figure out the main idea, make an extra notation on your paper, if necessary (for instance, circling something you've already written, or joining two ideas with an arrow). A main idea should be a complete sentence—it should have a verb!

This wil be discussed more in a later section.

Phase 3: Rephrase the Question, Anticipate the Answer

Once you have read, diagrammed, and stated the main idea to yourself, attack the first question. Most questions are easier to understand if you rephrase them mentally. Even a straightforward question can benefit from a rephrasing. For example:

> The primary purpose of the passage is to:

That "question" isn't even a question! Mentally rephrase as, "What is the primary purpose of the passage?"

Some questions need much, much more rephrasing. For instance:

> All of the following are considerations that support the main idea advanced in the
> second paragraph EXCEPT:

In order to rephrase (or even remotely understand) this question, you need to know what the main idea of the second paragraph is. Say you look back and determine that the main idea of that paragraph is *Westward migration led to the emergence of democratic reforms.* Now you can rephrase:

> All of the following are considerations that support the idea that Westward migration
> led to the emergence of democratic reforms EXCEPT:

You're still not done—it's still not a question, and the EXCEPT is confusing. Here's your final rephrase:

> Which does NOT support the idea that Westward migration led to the emergence of
> democratic reforms?

Now that's an understandable question!

12

Next, you want to anticipate the answer. If the question is something like "What is the main idea?" or "According to the information on lines 22–23, how does the wasp parasitize bird eggs?", then you can probably anticipate what you're looking for pretty precisely, because those questions are direct and specific.

For some other questions, though, such as the one above, the best you can do is probably to anticipate the *types of things* that would satisfy the requirements.

For this question (Which does NOT support the idea that Westward migration led to the emergence of democratic reforms?), you might say to yourself, "Okay, I'm looking for an answer that either says the migration led to LESS democracy, or maybe an answer that says that something else caused the democratic reforms." Once you've laid that out, it seems pretty likely that you'll find one of those in the answer choices.

Phase 4: Use Process of Elimination

On a practical level, process of elimination means writing A B C D E on your paper and crossing off answer choices as you find errors in them (you also do this for Sentence Correction and Critical Reasoning).

On Reading Comp, many students find that they are able to get down to just two answer choices—but then they seem to always pick the wrong one.

This is usually because students are not reading the choices *on a word-for-word basis*. A wrong answer choice is often wrong because of *just one word*. It is your job to "vet" your choice before you hit "submit."

"Vet" is a verb meaning "to appraise, check for accuracy, examine, etc." The word is most often used in politics or business when someone is being elected or hired. Just as you want to *vet* a new Supreme Court justice before appointing him or her to the bench for life, you want to *vet* your answer choice before you commit.

On a practical level, you do this by reading three or four words at a time, looking for a tiny word or phrase that makes one of the remaining choices incorrect. Just as a political appointee can lose the job when the vetting process brings a scandal to light, a seemingly good answer can sometimes be revealed to be too extreme, or have a cleverly-inserted "not" that changes the meaning completely.

Practicing the Four Phases of Reading Comprehension

If the four phases sounded complicated, don't worry—sometimes the best way to start learning something is to watch someone else do it well.

This section will model how to go through the four phases on the very first reading passage in the *Official Guide, 13th Edition*—below is a genuine, thought-by-thought example of a test-taker's mental processes as she read and diagrammed the passage, and then attacked the questions. Since there are three questions for this passage, the total time is six minutes.

For copyright reasons, it is not permissable to reprint the passage or questions here, so you will need to go get your *Official Guide* now in order to follow along.

What's written below might look really long, as though it would take a long time to diagram the passage and answer the questions the way the test-taker did. Don't worry! When you write out every single thing you think for six entire minutes, it takes up a lot of paper! What is being described below is a process that it is totally possible to complete accurately in six minutes.

And finally, the way someone diagrams and thinks about a reading passage is highly individual. Other top scoring test-takers might diagram the passage in a totally different way (although all would have a fairly similar phrasing of the main idea). Allow yourself some flexibility here; the goal is not to think exactly like the test-taker, but to take away some techniques that will work for you.

Official Guide 13th Edition
2nd Reading Passage ("Ecoefficiency"), page 366

Lines 1–5:   Ecoefficiency? I've never heard of that. Whatever, I'm sure they're going to tell me what it is. Oh look, they give the definition in parentheses. I'm not going to bother to write that down because, after reading most of a passage about ecoefficiency (I'll call it "EE"), I'm sure I'll remember what it is. Also, definitions are usually not really a part of the argument or main point—they're just background information. So I'll just write:

12

EE goal of co's

(That's my shorthand for "ecoefficiency is the goal of companies.")

Lines 5–9:   Then I see that these two guys—I'll call them S & C—say that EE is laudable but could WORSEN environmental stresses. Interesting! (And weird!) I think this is the main point right here. Something most people think of as good for the environment is actually bad! I've gotten the "change" or the "twist." (Not all passages have a change or twist, but most do.)

By the way, "laudable" means "praiseworthy," but you could definitely get the context of the sentence without knowing that.

I'm going to write:

EE goal of co's
S&C: EE laudable BUT could ↓ enviro

I'll put BUT in capitals because it shows the "twist" or main point.

Lines 9–12:   I now get an explanation of why EE can be bad—it reduces waste from making products, but it doesn't reduce the number of products made, or the waste from people using those products and throwing them away. I'll arrange it like a list.

EE goal of co's
S&C: EE laudable BUT could ↓ enviro
↓
reduce prod. waste BUT — same prod manuf.
— same waste from use & discard

I like to use arrows pointing from words I've already written so I don't have to write the words again, and so I can show how different ideas are related.

Lines 12–19:   Next, the passage says that companies do EE to make more profit, and they can use the profit for non-EE industries. (That sounds bad for the environment!)

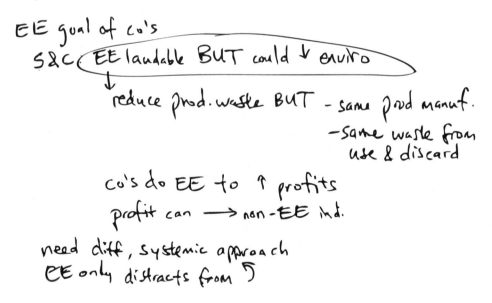

Lines 19–end: At this point, it looks like the passage is just giving more examples of the same thing—it says that more EE could lead to even more environmental destruction. I don't need to write that down. I'll skim to the very end.

S&C want a "new systemic approach." I don't know exactly what that is, but I get their point: EE isn't really helping the environment as much as people thought, so we need a new way for businesses to help the environment. I'm ready to go to the questions. Here's my complete diagram (I went back and circled the main idea):

Now I'm ready for phases 3 and 4—rephrasing the questions and anticipating the answers, then using process of elimination to get down to a single, correct answer.

Question 5
Rephrase the Question and Anticipate the Answer:

The question asks about the main point. I'm going to say the main idea for myself, in my head, before I read the answers: *some people think EE is good, but EE could actually be bad for the environment.*

12

The Choices:

(A) is a possibility, although I feel weird about "successful." Successful at what? Whatever the goal is the strategy is, I guess. I think this might be the answer, but I'm going to check the others.

(B) isn't bad, but I've seen a lot of GMAT questions and know to look out for the tricks being played here. Is the main point to "propose an alternative"? S&C say that we need a "new systemic approach," but they don't say what it is (I think that to "propose an alternative" you'd have to suggest something more specific), and that part of the passage was just one tiny part. Also, the passage says EE "could" cause damage, not that is already has. (B) is too extreme and cannot be justified by the passage. Also, I know I got the main idea right in my diagram, so I want to say that EE could actually be bad for the environment. I'm going to stick to what I know I'm looking for.

Oh, now I like (C) better than (A)! Here's why—I can break the answer choice into several little parts and justify each one. The passage definitely "presents a concern." It definitely talks about "possible consequences" (again, the passage keeps saying "could" cause damage, so this is a good match for something that is a possible damage but hasn't actually happened). And EE is definitely a "particular business strategy." I can't find a problem here—every single word of this choice is accurate. Now that I've checked out (C), I realize the problem with (A)—choice (A) says that the strategy "has been" less successful. Actually, the damages "could" happen but haven't actually happened, so (A) goes too far. Also, (C) matches with what I said I was looking for (that EE could actually be bad for the environment). (C) just said it in a really generic way to try to hide the answer from me.

(D) is the opposite—no one is making a case for *more* EE (nor is the main point to argue that a "new systemic approach" should be practiced on a wider scale—the new approach isn't currently practiced at all).

(E) popped out as wrong right away, because of the word "economic." The main idea is definitely not about the "economic" impact of EE, it's about the environmental impact.

The answer is (C).

Question 6
Rephrase the Question and Anticipate the Answer:

The question wants to know about a possible consequence of companies figuring out they can make more profit from EE. That's in my diagram:

co's do EE to ↑ profits
profit can ⟶ non-EE ind.

If companies do EE to make money and it works, they could use the money to do all kinds of non-EE business, and really damage the environment.

The Choices:

(A) is irrelevant. I want something about the environment, or non-EE businesses.

(B) is irrelevant. Again, I want something about the environment, or non-EE businesses.

(C) is living in a dream world! The whole point is that the companies might put their profits in NON-EE businesses and therefore harm the environment.

(D) Yes, this is just what I was looking for!

(E) is a lot like (C). This would be nice for the environment, but goes against one of the main points of the passage.

The answer is (D).

Keep in mind that ALL of the choices could possibly happen in real life. It's also true that companies that make more money from EE could choose to spend it in environmentally friendly ways. But that doesn't matter. The question asks *what consequence the passage mentions.* You only care about the consequence specifically written in the passage. You're just being asked to repeat what the author says.

Question 7
Rephrase the Question and Anticipate the Answer:

Wow, this question is really similar to the last one. That can happen in a fairly short passage that just has one big idea in it.

The question asks about "a possible consequence" of EE. The passage says up towards the top that EE can result in *not* reducing the number of products manufactured and *not* reducing waste from people using and discarding the products. There's also the main idea—that companies could reinvest their profits in non-EE businesses. So I think the answer could be about any of those things (although I'm not sure the first two are "consequences"—they're just things that EE isn't helping).

The question also says "implies," so this is an Inference question. On these types of questions, the GMAT acts like it wants me to think for myself, but it doesn't really. It wants me to take a fact from the passage and "flip it" in a way that generates an answer that can still be proven. For instance, if the passage says that more widgets are blue than red, the answer to an Inference question about that fact would probably say that fewer widgets are red than blue. A correct Inference answer *has* to be true, based on what I was told in the passage.

12

So, I might be looking for something about companies reinvesting their profits in non-EE businesses, but I might also be looking for something that wasn't stated directly in the passage, but still has to be true.

The Choices:

(A) is a pretty good match for a sentence in the passage: "there is no guarantee that increased economic growth from ecoefficiency will come in similarly ecoefficient ways." However, I feel a little weird about how the answer choice says "further improvements" in EE. The passage never says anything about improving EE—the passage makes EE sound like something you either do or don't do (there's nothing about doing it well or doing it poorly). So, I think that's a flaw in (A). I'll put a squiggle next to it on my paper—I'm pretty sure I'll find something better.

(B)… Hmmn. The passage didn't mention this, but it didn't mention that EE doesn't reduce waste from product use and discard, and that companies do EE to make more profits, and that there's "no guarantee" that the profits will go into EE industries. This seems to imply that the profits could be reinvested basically anywhere—which would include manufacturing a greater number of products to be used and discarded. I think this is a very GMAT-type Inference answer. The passage didn't say this directly, but based on the facts that were given in the passage, this answer really can't be wrong.

(C) talks about companies that don't realize cost savings. The passage never talks about this.

(D) is completely irrelevant to the passage, which never talks about companies developing dependency or having to compete with non-EE businesses.

(E) mentions "ecoefficiency goals," which I find a little confusing—are those goals for the environment or for profit? In any case, "unlikely" is too strong. The passage simply says that there is "no guarantee" that companies will reinvest in EE businesses ("unlikely" would imply a less than 50% chance of their doing so). Also, the passage makes no mention of "new and innovative" EE measures. Again, EE has been presented as something a company either does or doesn't do—there's no mention of needing to get better at it over time. For all I know, EE measures could have been the same for a long time.

The answer is (B).

That's how to do a GMAT Reading Comprehension passage!

> ### Grade Yourself
>
> How did you do in this section?
>
> ☐   **A** - I totally get this!
> ☐   **B** - I'm okay with this. Maybe review later if there's time.
> ☐   **C** - I'll make a note to review this later.

Chapter 13
of
Foundations of GMAT Verbal

Main Ideas & Difficult Information

In This Chapter...

Chapter 13:
Main Ideas & Difficult Information

What Is a Main Idea?

While you've just seen the entire Reading Comprehension four-step process laid out for you, you're going to spend the next few sections breaking it down in a little more detail. What does a main idea look like on the GMAT, and how can you be sure you've found it?

GMAT main ideas are not quite the same as "real world" main ideas.

Non-GMAT reading passages—including news articles, editorials, and academic papers—often have pretty straightforward main ideas, such as:

- Let's explain how bees pollinate certain plants.
- There are several different methods for seeding a cotton field (and here are the options).
- The death penalty should not be applied to mentally disabled criminals (and here are some reasons why).

NONE of these are GMAT-like main ideas. A GMAT main idea is not likely to take the form "Here are some facts," or "Let's contrast two equally good things," or "Here is my argument and here are the reasons."

GMAT main ideas are different. They are *nuanced*. They are very diplomatic—that is, even a writer arguing "for" something will usually give ways that he or she might also be wrong. (Being open to revision based on new information is an important part of the scientific method, and thus of much modern thought even outside of science.)

In the previous section, the main idea was something like, "Ecoefficiency is laudable but could actually HURT the environment." Note that there was a *twist*—something unexpected.

What to Look For

Most main ideas will fall into one of these three categories:

1. A Change (Here's a situation—but now it's different!)
2. A Twist (Here's something that seems straightforward—but it's not what you think!)
3. A Judgment Call (Here are two options—and now I'm going to tell you which one is better!)

So, to be clear: a main idea should contain, at very minimum, a topic and a *verb*. What is the topic *doing?* But there will probably be even more than that.

Many main ideas take the form, "The topic was doing something, but now it's doing something else," or "A group of people thought something for a particular reason, but now the reason is wrong, so maybe the thing they were thinking isn't really true (but we need more information to find out)." Some GMAT main ideas do give opinions, but the opinion will usually be contrasted against a view presented in the first paragraph ("A certain group of people have traditionally thought X—but actually, Y!").

So, now you know what you're looking for—a *change*, a *twist*, or a *judgment call*. So, if you're reading a GMAT passage and all you're reading is facts… you almost certainly haven't gotten the main idea yet.

Where to Look

The main idea of a passage can be located in the first paragraph, but is also very commonly located in the beginning of the second paragraph. Of course, you need to read the first paragraph to understand that the second paragraph is presenting a *change, twist,* or *judgment call.* Often, the first paragraph sets up an idea or situation, and then the second paragraph provides a contrast with the contents of the first paragraph.

Sometimes, it takes more than one paragraph to set up the initial situation (especially if the paragraphs are very short), so the *change, twist,* or *judgment call* doesn't happen until after the second paragraph.

An exception to that is when a contrast is presented right away. For instance, if the first line begins, "A stunning new theory has changed everything we thought we knew about the rotation of the Earth around the Sun," then that's almost certainly the main idea right there. It's pretty likely that the passage will tell us a little bit about what people have traditionally thought, before returning to explaining the "stunning new theory."

Knowing When You've Got It

Have you ever had someone break up with you by making a speech that began, "You are really amazing, and I've had such a wonderful time with you…"—but you can tell that the conversation isn't going anyplace good?

Then the person continues, "I really wish you the best in everything that you do, and you're such a nice person..."—but you're absolutely sure that there's a "but" about to happen? (As in, "BUT, I've met someone else" or "BUT, I just don't think this can work.")

GMAT passages are like that. Except they're often about things like sea urchins, which breakups rarely are.

While you are reading (and paying close attention) to a GMAT passage, a small voice in the back of your mind should be saying something like, "Facts facts facts facts facts! BUT WHAT?!" (Imagine that in a silly voice. *Facts facts facts facts facts!* The facts are not the main idea—keep looking!)

Very often, the main idea takes the form of "BUT actually, it's a little different from what this passage started off saying."

Drill 13.1 — Main Idea

In order to complete this drill, you'll need your *Official Guide, 13th Edition* and a timer.

Following are five *Official Guide* passages to give a variety of different kinds of main ideas. For each question below, go to the page numbers referenced and read the first two paragraphs or so. Time yourself—you should only spend 1.5–2 minutes reading. Stop when you think you have the main idea. Remember, you are looking for a *change*, a *twist*, or a *judgment call*.

Fill in the blanks for each main idea, then check your answers.

1.   Page 394 ("Two works published in 1984...")

        Main Idea: Two works give different approaches to writing the history of U.S. women. BUT Lebsock's _____

        _____

        _____.

        Where did you find the main idea? First paragraph ☐ Second paragraph ☐
        Somewhere else ☐

2.   Page 396 ("It was once believed...")

        It was once believed that _____. BUT _____

        _____.

        Where did you find the main idea? First paragraph ☐ Second paragraph ☐
        Somewhere else ☐

3.   Page 402 ("The majority of successful senior managers...")

Most successful senior managers _____.
Management writers have recognized this, BUT _____
_____. ACTUALLY, Isenberg tells
us that _____
_____.

Where did you find the main idea? First paragraph ☐ Second paragraph ☐
Somewhere else ☐

4.   Page 406 ("According to a recent theory...")

A widely held view says _____,
BUT a recent theory says _____. This theory is important because _____.

Where did you find the main idea? First paragraph ☐ Second paragraph ☐
Somewhere else ☐

5.   Page 416 ("In the two decades...")

From 1910–1930, _____. It has been
assumed that _____and were motivated by
_____ and _____, and therefore that
the migrants' problems were related to _____. BUT ___
_____
_____.

Where did you find the main idea? First paragraph ☐ Second paragraph ☐
Somewhere else ☐

Answers can be found on page 281.

Organizing Difficult Information

The last section discussed finding main ideas, and you wrote them down in sentence form. On the real test, you want to record this information—along with other important information about the passage—in a quick, clear, abbreviated format. But how can you do this when you don't fully understand what you're reading?

Reading passages often seem intimidating or confusing because you don't know anything about the subject matter. However, while a high school level of knowledge about science and history might be helpful, many Reading Comprehension questions are really more about your ability to organize the information you are told, and to spit it back in slightly different formats.

For example, consider this extremely brief passage:

> All terrichnoderms are classified by biologists as members of the phylum Aeridae. As opposed to members of the phylum Aeridae, phractopods do not have tails that can be used for balance, stability, and navigation.

That's all the information you get. Below is an example of a question that can be answered with only the two facts above, and no outside information.

Which of the following can be inferred from the passage?

- (A) Because geckos have tails that can be used for balance, stability, and navigation, they are members of the phylum Aeridae.
- (B) Because phractopods do not have tails, their balance and navigation abilities are less developed than those of animals in the phylum Aeridae.
- (C) Terrichnoderms were not always classified by biologists as members of the phylum Aeridae.
- (D) Terrichnoderms have tails that can be employed for stabilizing and balancing.
- (E) The focus of biology is classifying creatures based on characteristics such as the presence of tails that can be used for balance, stability, and navigation.

Whoa, that's kind of hard! Do not make wild guesses. Instead, go back and organize the information in this passage. You can use T for terrichnoderms, A for Aeridae, and and P for phractopods.

You are first told that "All T are A." Easy.

Then, you are told, "As opposed to A, P do not have tails that can be used for balance, stability, and navigation."

A lot of people write that down and stop there:

all T are A

as opp to A.,

P. ≠ tails for balance, stab., nav.

But you can do better than that.

The "as opposed to A" part is underlined above, because that type of language usually indicates something important in a passage—a contrast or a "twist."

> Imagine that you read an ad that says, "Unlike our competitor's yogurt, ours is organic." The implied meaning is obviously that "our competitor's yogurt is not organic." This little mental "flip" is a very important skill for GMAT inference questions (you'll learn more about this soon).

So, when the passage says, "As opposed to 'A', 'P' do NOT have these kinds of tails," that means that members of "A" *DO* have these kinds of tails. Thus:

all T are A

as opp to A.,

P. ≠ tails for balance, stab., nav.

∴ A <u>Do</u> have tails ...

The three dots arranged in a triangle pattern are a symbol that means "therefore," as was introduced in the Critical Reasoning section.

The information in the passage is deliberately feeding you a particular conclusion—a conclusion that *must* be true based on the information in the passage.

Now revisit the question.

Which of the following can be inferred from the passage?

(A)   Because geckos have tails that can be used for balance, stability, and naviga-tion, they are members of the phylum Aeridae.

(B)   Because phractopods do not have tails, their balance and navigation abilities are less developed than those of animals in the phylum Aeridae.

(C)   Terrichnoderms were not always classified by biologists as members of the phylum Aeridae.

(D)   Terrichnoderms have tails that can be employed for stabilizing and balancing.

(E)   The focus of biology is classifying creatures based on characteristics such as the presence of tails that can be used for balance, stability, and navigation.

Next, go through the answers one by one:

(A)   INCORRECT. You do know that "A" have tails that can be used for balance, stability, and navigation, but you do NOT know that anything that has such a tail is therefore "A". (For instance, all mammals have bones, but not everything with bones is a mammal).

(B)   INCORRECT. You don't know this! All you are told is that "phractopods do not have tails *that can be used for balance, stability, and navigation.*" Maybe they DO have tails (the tails just can't be used for balance, stability, and navigation). And, of course, they might have other, perfectly good body parts (other than tails) that they can use for balance and navigation. You can't infer things you just weren't told about.

(C)   INCORRECT. You have absolutely no information about the history of biologists' clas-sifications of anything. Perhaps you could argue that many thousands of years ago, there were no biologists and thus biologists could not have classified "T" as "A," but that idea is just not based on the passage.

(D)   CORRECT. You wrote at the bottom of your diagram that, "A have tails that can be used for balance, stability, and navigation." Answer choice (D) is about T, though, not A. But wait a minute! Your diagram says, "All T are A"! If all T are A, and A have these special tails, then T have these special tails! (This is like the transitive property in math!) This answer is a direct match with the information in the passage and the conclusion you drew in our diagram.

(E)   INCORRECT. You can stop reading after "the focus of biology." The focus of the entire field of biology? Way outside the scope of the passage. You certainly haven't been told anything about that.

The answer is (D).

Oh, by the way: There's no such thing as a terrichnoderm, a phractopod, or a phylum called Aeridae. It is all made up in order to show you that you can succeed simply by organizing the information you were given. (Just to be clear, the GMAT does not make up information—the makers of the exam pull the information from previously published sources. Here, it was just making a point.)

Grade Yourself

How did you do in this section?

- ☐   **A** - I totally get this!
- ☐   **B** - I'm okay with this. Maybe review later if there's time.
- ☐   **C** - I'll make a note to review this later.

Organizing Difficult Information

Here is a short passage on what most people would consider a difficult and unfamiliar topic (this time, it's all true!) Give the passage a quick read, then you'll diagram it.

> Is the rightness of an action determined by its consequences, or by the intentions of the agent behind the action? Deontological ethics, in contrast to teleological or utilitarian ethics, asserts the latter. For example, Immanuel Kant argued that the only absolutely good thing is a good will, and thus that the only means of determining the rightness of an action is the motive of the person performing that action. Thus, if a person is acting on a bad maxim ("Stealing is good"), then the action is wrong, even if it produces some good consequences (e.g., stealing from the rich and giving to the poor). However, not all deontologists are absolutists: W.D. Ross, for instance, holds that lying is sometimes the right thing to do if the results of the action are likely to be beneficial.
>
> A criticism levied by Jeremy Bentham, a utilitarian philosopher, is that deontological ethics were merely a dressed-up version of popular morality, wherein the ostensible "universal laws" were actually merely subjective opinion. A separate critique of deontology comes from aretaic theories, which hold that it is not the good will of the agent nor the consequences of the action that determine the moral rightness of that action— rather it is the character of the person performing the action. This is by no means a new idea: the ancient Greek philosopher Aristotle is considered the founder of virtue ethics, which seeks to describe the traits of an ideally virtuous person, and then posit that we should act in accordance with those traits.

Whoa, that was complicated! However, parts of it are very easy to understand: W.D. Ross thinks it's okay to lie for a good cause.

Do not simply ignore the parts you don't understand and think that you'll be able to "work it out" based on the parts you do understand. That approach will not work.

You don't have to understand everything here simply to organize the information. While there are many ways to diagram a reading passage, when a particular reading passage seems to be related to contrasting two things, a T-chart is a great way to lay out the information. You don't need to understand everything in order to simply put the information in the correct part of the chart.

You begin with a question: Is the rightness of an action determined by its consequences, or by the intentions of the agent behind the action? You're already setting up a contrast.

In the next sentence, you find that "Deontological ethics" (let's just call that "D") "asserts the latter." The latter means "the last one in the list" (the phrase for "the first one in the list" is "the former").

Therefore, "D" is on the side of "the rightness of an action is determined by the intentions of the agent behind the action." Now, make a chart.

$$\text{D.}$$
$$\text{rightness determined by intentions} \quad \Big|$$

That same sentence about "D" also says "in contrast to teleological or utilitarian ethics." Therefore, teleological or utilitarian ethics (you can call that "T or U") is NOT on the side of "the rightness of an action is determined by the intentions of the agent behind the action."

You can infer, then, that "T or U" is on the *other* side of the question in the first sentence—the rightness of an action is determined by its consequences.

$$\text{D.} \qquad\qquad\quad \Big| \qquad \text{T. or U.}$$
$$\text{rightness determined by intentions} \quad \Big| \quad \text{rightness determined by consequences}$$

13

After that, you are told about Kant and given an example that matches pretty well with the idea that "the rightness of an action is determined by the intentions of the agent behind the action." You can put "Kant" on the "D" side of your chart.

You then find out that W.D. Ross is also a "D" philosopher. Since the part about W.D. Ross is given as an example of "not all deontologists are absolutists," put "not absolutist" with his name.

But wait! You can get even more information from that sentence! Notice that "However, not all deontologists are absolutists" came directly after the part about Kant. *The word "however" allows us to infer that Kant was an absolutist.* Add that to the chart.

D.
rightness determined
      by intentions

Kant - abs.
W.D. Ross - not abs.

T. or U.
rightness determined
      by consequences

The second paragraph tells us that Bentham was a utilitarian. Put him on the other side of your chart (in "T or U"). You also learn that a "separate" critique of "D" comes from "aretaic theories." So, it sounds like aretaic theories (let's call that "A") isn't on either side—so put it here:

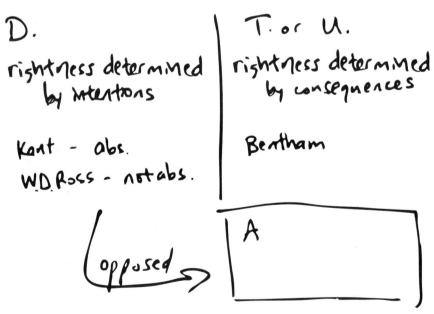

The rest of the paragraph tells you that Aristotle was on the side of "A", which is apparently the same as or similar to "virtue ethics." So add that.

MANHATTAN
GMAT

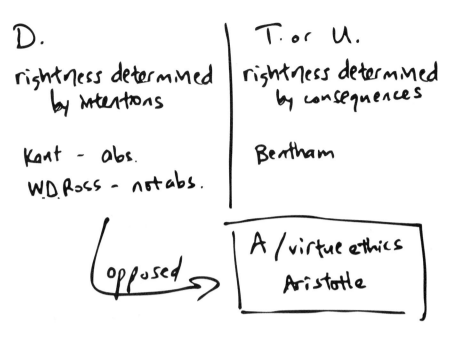

That's everything! Note that you really haven't said much about the actual philosophical ideas in this passage. If you were asked about Kant's ideas, for instance, you would use your chart to remind yourself that Kant is on the "D" side and is an absolutist, and then you'd go back to the first paragraph and carefully read the sentence about Kant.

The point here is that you can do very well simply by organizing the information. You can even do that without understanding all of the words—as long as you can get those words into an appropriate place on a chart or diagram.

Try three questions. Use the above chart (and refer back to the passage) to help you select your answers.

Drill 13.2 — Solve Three Questions

Using the passage, answer the following questions.

1. Which of the following best describes the function of the first paragraph?

    (A)   It poses a question to be answered.
    (B)   It outlines a process and contrasts it with an opposing process.
    (C)   In introduces a theory and indicates that variations in that theory exist.
    (D)   It advances an argument to be disputed later in the passage.
    (E)   It introduces a philosophy and attempts to reconcile it with another philosophy.

13

2. Which of the following can be inferred about teleological theories of ethics?

    (A)   Unlike utilitarian theories, they are in opposition to the main idea of deontological ethics.

    (B)   Like utilitarian theories, they are in opposition to the main idea of deontological ethics.

    (C)   Unlike deontological theories, they are in opposition to the main idea of virtue ethics.

    (D)   Like deontological theories, they are in opposition to the main idea of utilitarian ethics.

    (E)   Unlike deontological theories, they are widely taught in philosophy programs.

3. According to the passage, virtue ethics:

    (A)   suggests that individuals should behave like a person whose character matches an ideal

    (B)   purports that those acting on a bad maxim can still be morally correct

    (C)   has been more influential in society than deontological ethics

    (D)   is more widespread in modern-day Greece than elsewhere

    (E)   contrasts with teleological ethics in its view of the human will

Answers can be found on page 282.

Grade Yourself

How did you do in this section?

☐   **A** - I totally get this!

☐   **B** - I'm okay with this. Maybe review later if there's time.

☐   **C** - I'll make a note to review this later.

Chapter 14

of

Foundations of GMAT Verbal

Inferences & Improving Your Reading

In This Chapter...

Chapter 14:
Inferences & Improving Your Reading

Inference Questions

In the last exercise, you were asked to make an *inference* about teleological ethics. In order to get the right answer, though, you had to use only the information from the passage (which you had helpfully organized in a chart). You didn't add your own ideas or draw your own conclusions.

An inference sticks pretty closely to the facts.

Many people, however, incorrectly use the word *infer*.

First of all, *infer* is definitely not the same as *imply*. To *imply* is to *hint at* something. To *infer* is to draw a conclusion. If your friend *implies* something, you might *infer* her meaning.

But on the GMAT, you must be even more strict in your interpretation of the idea of *inference*. To *infer* for GMAT purposes is to use ONLY the information in the passage in order to **draw a conclusion that cannot be wrong.**

That is, drawing an inference is NOT the same as making an assumption about something that a normal person would assume is probably true. Making assumptions will get you a wrong answer! Picking something that is *probably* true will also get you a wrong answer!

When answering an Inference question, the following are indicators of a WRONG answer:

- Answers that are *probably* true (but not definitely)

- Answers that require additional assumptions (such as about what people might have been thinking when they did something, or about what will happen in the future)

14

So, what kind of conclusion could you possibly draw from a GMAT passage, using only the information in the passage and not assuming anything?

A really boring, trivial, not very insightful one. Seriously.

For instance, if a teacher tells you that "Joey failed the test." What can you infer?

That Joey didn't study? No, maybe he did study and still failed. That the test was hard? Not necessarily.

The only thing you can infer is that *Joey did not pass the test.*

That's kind of stupid, isn't it? But it certainly isn't wrong. Try to argue with *"Joey did not pass the test."* You can't. That's why it's an inference.

The idea of "flipping" something you just read is going to be very helpful in Inference-type questions.

By the way, not every Inference question uses the word *infer*. Many questions use words such as *suggest* or *imply*. Although you just noted the difference between inferring and implying, for purposes of the GMAT, all these questions will be treated the same way: **find the relevant information in the passage and pick something that MUST be true based on that information.**

Words that indicate that you are dealing with an Inference question:

- Infer
- Imply
- Suggest

Here's an example:

> In the early 1940s, women's participation in the U.S. labor market changed dramatically as a result of the labor shortages resulting from the drafting of men to fight in World War II. While persistent and institutionalized discrimination had discouraged women from paid work in the Depression era, the wartime government used patriotic propaganda to encourage women to work in defense industries. While women's employment was still viewed as an extraordinary measure for extraordinary times—and the woman worker as merely filling in for "some soldier" to whom the job properly belonged—gender barriers were lowered somewhat during this period, and pay began to equalize. Despite these moves towards women's participation in the workforce, however, shifting forces in the postwar labor market meant that fewer American women worked outside the home in 1952 than in 1942.
>
> Which of the following can be inferred regarding women's employment during the period discussed in the passage?

(A) Discrimination against women in the workplace increased between 1942 and 1952.
(B) Women's job qualifications decreased during the period 1942–1952.
(C) The end of World War II caused many men to come home and take back jobs they had once held.
(D) Increased economic prosperity in the 1950s meant women didn't have to work.
(E) More women worked outside the home in 1942 than ten years later.

What do you know from the passage? Not much: fewer women worked in 1952 than in 1942, and the cause of this is "shifting forces in the postwar labor market." You need to pick an answer choice that MUST be true, based on only those facts. You should examine the choices.

(A) INCORRECT. You have no way to know that. You were told that employment decreased during that period, but you don't know why.

(B) INCORRECT. Again: You have no way to know that. You were told that employment decreased during that period, but you don't know why.

(C) INCORRECT. This is a trap. You are told that the drop in employment is due to "shifting forces in the postwar labor market," and the idea of men coming back from war and taking back jobs is certainly *consistent* with that, but *consistent* isn't enough. You need a choice that *must be true*. Note that this choice might also mirror something you learned in an American history class. That's because it's true! That's exactly what happened! But it's not the answer to the question, *because you cannot infer it from the information in the passage.*

> **MEMORIZE IT:**
>
> If a passage tells you that something happened, and an Inference answer choice gives a *possible reason* why that thing happened, that choice is wrong! Do not assign causes for things you are told have happened.

Do not bring in outside information. Even if you are certain that something is true in real life, that does not make it the answer to the question at hand. You must pick a choice *that MUST be true based on only the information in the passage.*

(D) INCORRECT. Once again: You have no way to know that. You were told that employment decreased during that period, but you don't know why.

> **MEMORIZE IT:**
>
> Do not pick an answer that is merely "consistent with" something you were told in the passage.

(E) CORRECT. If fewer women worked in 1952 than in 1942, then MORE women worked in 1942 than in 1952. That's a pretty trivial observation. But it MUST be true, based only on the information in the passage. That's why it's the answer.

Once you get the hang of drawing inferences, you can do it very quickly and easily. For instance, what can you infer from this sentence?

> In 2008, Ecuador became the first nation in the world to pass a Constitution codifying the rights of nature.

14

The inference is such as this: *Prior to 2008, no nation had passed a Constitution codifying the rights of nature.* You could even infer something like: *As of 2007, the United States Constitution did not codify the rights of nature.* That's kind of random, but definitely true based only on the information presented. If you are able to draw a general inference (*no nation has passed a Constitution*), then you can often infer a particular case as well (*the United States Constitution did not pass*).

Here's another example. What can we infer from this sentence?

> Because of monumental shifts in the social behavior the researcher studied in the 1970s, the researcher's methodology has proved to be of more lasting value than her results.

It might be helpful to paraphrase the original information first. Maybe something like, *Since a lot has changed since the '70s, the researchers methodology is still valuable, but the results are less valuable.*

The inference is something like, "The results are out of date."

One more. What can you infer from this sentence?

> As opposed to typical artifacts from the period, the newly-named Rozzi Urn depicts a battle scene.

The inference is that *Typical artifacts from the period do not depict battle scenes.*

Now try a drill.

Drill 14.1 — What Can You Infer?

For each statement, fill in the blanks in the inference below. Remember, an inference is something that *must* be true based on the information presented. Try "flipping" the information you've been given.

1. Toads, unlike frogs, lack teeth and spend most of their time on land.

    Inference: Frogs _____ and
    _____ .

2. Irish-American groups pressed for a more accurate treatment of the Irish Potato Famine in textbooks used in American schools.

    Inference: Irish-American groups thought _____
    _____ .

3. The company's household products division was responsible for 40% of its profits in 2010. The balance of its profits came from its beauty products, baby care, and health products divisions, with 25% of the balance coming from the baby care division.

Inference: The 2010 profits from the household care division are _____ than the combined profits of the beauty products and health products divisions.

4.   Unlike most skinks, the crocodile skink of Papua New Guinea is nocturnal or crepuscular (active in the early mornings and at dusk).

   Inference: Most skinks are active _____.

5.   In 1980, Canadian expenditures on these measures were only slightly lower than American expenditures on these same measures. Throughout the 1980s and early 1990s, the Canadian expenditures increased by a constant rate of 2% per year and the American expenditures by a constant rate of 3% per year.

   Inference: Throughout the 1980s and early 1990s, _____

   _____.

Answers can be found on page 285.

Grade Yourself

How did you do in this section?

❑   **A** - I totally get this!
❑   **B** - I'm okay with this. Maybe review later if there's time.
❑   **C** - I'll make a note to review this later.

Reading Comprehension Drill

From now on, you must use a timer to time every GMAT reading passage you read. Four minutes is an absolute maximum for reading—3 or 3.5 minutes is more appropriate for a short or medium-length passage.

Go get a timer right now, before reading this passage. See how much you can read and understand in 3.5 minutes. You may find that 3.5 minutes is actually longer than you think!

After each passage is a "Hint" section that asks you to consider the main idea and structure. Over time, this should become an automatic part of reading for the GMAT.

Time to start!

Passage 1: Padua's Supernova Sighting

A supernova is a brief stellar explosion so luminous that it can briefly outshine an entire galaxy. While the explosion itself takes less than fifteen seconds, supernovae take weeks or months to fade from view; during that time, a supernova can emit an amount of energy equivalent to the amount of energy the Sun is expected to radiate over its entire lifespan. Supernovae generate enough heat to create heavy elements, such as mercury, gold, and silver. Although supernovae explode frequently, few of them are visible (from Earth) to the naked eye.

In 1604 in Padua, Italy, a supernova became visible, appearing as a star so bright that it was visible in daylight for more than a year. Galileo, who lectured at the university, gave several lectures widely attended by the public. The lectures not only sought to explain the origin of the "star" (some posited that perhaps it was merely "vapour near the Earth"), but seriously undermined the views of many philosophers that the heavens were unchangeable. This idea was foundational to a worldview underpinned by a central and all-important Earth, with celestial bodies merely rotating around it.

Hint: Before answering the questions, ask yourself: *What was the purpose of the first paragraph? What was the purpose of the second paragraph? What was the main idea overall? Was there a "twist"?* For instance, after you read the first paragraph, were you surprised that the second paragraph went in a different direction? Make sure you are clear about what Galileo thought or suggested, and what the philosophers thought.

1. The primary purpose of the passage is to

    (A) give the history of supernovae.
    (B) describe a shift in thought as a result of a natural event.
    (C) juxtapose two opposing views about supernovae.
    (D) corroborate the view that the Earth is not central to the universe.
    (E) explain how science and philosophy interrelate.

2. Which of the following can be inferred by the passage:

    I.   Supernovae can take over a year to fade from view.
    II. Prior to 1604, no one had even seen a supernova.
    III. Galileo convinced philosophers of the incorrectness of their views.

    (A) I only
    (B) II only
    (C) I and II
    (D) II and III
    (E) I, II, and III

3.   The author mentions which of the following as a result of the supernova of 1604?

(A)   The supernova created and dispersed the heavy elements out of which the Earth and everything on it is made.
(B)   Galileo explained the origin of the supernova.
(C)   The public was interested in hearing lectures about the phenomenon.
(D)   Galileo's lectures were opposed by philosophers.
(E)   Those who thought the supernova was "vapour" were proved wrong.

14

Passage 2: *Don Giovanni*

By 1784, Wolfgang Amadeus Mozart was internationally renowned as the composer of *Marriage of Figaro*, and consequently received a commission from the Prague Opera House to compose another opera. The resulting product was *Don Giovanni*, which tells the tale of a criminal and seducer who nevertheless evokes sympathy from audiences, and whose behavior fluctuates from moral crisis to hilarious escapade.

While *Don Giovanni* is widely considered to be Mozart's greatest achievement, eighteenth century audiences in Vienna — Mozart's own city — were ambivalent at best. The opera mixed traditions of moralism with those of comedy — a practice heretofore unknown among the composer's works — creating a production that was not well liked by conservative Viennese audiences. Meanwhile, however, *Don Giovanni* was performed to much fanfare throughout Europe.

Hint: Before answering the questions, ask yourself: *What was the purpose of the first paragraph? What was the purpose of the second paragraph? What was the main idea overall? Was there a "twist"?* Note that the second paragraph "flip-flops" a few times — note on your paper which people liked *Don Giovanni* and which people did not. ("*Don Giovanni* was performed to much fanfare" means that the opera was met with a very positive response — "fanfare," sometimes used metaphorically, is literally a "spectacular public display.")

4.   The primary purpose of the passage is to

(A)   relate the story of a somewhat likable antihero.
(B)   discuss how a work of art has been met by diverging responses.
(C)   give a history of the work of Mozart.
(D)   make a case for the renown of *Don Giovanni*.
(E)   emphasize the moral aspects of a musical work.

5.   The author mentions the mixing of "traditions of moralism with those of comedy" primarily in order to

(A)   explain a work's cool reception among a particular group of people.
(B)   remind the reader of the plot of *Don Giovanni*.
(C)   highlight a practice common in contemporary opera.
(D)   argue for an innovative approach to opera.
(E)   undermine a previously presented assertion.

6.   It can be inferred from the passage that which of the following is true about the response of Viennese audiences to *Don Giovanni*?

(A)   The audiences preferred purely moralistic works.
(B)   The response was unequivocally positive.
(C)   They did not know that the composer was attempting to mix musical styles.
(D)   The play's moral themes were offensive to Viennese audiences.
(E)   To say that the response was "mixed" would be a generous interpretation.

Passage 3: Cargo Cults

Cargo cults are religious movements that have appeared in tribal societies following interaction with technologically advanced cultures whose representatives have arrived bearing manufactured goods, or "cargo." These cults were known in the late nineteenth century, but arose in earnest in the years following World War II, as members of tribal societies came into contact with radios, televisions, guns, airplanes, and other goods brought to New Guinea and other Micronesian and Melanesian countries as part of the Allied war effort. Members of native societies, having little knowledge of Western manufacturing, found soldiers' explanations of the cargo's provenance unconvincing and drew the conclusion that the "cargo" had come about through spiritual means. Some concluded that the cargo had been created by the deities and ancestors of the native people, and that the foreigners had attracted the cargo to themselves through trickery, or through an error made by the deities and ancestors. Cargo cults arose for the purpose of attracting material wealth back to its "rightful owners" via religious rituals that sought to mimic the actions of the foreigners in order to attract cargo. The most famous of the cargo cults still exists on the island of Tanna in Vanautu, where cult members have constructed elaborate airstrips and control towers intended to attract airplanes, and where an annual celebration features barefoot soldiers in re-created U.S. Army uniforms conducting military exercises. Cult members wearing "headphones" made of wood can be observed speaking into "radios" made of coconuts and straw, mimicking actions observed by Allied troops during the war.

Members of cargo cults commit the fallacy of confusing a *necessary* condition with a *sufficient* one. It is true, of course, that an airstrip and a control tower are

14

necessary for executing a safe landing of a military airplane; they are not, of course, sufficient to attract an airplane in the first place. Communicating with a radio tower may bring new supplies; speaking gibberish into a straw replica of a radio, of course, will not bring the desired cargo. Thus, the term "cargo cult" has arisen as an idiom in English to describe those who mimic the superficial appearance of a procedure without understanding the underlying purpose, meaning, or functioning of that procedure.

In the book *Surely You're Joking, Mr. Feynman!*, physicist Richard Feynman dedicates a chapter to "cargo cult science," the product of researchers who create the appearance of real science — even with the fastidiousness of those who create a full-size Jeep from bamboo and straw — but without an understanding of the underlying workings of real science. Feynman gives the example of experiments involving running rats through a maze. In 1937, a researcher named Young discovered that rats who had run a maze previously were using some hidden cue on subsequent runs that invalidated the results of those trials. Through meticulous experimentation, Young discovered that the rats could use the sounds made by the maze's floorboards to memorize positions within the maze; when the maze was put on a floor of sand, this cue was removed, and future experiments could be conducted untainted by the "floorboard problem." However, Young's research made no impact whatsoever; other scientists — cargo cult scientists — went on running rats through the maze just as they had before, publishing their results and going about the motions of science without, as Feynman argues, actually doing science.

Hint: This is obviously a harder and longer passage than the other two. It's okay if you can't read this much in 3.5 minutes. If you read the first paragraph, the short second paragraph, and the first sentence of the last paragraph, that would be enough to figure out that *everything in the passage was leading up to talking about some not-very-good scientists.*

Before answering the questions, ask yourself: *What was the purpose of the first paragraph? What was the purpose of the second paragraph? The third paragraph? What was the main idea overall? What was the "twist"?* After you read the first paragraph about the islanders, were you surprised that the third paragraph was about scientists?

Note how the second paragraph (especially the part about the "idiom" — that's the "twist!") ties together the first and third paragraphs. If you didn't catch that, go back now and re-read paragraph 2 to find exactly where it stopped talking about the people on the island, and began talking about something else.

Finally, a word of warning: at the beginning, this passage was about islanders, but in the end, it was about scientists. *The islanders are merely a warmup on the way to the real topic.* Do not be tricked into thinking that the main idea of the passage is about the islanders! It is not. You must take the "twist," and the subject matter of the third paragraph, into account.

7.   The primary purpose of the passage is to

      (A)   offer a suggestion for improving the results of scientific experiments.
      (B)   suggest that two disparate groups of people share similar logical errors.
      (C)   explain that cargo cults mistakenly confuse preceding events with causal
            events.
      (D)   argue that it is important for scientists to take into account the research of
            other scientists in their fields.
      (E)   imply that the cargo cult members' mistakes in logic could be remedied
            through the scientific method.

8.   The passage suggests that resident of Tanna concluded that they were the "rightful
      owners" (lines 28–29) of the "cargo" because

      (A)   they found stories of the goods' actual origins to be incredible
      (B)   they believed all possessions were created by deities
      (C)   they believed they were owed a debt by their ancestors
      (D)   Allied forces had given them the cargo
      (E)   guns and airplanes were unknown to them prior to World War II

9.   According to the information provided by the passage, which of the following would
      critics such as Feynman most likely describe as practitioners of "cargo cult science"?

      (A)   Scientists who create a sufficient cause for an event rather than a necessary
            one.
      (B)   Residents of Tanna who attempt a scientific experiment with only primitive
            equipment.
      (C)   Researchers who are unsuccessful in causing a desired phenomenon to
            occur.
      (D)   Westerners who believe in supernatural phenomena despite overwhelming
            evidence to the contrary.
      (E)   Scientists who receive recognition for their work without disclosing possible
            flaws in the design of their experiments.

10.   According to the passage, the similarity between cargo cult members and practi-
      tioners of "cargo cult science" can most appropriately be described in which of the
      following ways?

      (A)   Both use inappropriate equipment in trying to cause a phenomenon.
      (B)   Both refuse to accept the principles of the scientific method.
      (C)   Both adhere to processes that lack scientific rigor.
      (D)   Both have no logical basis for their actions.
      (E)   Both would benefit from enhanced scientific education.

Answers to Reading Comprehension Drill Sets

Answers to Drill 13.1 — Main Idea:

Obviously, you will have phrased your answers differently from the answers below, so don't worry too much about that. Were you able to paraphrase in order to state the main idea concisely? And, more importantly, did you get the basic idea of what comes after the "BUT"?

1. Page 394 ("Two works published in 1984...")

   Main Idea: Two works give different approaches to writing the history of U.S. women. BUT Lebsock's <u>deals DIRECTLY with the controversy regarding whether women gained or lost status from the 18th to the 19th centuries.</u>

   Where did you find the main idea? First paragraph (but, of course, the entire passage is one long paragraph—you have to read down to about line 14 to get the main idea).

2. Page 396 ("It was once believed...")

   It was once believed that <u>the brain functioned independently of metabolic processes in the body.</u> BUT, <u>serotonin in the brain depends on food.</u>

   Where did you find the main idea? First paragraph.

   After getting what you were pretty sure was the main idea—that serotonin in the brain actually depends on food—you should have kept reading a little bit to make sure that there wasn't *another* twist. There wasn't. The second paragraph simply explains how "serotonin depends on food" was discovered.

3. Page 402 ("The majority of successful senior managers...")

   Most successful senior managers <u>use intuition (rather than the classical, logical model).</u> Management writers have recognized this, BUT <u>they don't understand intuition & they see it as bad.</u> ACTUALLY, Isenberg tells us that <u>intuition is NOT bad, irrational, etc.</u>

   Where did you find the main idea? Somewhere else (third paragraph).

   In order to really get the main idea, you need to interpret the phrase "neither of these" in line 20. Isenberg says that intuition is "neither of these." Neither of *what?* Isenberg's thesis is placed in contrast to information in the previous paragraph—the management writers saying that intuition is "the opposite of rationality" or "an excuse for capriciousness." So Isenberg is refuting those two ideas.

14

4. Page 406 ("According to a recent theory...")

> A widely held view says <u>gold-quartz systems were deposited from metamorphic fluids</u>, BUT a recent theory says <u>the gold-quartz systems were formed more than a billion years ago from magmatic fluids deep below the Earth's surface</u>. This theory is important <u>because it could help find gold.</u>

Where did you find the main idea? Second paragraph.

The main idea is mostly expressed in lines 10–11 ("The recently developed theory has considerable practical importance"), but you have to keep reading in order to find out *why* it has practical importance—because "simple prospecting methods" aren't finding much gold these days, as gold deposits "have no surface expression."

Note that the author never says that the new theory is *true*. The meaning is more like, *IF the new theory were true, that would be super great for helping us find some gold.*

5. Page 416 ("In the two decades...")

> From 1910–1930, <u>more than 10% of the black population moved from the South to the North</u>. It has been assumed that <u>the migrants came from rural areas</u> and were motivated by <u>cotton industry collapse</u> and <u>Northern demand for labor</u>, and therefore that the migrants' problems were related to <u>being from rural places</u>. BUT <u>these assumptions have never been proven.</u>

Where did you find the main idea? Second paragraph.

Notice that the author never says that the idea that the migrants were rural is *wrong*. The author simply says that this idea has not been proven, and then goes on to suggest that urbanized, skilled, employed black workers *could* have made up most of the migrant population. This level of uncertainty is very GMAT-like.

Answers to Drill 13.2 — Solve Three Questions

1. In this particular chart, information from paragraph 1 and paragraph 2 isn't physically separated, but, by this point, it should be pretty clear that the first paragraph set up the contrast and the second paragraph gave criticisms of "D." Here is the chart from just the first paragraph:

D.   T. or U.
rightness determined | rightness determined
     by intentions | by consequences

Kant - abs.
W.D Ross - not abs.

(A) Answer choice (A) is attractive—the first sentence of the passage is, indeed, a question! However, *answer choice (A) is a trap*. You have to have read (or at least scanned) the rest of the passage to know that the question "Is the rightness of an action determined by its consequences, or by the intentions of the agent behind the action?" is never answered. The author simply describes philosophers' views on the topic (the author does not take a side). Also, the *point* of the paragraph is not to ask the question. The question is just a small introduction to explaining deontological ethics.

(B) Answer choice (B) refers to a "process." What process? Two (or more) ethical theories are being talked about.

(C) The first paragraph does "introduce a theory" (the theory of deontological ethics). Does the paragraph "indicate that variations in that theory exist"? Look at your chart—Kant is an absolutist, and W. D. Ross is not. Choice (C) is correct. Note that if you had *not* made a chart, you might think that Kant and W. D. Ross were on totally opposite sides, so it might have been very difficult to realize that their ideas are really "variations" on the same idea.

(D) Choice (D) says that the passage "advances an argument." This implies that the author is actually advocating a position (to "advance" is to argue for). The author is simply describing philosophers' views, not arguing in favor of anything.

(E) "Introduces a philosophy" sounds okay, but the author does not "reconcile" deontology with another philosophy (to "reconcile" two ideas would be to show that the ideas are compatible with one another). You can see from your chart that the contrast remains throughout the passage.

The answer is (C).

14

2. When you "infer" on the GMAT, you must not make additional assumptions. You must pick an answer *directly* supported by facts from the passage. Before looking at the choices, it would be helpful to look at your chart and rephrase what you know about "T":

"T" is on the same side as "U"—they are the same or pretty similar.

"T" (and "U") are on the opposite side of "D."

"T" says that rightness is determined by consequences.

"T" is supported by Bentham.

"T" and "A/virtue ethics" are both opposed to "D" (but you don't know whether "T" and "A/virtue ethics" have anything else in common with each other).

That is all the information you have. Nothing else.

(A) INCORRECT. Choice (A) is wrong because of the first word, "unlike." Teleological theories *are* opposed to the main idea of deontological ethics, but so are utilitarian theories.

(B) CORRECT. Choice (B) matches what you just said above: "T" (and "U") are on the opposite side of "D".

(C) INCORRECT. You don't know whether "T" is opposed to the main idea of virtue ethics, and also because "D" and virtue ethics are on opposite sides.

(D) INCORRECT. As was just said above, "T" is on the same side as "U".

(E) INCORRECT. Choice (E) is wildly out of scope—you have absolutely zero information about what is taught in philosophy programs.

The answer is **(B)**.

3. This is just a "detail question," asking about something specific in the passage. You know from the last sentence of the passage that "seeks to describe the traits of an ideally virtuous person, and then posit that we should act in accordance with those traits." You also know that virtue ethics is on the same side as aretaic theories, and that these theories are on the opposite side of deontology.

(A) CORRECT. "Suggests that individuals should behave like a person whose character matches an ideal" is a very good match with "seeks to describe the traits of an ideally virtuous person, and then posit that we should act in accordance with those traits." This is just a paraphrase of a fact from the passage. Thus, choice (A) is correct.

(B) INCORRECT. This idea (about the "bad maxim") is from paragraph 1, about W.D. Ross. It is not in regard to virtue ethics.

(C) INCORRECT. Out of scope. You have no way to know what has been influential.

(D) INCORRECT. Out of scope. You are never told which theories are more widespread, and certainly mentioning one ancient Greek philosopher doesn't tell you anything about modern-day Greece.

14

(E) INCORRECT. You only know similarities between virtue ethics and teleological theories; you weren't told of any differences.

Answers to Drill 14.1 — Inference Drill

1. Since the facts about toads are "in contrast to frogs," you can infer that **Frogs have teeth and do NOT spend most of their time on land**. (If you said "frogs spent most of their time in the water," then you were using outside information—for all you know from the sentence, frogs spend most of their time in the air.)

2. If Irish-American groups "pressed for a more accurate treatment," they must have thought that **the treatment of the Irish Potato Famine in textbooks used in American schools was *not accurate enough***.

3. "The balance" means "the rest" or "the remainder." So if household products accounted for 40% and baby products for 25% "of the balance," then baby products accounted for 25% of the leftover 60%. One-fourth of 60% is 15%. Thus, household = 40%, baby = 15%, and beauty and health combined = 45%. Thus, **the 2010 profits from the household care division are *lower* than the combined profits of the beauty products and health products divisions**. (Note: If there's ever even a tiny bit of math in a Critical Reasoning or Reading Comp question, *do the math*—it's going to be much easier than the math you're already doing for the Quant section of the GMAT anyway.)

4. Your clue is "unlike most skinks." Since the crocodile skink is active at night ("nocturnal") or in the early morning or at dusk, pretty much the only time that leaves for the regular skinks is daytime. Thus, **most skinks are active *in the daytime***. (If you've never heard of a skink, don't worry—almost no one has. No previous knowledge of skinks is required here.)

5. The Canadian expenditures were lower in 1980 and then grew at a slower rate than the already-higher American expenditures. **Throughout the 1980s and early 1990s, *American expenditures were consistently higher*** (or Canadian expenditures were consistently lower).

Think a little more about #5. If you know for sure that American expenditures throughout the period were always higher (and you do know that), you could also infer some fairly random-sounding (but not really random) facts, such as:

Canadian expenditures in 1987 were lower than American expenditures in 1989.

That sounds out of scope, but actually, that statement **must be** true based on the original information—if American expenditures are higher throughout the entire period, and the gap between the

14

American and Canadian expenditures only widens every year, then you can safely conclude that American expenditures will always be greater than Canadian expenditures from the same or an earlier year.

However, you could NOT conclude that American expenditures from an EARLIER year would be greater than Canadian expenditures from a LATER year. "American expenditures in 1980 were greater than Canadian expenditures in 1983" would be an INCORRECT answer because, while that *might* be true, you do not have enough information to *infer* it (that is, to know it for sure).

If it seems like you're doing Critical Reasoning again instead of Reading Comprehension, that's because there is a large overlap in the reasoning required for Critical Reasoning questions that ask you to draw a conclusion and Reading Comprehension questions that ask you to draw an inference.

Passage 1: Padua's Supernova Sighting

Sample diagram:

1. **(B)**

Before reading the choices, it is helpful to state in your head—or refer back to your diagram—to determine for yourself what the main idea is. Is the passage really about supernovae, or is it about Galileo, the philosophers, and the ideas being discussed? The fact that the "twist" occurs in paragraph 2 (it's not talking just about science—now it's talking about history and philosophy) should tell you that paragraph 2 is more central to the main idea and paragraph 1 is just background information.

Choice (A) is wrong because it does not mention the main content of paragraph 2, the ideas and assumptions that became controversial. It is also *much* too broad—giving a history of supernovae would take a lot more than two paragraphs.

14

Choice (B) is correct—the passage does describe a "shift in thought" (from an unchangeable "heavens" to a more scientific view), and this shift (at least among intellectuals in Padua) was prompted by a "natural event" (the supernova).

Choice (C) is attractive ("juxtapose" means to put next to one another or to compare), but does not describe the main idea. While Galileo and the philosophers certainly had different views about the bright light they saw in the sky, it's not clear that you can say that the philosophers had "views about supernovae" in general. It is also clear from the historical aspect of the passage (Galileo clearly "won") that the purpose is to give a history of a breakthrough in thinking about a topic in astronomy.

Choice (D) can be stricken simply due to "corroborate" (to prove true or support with evidence). The passage is describing, not making an argument.

Finally, choice (E) is *much* too broad! You could spend an entire career discussing "how science and philosophy interrelate." This passage covers a much more narrow topic.

2. **(A)**

Remember that Inference questions are *not* asking you to think for yourself. You must not make any assumptions or go beyond the information in the passage.

Statement I is true because you can prove it with the first sentence of paragraph 2: "In 1604 in Padua, Italy, a supernova became visible, appearing as a star so bright that it was visible in daylight for more than a year." Since this supernova was visible for more than a year, it is possible for supernovae to "take more than a year to fade from view." Note that paragraph 1 says "supernovae take weeks or months to fade from view"—apparently, according to paragraph 2, the number of months can be more than twelve. (Note that if Statement I said "Supernovae *always* take more than a year to fade from view," it would be wrong.)

Statement II cannot be proven. Just because you are told that a supernova in 1604 caused a stir doesn't mean no one else had ever seen one before.

Statement III also cannot be proven. You know that Galileo disagreed with the philosophers; you don't know that those particular philosophers ever changed their minds.

3. **(C)**

Try to answer questions like this in your head before reading the choices. What happened as a result of the supernova in 1604? Galileo gave popular lectures in which he "sought to explain" the origin of the "star" and which "undermined the views" of some philosophers. That's all you know.

Choice (A) is a bit silly—was the Earth created after 1604? This choice took some wording from the paragraph and twisted it around to trick us.

Choice (B) is too extreme—you know that Galileo "sought to explain" the origin of the supernova, but you don't know that he succeeded.

Choice (C) is true—you are told that the lectures were "widely attended by the public." (A very picky person might point out that just because people go to a lecture doesn't mean they are interested, but all of the other answers are definitely wrong, so that confirms that this is a reasonable—that is, very tiny—leap.)

Choice (D) is attractive, but is a trap answer. You know that Galileo, in his lectures, "undermined" (weakened) the views of the philosophers. But you don't know what the philosophers' response was, and you certainly don't know whether the philosophers were opposed to the lectures themselves (a person could be opposed to the ideas in a lecture but still think the lecturer should be allowed to lecture).

Choice (E) is also attractive because you, as a modern reader, know this to be true in real life. However, the question *does not* ask, "What really happened?" It asks, "*The author mentions which of the following as a result of the supernova of 1604?*" *The author does not mention* that the philosophers were "proved wrong." (Their views were "undermined, which is much less extreme.) You cannot validate this answer choice with evidence from the passage.

Passage 2: *Don Giovanni*

Sample diagram:

4. **(B)**

In main idea questions, you can often eliminate one or more answers just based on the first word or phrase: *relate, discuss, give a history, make a case, emphasize.* Does the passage "make a case"? It doesn't—like almost all GMAT passages, it is merely reporting facts and/or the opinions of others. *Emphasize* is also a bit strange—usually, the purpose of a passage is something a little bigger than just "emphasizing" something.

When you read and diagrammed the passage, you may have determined that paragraph 1 simply gives background information about *Don Giovanni*, while paragraph 2 gives the "twist"—even though almost the whole world loved *Don Giovanni*, people in Mozart's own hometown were a lot less into it. Choice (B) matches this: the passages discusses how a work of art (the opera) has been met by diverging (different, diverse) responses, specifically those of Viennese audiences versus those of everyone else.

14

5. (A)

The full sentence is, "The opera mixed traditions of moralism with those of comedy—a practice heretofore unknown among the composer's works—creating a production that was not well liked by conservative Viennese audiences." You can get two facts about "mixing traditions of moralism with those of comedy":

- "a practice heretofore unknown among the composer's works" = Mozart had not done this before

- "not well liked by conservative Viennese audiences" = Viennese audiences did not like this because it was a departure from tradition

Correct answer (A) is a good match—a "cool reception" means that those who "received" something (the audience) were holding back or hostile (think "emotionally cold.") Note that the GMAT is trying to hide the correct answer from you a little bit by saying "a particular group of people" for "Viennese audiences."

Also note that (D) and (E) could be eliminated straightaway—the author does not "argue" or "undermine" (which would mean the author was arguing) at any point. Obviously, talking about moralism and comedy doesn't "remind the reader of the plot" (choice B), and you have no idea (from the passage, at least) what is common in contemporary (modern) opera, so (C) is out of scope.

6. (E)

You know that Viennese audiences did not like the (new) mixing of moralism and comedy because the audiences were "conservative." But there's an even better clue: the passage says "eighteenth century audiences in Vienna—Mozart's own city—were ambivalent at best."

Ambivalent means *having mixed feelings or undecided. At best* is an expression meaning *or worse.* The expression *a generous interpretation* has a similar meaning (*To say he manages by intuition rather than logic is a generous interpretation* means the manager is probably an irrational person who just goes with his feelings, in a bad way).

(E) is a direct match with a sentence from the passage.

Note that (A) and (B) contain extreme language (purely, unequivocally). Choices (C) and (D) go too far. You have no indication that audiences were confused or offended, merely that they didn't like or had mixed feelings about a work of art.

Passage 3: Cargo Cults

Sample diagram:

I def of CC
   arose following WW II
   native societies = C comes from deities, ancestors
          Westerners got thru "trickery"
   cult = attract wealth back
   rituals mimic Westerners' actions (coconut radios!)

II confuse nec w/ suff condition
☆ CC is IDIOM for mimic procedure w/out
        underlying meaning, purpose, etc.

III Feynman: CC scientists
        young, rat maze

7. **(B)**

A quick scan of the opening verbs or phrases — *offer a suggestion, suggest, explain, argue, imply* — should eliminate choice (D), since the passage does not argue anything, but merely reports about cargo cults, the use of the term "cargo cult," and the views of Richard Feynman.

Choice (A) can be eliminated because the author does not "offer a suggestion" anywhere (if you are going to pick an answer that says the author offered a suggestion, you need to be able to actually put your finger on the suggestion written down in the passage).

Choice (C) is too narrow and only references the first paragraph. This is the trick answer! The passage is not really about the islanders; the islanders are being used as a metaphor to talk about the scientists.

Choice (E) is offensive! Also, GMAT authors rarely try to tell anybody what to do. This author certainly does not.

The correct answer is (B), which is a very good match with paragraph 2, which contains the "twist," and also nicely ties together the content of the entire passage. Note also that correct main idea answers often lack keywords ("cargo cults," "science," etc.) and therefore look "boring." This can sometimes be used as a hint.

14

8. (A)

The correct answer here hinges on knowing that "incredible" means "not believable." (In casual speech, it is used to mean "awesome," but just as *a credible story* is a believable one, *an incredible story* is an unbelievable one, probably a lie.)

The extreme word "all" completely eliminates choice (B). Sure, the cargo cult members thought that the cargo was created by deities, but *all possessions*? Even the stuff the islanders owned before the Westerners arrived? You don't know that.

(C) is a twisting of language in the passage. If someone (ancestors and deities) means to give you a gift and someone else (Westerners) "steals" it, that does not mean that the gift-giver "owes you a debt." This is a trap answer not indicated by the passage.

(D) and (E) may be true, but do not answer the question: *Why* did the islanders think the stuff came from deities and ancestors? *Do not fall for true or possibly true answers that do not answer the question!*

Correct choice (A) is *simply a sentence from the passage rewritten using synonyms*! Paragraph 1 says that the members of native societies "found soldiers' explanations of the cargo's provenance unconvincing." In other words, they "found stories of the goods' actual origins to be incredible" (*provenance* = origin and unconvincing = incredible).

9. (E)

If you did not read all of paragraph 3 early on, you would have to go back and dig into it now. That's fine—why waste the time earlier when you already had the main idea and you might not have gotten asked about that part anyway?

It will also be helpful here to say the answer in your own words before attacking the choices. The passage says Feynman thinks cargo cult scientists are "researchers who create the appearance of real science—even with the fastidiousness of those who create a full-size Jeep from bamboo and straw—but without an understanding of the underlying workings of real science." You need an answer that gives an example of scientists who "create the appearance of science" but without really doing science.

Start by killing (B) and (D)—keep in mind that to be a practitioner of "cargo cult science," you have to first be a scientist! (Feynman's book is specifically about scientists.) (B) and (D) are not even about scientists.

Choice (A) is a twisting around of wording from elsewhere in the passage. Also, what's wrong with creating a sufficient cause for an event? It's not clear that this is even describing something bad.

(C) is much too broad. What is the *desired phenomenon*? You don't know. A researcher who fails at creating a desired phenomenon isn't necessarily practicing bad science—trial and error, and failure, are a normal part of science. (This is why we haven't yet cured cancer.)

(E) is correct. Someone who takes recognition for their work even though he or she knows the work is based on a flawed design is putting on a show of science without really doing science.

10. **(C)**

This question is asking for the *best* description of what the islanders and the scientists from the passage have in common. Watch out for answers that are true, but don't answer the question. (For instance, both the islanders and the scientists have arms and legs, presumably, but that is obviously not a good description of why the author wrote about both of them in the same passage.)

Choice (A) is true—the islanders do things like talk into a coconut as though it were a radio; the scientists are using rat mazes that are flawed. But this is the trap answer. Using inappropriate equipment is not the main similarity the two groups have. Paragraph 2 contains the main idea of the passage, which is exactly the similarity you are being asked about—two seemingly different groups of people share the same logical flaw, that of engaging in the superficial performance of something without the real, meaningful, underlying functionality.

Correct choice (C) doesn't say exactly that, but "Both adhere to processes that lack scientific rigor" is a more general description of the two groups' problems. Note that this is a rather mild and polite (not extreme) way to discuss the two groups' flaws—rather than saying, "What you are doing is superficial and meaningless," it says, "What you are doing is not strictly scientific." This is a mild restatement of the main idea in paragraph 2.

Choices (B) and (D) are too extreme (it is doubtful that the scientists, at least, "refuse to accept" the scientific method, and the islanders may never have even heard of the scientific method). (D) is offensive and much too extreme.

(E) is a policy prescription not indicated by the passage, which offers no such prescriptions. GMAT authors rarely tell anybody what to do.

Grade Yourself

How did you do in this section?

- ☐ **A** - I totally get this!
- ☐ **B** - I'm okay with this. Maybe review later if there's time.
- ☐ **C** - I'll make a note to review this later.

Improving Your Reading in General

If you have six months or more until you need to take the GMAT, you have time to genuinely become a better (and faster) reader. A fellow instructor ,Stacey Koprince, has written an excellent article on the Manhattan GMAT blog on exactly this topic. Below is a reprint of Stacey's excellent advice.

14

Part IV of this book will address improving your vocabulary and understanding of idioms, which will also help immensely.

How to Improve Your Reading Skills for Reading Comprehension
by Stacey Koprince

Students often ask for non-GMAT reading sources that they can use to improve their reading skills in general, for comprehension and for speed. Recently, some students have asked for more: how should they read such material? Is it the same as reading for work or for pleasure? (Not entirely, no.)

Reading Passages on the GMAT

Several circumstances separate GMAT reading from real-world reading (whether for business or pleasure). First, we're severely time-constrained on the GMAT. It's rare that your boss will toss some reading material at you, instruct you to read it and report back to her, and then add, "By the way, I want your report in 3 minutes." (If this happens to you… maybe you need to find a new boss!)

Second, the material is often more dense than the kinds of things that we read in the real world. Third, the material is often excerpted or edited down from a longer work, so some of the transitions may be disjointed and the material may provide only bare-bones context.

Non-GMAT Reading Sources

For those who are learning English, and aren't planning to take the GMAT for at least six months to a year, you may want to begin with business and science articles in newspapers such as *The Wall Street Journal* or magazines such as *The Economist*. These sources are a bit too "casual" and easy to read compared to most GMAT material, but they can provide you with a good starting point if you feel you need it.

Sources that are closer to "GMAT-speak" include:

> *Scientific American* for the harder science passages
> *The University of Chicago Magazine* (particularly articles found in the Investigations tab)
> *Harvard Magazine*

But it's not enough just to read these the way that you read your regular news material.

14

How to Read from non-GMAT Sources

So what do we need to do to learn GMAT lessons from these non-GMAT reading sources? (Note: the things I'm going to recommend below are geared toward helping you prepare for the GMAT; I would recommend different strategies if you were looking for pure comprehension without artificial time limits.)

First, GMAT reading material rarely provides a long introductory section or much of a conclusion, but those features are quite common in news and magazine articles. Skip the first paragraph or two (possibly several) and dive in somewhere in the middle. Read approximately three to five paragraphs (depending upon the length: you want about 200 to 400 words), and give yourself a time limit. Give yourself 2 minutes for a shorter length and 3 minutes for a longer one.

Don't expect to get 100% comprehension from the three to five paragraphs you read initially; after all, you aren't actually reading the full text. Don't give yourself extra time; stop when that buzzer buzzes. Part of your task is to become comfortable with reading quickly and actually not fully comprehending what you just read.

Then, try to articulate:

- the main point of each individual paragraph
- the main idea of the entire article (or at least of this section of the article) without having to go back to the introductory paragraph; don't expect to get it exactly right, since you aren't actually reading the entire article
- "content" language (facts, historical information, processes, categories) and "judgment" language (opinions, hypotheses, comparisons)
- any "changes in direction" in the text that you read: "however" language, two differing points of view, etc.

Then, go read more and gauge your accuracy. Read a couple of additional paragraphs. Does that change your answers to the above? How? Why? Read a bit more and do the same. Finally, read the entire article.

When you start to feel more comfortable with this type of reading, add another layer of complexity: what might they ask you about the details of the article? What can you infer for GMAT purposes? (That is, what is not stated but must be true based upon information given in the article?) Do you understand the detail well enough that you could summarize it for someone else, possibly using easier language?

Content

To start, you might read articles that cover all kinds of content. GMAT Reading Comp passages come in one of four main categories: Physical Sciences, Biological Sciences, Social Sciences, and Business. As you study, ask yourself: is your RC ability the same regardless of the type of content? Or do you tend

14

to struggle more with certain kinds of content? If the latter is true, then start doing some more non-GMAT reading in those areas.

What do you do when you hit a particular sentence that makes you think, "What in the world does that mean?" You "unpack" the sentence into multiple simpler sentences. Use your grammar knowledge and find a noun that you understand. Look for actions that describe that noun (don't worry about what parts of speech are used—just articulate the action). Make a short sentence: that noun plus that action (in the form of a verb).

Then, create a second sentence that uses some new piece of info from the original and that relates to your first new sentence. Keep the sentence simple: one subject, one verb. Often, you can start these sentences with this or these: for example, "this caused…" or "these theories were tested…." If there are technical terms that you don't understand, abbreviate them to a single letter and don't worry about the meaning; use the rest of the sentence to understand what's going on. Keep going until you have "unpacked" the original sentence.

When studying, you may want to write out your "unpacking" of a sentence, but your goal is to get good enough that you don't need to write it all out (because you certainly won't have time to do that during the test).

Takeaways

1. If you are struggling with reading speed or comprehension, practice reading from non-GMAT sources. If necessary, build up from "lighter" sources, such as *The Wall Street Journal* and *The Economist*, to more GMAT-like material, such as scientific and university magazines.

2. Answer certain questions about the material that you read: what's the overall point? What's the purpose of each paragraph? What are the main pieces of content and the judgments made? What changes of direction exist?

3. If any specific content gives you trouble, practice that type more. Learn to "unpack" difficult sentences efficiently and effectively.

How to Study from the Official Guide

You will definitely want to use *The Official Guide for GMAT Review, 13th Edition,* to study Reading Comprehension (as well as the other sections of the exam).

Working out of a book is, of course, different from taking an exam or practice test on a computer. On the Reading Comp section, the difference is even more pronounced. Here are some important differences:

14

The *Official Guide (13th Ed.)*	The Real GMAT (a computer-adaptive exam)
You could theoretically write in the book	You obviously can't write on the screen
3–9 questions per passage (usually 5–7)	3–4 questions per passage
Questions at all levels of difficulty	Questions adapt to your level of ability
You can see all the questions at once	You can only see one question at a time
You can skip questions and go back to previous questions	As on all of the GMAT, you must answer every question and you cannot go back
You must time yourself	A clock on the screen counts down

Perhaps the most obvious difference between the *Official Guide* and the real exam is the number of questions per passage. The *Official Guide* gives as many as nine questions for a single passage, but on a computer-adaptive exam, you would see only the three or four questions that have been selected for your level of performance (based on how well you've been doing on the verbal section in general).

You want to make your *Official Guide* practice as much like the real GMAT as possible. Therefore, here are some instructions for studying from the *Official Guide*.

Always use a timer. On the real exam, a section will have 3–4 questions, so you should allot 6–8 minutes for the section (3–4 minutes to read, and about 1 minute per question). On *Official Guide* passages, allow yourself 3–3.5 minutes to read a short passage and 3.5–4 minutes to read a long passage. Then allow an average of 1 minute per question (so if a section has six questions, allow 6 minutes). Some questions do take longer than others, so it is not important to make sure you can do each one in exactly 1 minute, so long as the timing works out overall. Questions that say EXCEPT or NOT in the stem usually take longer.

Do not write in the book. Treat the book like a computer screen. Do everything on separate paper.

Do not skip questions. Do not go back. You must answer every question, *in order*. (If you have to guess on a problem, make a note on your paper that your answer was a guess—that will remind you to really go over that question later.) Once you move on to a new question, you may not change your answer to an old question.

> **MEMORIZE IT:**
> Imagine that, on every question, you have to argue with four other people, each of whom insists that one of the other answers is correct. Imagine convincing each of those people why he or she is wrong.

If you wish, you may read the first question before you read the passage. But do not read the other questions. On the real GMAT, you will see a passage and one question only. If you wish, you can read that question (it is recommended to preview the question stem only, not read all the answer choices) before you read the passage. But on the real exam, not only can you not see any other questions, but you don't even know how many questions there are going to be.

Once you finish a passage, go to the answer explanations and read *everything*. Even if you got a question right, you want to know *why the GMAT thinks the other answers are wrong.*

How to Diagnose Problems in Your Reading Comp Process

For every answer you get wrong, figure out *why that happened.* **Do not just say, "Oh, I get it now."** That is not good enough! You must *diagnose* the problem so it does not happen again. For each question you missed:

- Did you not read the question carefully enough?
- Did you not "vet" your answer choice by reading it word for word?
- Did you pick an answer choice that is a true statement—but not the answer to the question being asked?
- Did you miss a question because you didn't understand the vocabulary?
- Did you pick an Inference answer that introduced a new assumption or couldn't be proven with evidence from the passage?
- Did you answer a detail question without looking back at the right part of the passage to find proof?

Every question you miss is a chance to improve—IF you take the time to figure out *why* you missed the question. Then, reflect. How can you make sure that doesn't happen again? Maybe you could write yourself a note ("What is the question *really* asking?" etc.).

How to Plan Your Study Sessions

There's no need to do more than one passage at a time. The *Official Guide (13th Edition)* contains only 29 reading passages, so there's no need to plow through them too quickly. (The supplementary book, *GMAT Verbal Review, 2nd Edition,* contains 18 more passages.)

A good study session for Reading Comp might consist of the following:

- Make 10–15 new flashcards from Part 4 of this book (Vocabulary and RC Idioms) and quiz yourself on the flashcards you've just made.
- Read 1–2 non-GMAT articles using Stacey's instructions from the previous section.
- Do 1 *Official Guide* (or *GMAT Verbal Review*) passage according to the instructions above, including reading all of the explanations afterwards.
- Quiz yourself on your new flashcards again, as well as your flashcards from previous days.

Could you do that every day for 24 (or 42) days? If so, you will do much better on GMAT Reading Comprehension.

Reading Comp Wrap-up

Congratulations! You have finished the Reading Comprehension portion of this book! Reflect back on how much more rigorously you are able to approach a reading passage now than you were before you read this book—isn't it an enormous and wonderful difference?

Go online and access the Question Banks that are included with your purchase of this book. You'll gain practice with doing Reading Comp passages in an online format—and the explanations will help guide your improvement.

But don't stop there. There is another secret weapon about to be shared! Part 4 of this book is chock full of powerful GMAT vocabulary words and idioms. Improving your understanding of the small parts of passages—individual words and phrases—will greatly improve your understanding of the "big picture" of passages.

MANHATTAN
GMAT

Chapter *of* 15

Foundations of GMAT Verbal
Part 4: **Vocabulary & RC Idioms**

Vocabulary & RC Idioms

In This Chapter...

Chapter 15:

Vocabulary & RC Idioms

Why Learn Vocabulary for the GMAT?

At the simplest level, it's pretty hard to do well on Reading Comprehension (or Sentence Correction or Critical Reasoning for that matter) if you can't comprehend what you're reading.

The vocab list in this section contains words that have appeared in the *Official Guide* or other official GMAT materials in the Reading Comprehension, Critical Reasoning, and Sentence Correction sections, as well as words from other sources at the same reading level. Following the vocab list is an RC idioms guide, which serves the same purpose as the vocab list, but focuses on expressions or phrases rather than single words.

This list includes only words and phrases that are general enough that they are likely to appear again. For instance, a GMAT reading passage about sea urchins might contain many biology terms that would be defined within the passage (or else would not be needed to answer the questions). Those words would not be included here.

Another type of word you will likely see on the GMAT but not on the list is "glued-together" words— words that hardly anyone has seen before, but that can be puzzled out by looking at the component parts. Don't let these kinds of words shake your confidence. Each one is just two easy or medium-level words or word parts stuck together. For example:

Circumstellar – around a star
Deradicalized – something made not radical or extreme
Historicophilosophical – both historical and philosophical
Knowingness – quality of knowing something
Presolar – before the sun
Spherule – tiny sphere or globule

15

Thus, the compiled list does not include super-specialized words like those above, while it includes many abstract words about ideas and arguments.

While this book is meant for everyone, this portion of the book is geared mostly for non-native speakers. If you are a native speaker of English and don't feel that you have issues with vocabulary, still take a quick look over both lists—you will probably discover some new things. Or you could skip straight to the drills at the back of this section to make sure that you're on the right track.

While these lists are most tied to Reading Comprehension, learning these words will also help your Critical Reasoning and even Sentence Correction. There have been students who have eliminated a correct Sentence Correction answer choice because they didn't know how to use the word *seemingly*, or because they didn't know that you could use the word *ranks* in the sense of *Our university has many distinguished people among the ranks of our alumni.*

Finally, learning these words will not just improve your GMAT score, but will serve you well for the rest of your life.

Many of these words are words that people just "read over" without even realizing that they don't know. If you saw a word like *omphaloskepsis* somewhere, you would definitely realize you didn't know it, and you might look it up (it means the contemplation of one's bellybutton as a meditation aid). But if you saw a much more boring, familiar-looking word used in a new way, as in *Her work is **informed** by a background in ancient Greece* or *The board won't **condone** noncompliance,* you would be much more likely to just pass over those words—at the expense of your comprehension. (Both *inform* and *condone* appear in the list.)

If you see an easy looking word in the list, don't skip over it! There's a good chance it's here because it has another meaning that not everyone is aware of. For instance:

*   A *novel* is a book, but as an adjective, *novel* means "new and original."

*   *Conversant* looks like *converse,* but does it really mean the same thing? (Actually, it means "knowledgeable.")

*   Everyone knows the word *qualified,* right? Then how about the use of *qualified* in "Dr. Wong could give only *qualified* approval to the theory, as the available data was limited in scope." Why is Dr. Wong's approval "only" qualified? *Qualified* is good, right? *Qualified* here means "limited, conditional, holding back."

Some of the definitions you learn may surprise you.

Of course, if you have an impending GMAT deadline, you may not have time to learn vocabulary. It is more important that you spend time on things on which you are tested directly. If you have limited time, at least look over this list. You will probably see a few words you have always wondered about!

MANHATTAN
GMAT

How to Learn Vocabulary for the GMAT

You should be making flashcards for vocabulary words. However, many of the words in the list are words that you won't need special efforts to memorize because they just *make sense*. For instance, if you know that a *blunt* knife is bad at cutting, then it shouldn't be a big surprise that *blunt* as a verb means *weaken* or "take the edge off"—for example, you can *blunt* criticism by also offering praise. A good number of the words on the list may stick with you after just a single read.

In order to keep the list a reasonable length, if a word has been included because of a less common meaning, the common one will *not* be included, too. So, for instance, when it says that *grade* means *blend into* or *slant,* don't worry that you're going crazy—of course, *grade* can also refer to what teachers do when they mark your papers.

While some of the words on the list might just stick, some of the words will take some memorization. To make a good vocabulary flashcard, put the word on the front (and the part of speech, if it helps you). Put the definition on the back. It might be helpful to write an example sentence. It's fine if the example sentence illustrates the meaning of the word only to you—in fact, the more personal it is, the more likely you are to remember. If you've written, "I can't *countenance* my spouse's tantrums" on a flashcard, you're pretty likely to remember the meaning of *countenance*.

Here is a sample flashcard:

Aberrant
(adj)

Also *abberration* (noun)

Abnormal, deviant

Losing rather than gaining weight over the holidays is certainly an aberration.

15

This student happened to include some extra information—the noun form of *aberrant*. The richer your flashcards, the more likely you are to learn from them (even from the act of making them)!

Many students make the mistake of memorizing dictionary definitions of words without really understanding those definitions or being able to comfortably use those words in sentences.

You want to learn words such as *advent* and *dubious* the same way you know words such as *study* and *mistake*—that is, you use those words all the time, effortlessly, and in a variety of situations. Because you will not be taking a vocabulary test, but rather using vocabulary in understanding other types of verbal problems, you need to be able to read and understand these new words quickly and normally.

Memorization is important. But while vocabulary lists, flashcards, and the like are excellent tools, some of the best vocabulary accrual occurs when you are reading difficult material and you go look up a word you just read in context. For sources of difficult material, try *The Economist, Scientific American,* or the articles posted on aldaily.com (that's "Arts and Letters Daily").

If you read a definition and you don't really understand it, look the word up someplace else! One great place is www.learnersdictionary.com, which defines words in a simple way for English language learners.

It can also be helpful to ask someone, or to simply Google the word to see how other people are using it. Some students have had success typing the word into an online translation engine and reading a definition in their native language (only do this if you don't understand the English definition).

TIP:

You can easily look up words on dictionary. com, thefreedictionary.com, or m-w.com, but if you want simpler definitions, try learnersdictionary.com.

Finally, of course, you will learn words much better if you use them. Try pairing up with a study partner and sending each other emails using words off your list (you can probably think of plenty of other ways to use technology to practice vocab socially).

Once you have studied the definition, read the word in context, and worked the word into conversation three times (this can cause your friends to look at you funny, but it'll be worth it!), that word is probably yours for life.

Vocabulary List for the GMAT

Abate – Reduce or diminish.

> Her stress over spending so much money on a house **abated** when the real estate broker told her about the property's 15-year tax **abatement**.

Aberration, Anomaly – Something that stands out or is abnormal. *Outlier* is similar.

> The election of a liberal candidate in the conservative county was an **aberration** (or **anomaly**), made possible only by the sudden death of the conservative candidate two days before the election.

Acclaim – Great praise or approval.

Accord, Discord – Accord is agreement, and discord is disagreement.

> Our management is **in accord with** regulatory agencies about tightening standards.

Acquisitiveness – Desire to acquire more, especially an excessive desire.

> The firm did well in buying up its competitors as a means of growth, but its **acquisitiveness** ultimately resulted in problems related to growing too quickly.

Acreage – Land measured in acres.

> Our property is large, but much of the **acreage** is swampland not suitable for building.

Adhere to and **Adherent** – To adhere to is to stick to (literally, such as with glue, or metaphorically, such as to a plan or belief). An adherent is a person who sticks to a belief or cause.

> The **adherents** of the plan won't admit that, in the long term, such a policy would bankrupt our state.

> Employees who do not **adhere** to the policy will be subject to disciplinary action.

Ad-lib – 1) Make something up on the spot, give an unprepared speech; 2) Freely, as needed, according to desire.

> We have ended our policy of rationing office supplies—pens may now be given to employees **ad-lib**.

Adopt – Take and make one's own; vote to accept. You can adopt a child, of course, or a new policy. To adopt a plan implies that you didn't come up with it yourself.

15

Advent – Arrival.

> Before the **advent** of the Internet, people often called reference librarians to look up information for them in the library's reference section.

Adverse – Unfavorable, opposed.

> A noisy environment is **adverse** to studying, and lack of sleep can have further **adverse** effects.

Agency – The ability to use power or influence.

> Some global warming deniers acknowledge that the planet is heating up, but argue that human **agency** does not affect the climate.

Aggravate – Make worse.

> Allowing your band to practice in our garage has greatly **aggravated** my headache.

Altogether – Completely, overall. *Altogether* is an adverb, and is one word. It is not the same as *all together,* as in *Let's sing all together.*

> It was an **altogether** stunning new design.

Ambivalent – 1) Uncertain, unable to decide; 2) Wanting to do two contradictory things at once.

> The health care plan has been met with **ambivalence** from lawmakers who would like to pass the bill but find supporting it to be politically impossible.

Amortize – Gradually pay off a debt, or gradually write off an asset.

> A mortgage is a common form of **amortized** debt—spreading the payments out over as long as 30 years is not uncommon.

Analogous – Corresponding in a particular way, making a good *analogy.*

> Our situation is **analogous** to one in a case study I read in business school. Maybe what worked for that company will work for us.

Annex – To add on, or something that has been added on. An annex to a building is a part built later and added on, or a new building that allows an organization to expand.

Annihilate – Completely destroy.

Annul – Make void or null, cancel, abolish (usually of laws or other established rules). Most people associate this word with marriage—a marriage is annulled when a judge rules that it was invalid in the first place (because of fraud, mental incompetence, etc.), so it is as if it never happened.

> Can we appreciate the art of a murderer? For many, the value of these paintings is **annulled** by the artist's crimes.

Anoint – The literal meaning is "rub or sprinkle oil on, especially as part of a ceremony that makes something sacred." The word is used metaphorically to refer to power or praise being given to someone who is thought very highly of. For instance:

> After Principal Smitters raised test scores over 60% at her school, it was only a matter of time before she was **anointed** superintendant by a fawning school board.

Antithetical to – Totally opposed to; opposite.

> The crimes of our chairman are totally **antithetical** to what the Society for Ethical Leadership stands for.

Application – Act or result of applying. Of course, you can have an *application* to business school, but you can also say *The attempted application of American-style democracy in Iraq may ultimately prove unsuccessful.*

Apprentice – A person who works for someone else in order to learn a trade (such as shoemaking, weaving, etc.) from that person. Mostly historical, but still exists in the U.S., in a few industries, such as contracting and electrical wiring.

Arbiter – Judge, umpire, person empowered to decide matters at hand. *Arbitration* is typically a formal process in which a professional *arbitrator* decides a matter outside of a court of law.

> Professional mediators **arbitrate** disputes.

> The principal said, "As the final **arbiter** of what is and is not appropriate in the classroom, I demand that you take down that poster of the rapper Ice-T and his scantily clad wife Coco."

Archaic – Characteristic of an earlier period, ancient, primitive.

> The school's **archaic** computer system predated even floppy disks—it stored records on tape drives!

> Sometimes, when you look a word up the dictionary, certain definitions are marked "**archaic**"—unless you are a Shakespeare scholar, you can safely ignore those **archaisms**.

Aristocracy – A hereditary ruling class, nobility (or a form of government ruled by these people).

Artifact – Any object made by humans, especially those from an earlier time, such as those excavated by archaeologists.

> The archaeologists dug up countless **artifacts**, from simple pottery shards and coins to complex written tablets.

> The girl's room was full of the **artifacts** of modern teenage life: Justin Bieber posters, *Twilight* books, and a laptop open to Facebook.

Ascribe to/ascription – To *ascribe* is to give credit; *ascription* is the noun form.

> He **ascribed** his good grades **to** diligent studying.

> The boy's mother was amused by the **ascription to** his imaginary friend **of** all the powers he wished he had himself—being able to fly, having dozens of friends, and never having to eat his broccoli.

Assert – Affirm, claim, state, or express (that something is true).

Assimilation – The process by which a minority group adopts the customs and way of life of a larger group, or the process by which any new thing being introduced begins to "blend in." Words like *Westernization* or *Americanization* refer to the process of *assimilation* into Western culture, American culture, etc.

Attain – Achieve.

Attribute to – Give credit to.

Atypical – Not typical.

Backfire – To produce an unexpected and unwanted result. The literal meaning refers to an engine, gun, etc., exploding backwards or discharging gases, flame, debris, etc., backwards, thus possibly causing injury.

> The company's new efficiency measures **backfired** when workers protested and staged a walkout, thus stopping production completely.

Balance – The remaining part or leftover amount. This is related to the idea of a *bank balance*—a *balance* is what you have left after deductions.

> The publishing division accounted for 25% of the profits, and the film division for **the balance**. This means that the film division provided 75% of the profits.

Baldly – Plainly, explicitly. (This is the same word as in "losing one's hair.") To say something *baldly* is to be blunt. People are sometimes shocked or offended when things are said too bluntly or *baldly*.

> An article in *Mother Jones* explained that Maine is not very diverse: "It is, to put it **baldly**, one of the whitest states in the union."

Balloon – 1) Swell or puff out; 2) Increase rapidly. Also, in finance, a *balloon payment* is a single payment at the end of a loan or mortgage term that is much larger than the other payments.

> During the dot-com bubble, the university's investments **ballooned** to three times' their former value.

> When he won the award, his chest **ballooned** with pride.

Befall – Happen to (used with something bad). The past tense is *befell*.

> Disaster **befell** the company once again when the CEO was thrown from a horse.

Belie – Contradict or misrepresent.

> The actress's public persona as a perky "girl next door" **belied** her private penchant for abusing her assistants and demanding that her trailer be filled with ridiculous luxury goods.

> The data **belie** the accepted theory—either we've made a mistake, or we have an amazing new discovery on our hands!

Benevolent – Expressing goodwill, helping others or charity.

Benign – 1) Harmless; 2) Kind or beneficial; 3) Not cancerous.

> He was relieved when the biopsy results came back, informing him that the growth was **benign**.

> He's a **benign** fellow. I'm sure having him assigned to your team at work will be perfectly pleasant, without changing the way you do things.

Blight – Disease that kills plants rapidly, or any cause of decay or destruction (noun); ruin or cause to wither (verb).

> Many potato farmers have fallen into poverty as a result of **blight** killing their crops.

> Gang violence is a **blight** on our school system, causing innocent students to fear even attending classes. In fact, violence has **blighted** our town.

Blunt – To dull, weaken, or make less effective.

> The new therapy has severe side effects, but they can be **blunted** somewhat with anti-nausea medication and painkillers.

Blur – To make blurry, unclear, indistinct.

> In Japan, company titles are taken very seriously and roles are sharply defined, whereas in the U.S.—especially in smaller firms—roles are often **blurred** as everyone is expected to pitch in on a variety of projects.

Bogus – Fake, fraudulent.

> The back of this bodybuilding magazine is just full of ads for **bogus** products—this one promises 22-inch biceps just from wearing magnetic armbands!

Bolster – Strengthen or support.

> The general requested reinforcements to **bolster** the defensive line set up at the border.

> Many people use alcohol to **bolster** their confidence before approaching an attractive person in a bar.

Broad – Wide, large; in the open ("in broad daylight"); obvious, clear; liberal, tolerant; covering a wide scope of things. ("Broad" is also a mildly derogatory term for women, in case you're confused—of course, no one would ever be called *a broad* on the GMAT.)

> The panel was given **broad** discretionary powers. (That pretty much means that the panel can do whatever they want.)

Brook – Suffer or tolerate. Often used with the word *no*. You could say *The dictator will not brook dissent,* but a more common usage would be *The dictator will brook no dissent.*

Buffer – Something that separates two groups, people, etc., who potentially do not get along. When the U.S. was controlled by England, the state of Georgia was colonized as a *buffer* between the English colonies and Spanish Florida. A breakwater of rocks would act as a *buffer*, protecting the beach against crashing waves.

Bureaucracy – 1) Government characterized by many bureaus and petty administrators; 2) Excessive, seemingly meaningless requirements.

> Some nations have a worse reputation for **bureaucracy** than others—in order to get a Visa, he had to file papers with four different agencies, wait for hours in three different waiting rooms, and, weeks later, follow up with some petty **bureaucrat** who complained that the original application should've been filed in triplicate.

Bygone – Past, former; that which is in the past (usually plural, as in the expression "Let bygones be bygones," which means to let the past go, especially by forgiving someone).

At the nursing home, the time to reminisce about **bygone** days was pretty much all the time.

Bypass – Avoid, go around; ignore. The word can be a noun or a verb. Literally, a **bypass** is a stretch of highway that goes *around* an obstacle (such as a construction site). A synonym for *bypass* (verb) is *circumvent*, as in *to circumvent (or bypass) the normal approval process by going straight to the company president.*

Canon – Body of accepted rules, standards or artistic works; **canonical** means authorized, recognized, or pertaining to a canon. Note that the spelling of *canon* is not the same as *cannon* (a large weapon). The "Western canon" is an expression referring to books traditionally considered necessary for a person to be educated in the culture of Europe and the Americas.

School boards often start controversies when replacing **canonical** books in the curriculum with modern literature; while many people think students should read works more relevant to their lives, others point out that *Moby Dick* is part of the **canon** for a reason.

Chancy – Risky, not having a certain outcome. This word comes from the idea of "taking a lot of chances" or depending on chance.

Channel – To direct or guide along a particular course. Of course, *channel* can also be a noun (television channel, the channel of a river, channels of communication). As a verb, you might *channel* your energy towards productive purposes.

Checked – Restrained, held back. A *check* or *checks* can also be used to mean *safeguards, limitations.* This is the same *checks* as in *checks and balances,* which refers to an aspect of the American system of government in which the Executive, Judicial, and Legislative branches all have power over each other, so no one branch can gain too much power. The expression *held in check* means *restrained, held back.*

Once the economy took a turn for the worse, the investors began to **hold** spending **in check**.

The situation isn't so simple—while the warlords are surely criminals of the worst degree, they are the only force **checking** the power of the dictator.

Chronological – Arranged in or relating to time order.

Joey, I'm afraid you've done the assignment wrong—the point of making a timeline is to put the information in **chronological** order. You've made an alphabetical-order-line instead!

15

Clamor – Noisy uproar or protest, as from a crowd; a loud, continuous noise. (NOT the same word as *clamber,* "to scramble or climb awkwardly.")

> As soon as a scent of scandal emerged, the press was **clamoring** for details.

> The mayor couldn't even make herself heard over the **clamor** of the protestors.

Clan – Traditional social unit or division of a tribe consisting of a number of families derived from a common ancestor. Metaphorically, a *clan* could be any group of people united by common aims, interests, etc.

Cloak – To cover or conceal. Often used as *cloaked in.* (Literally, a *cloak* is a large, loose cape, much like a winter coat without arms.)

> Apple's new products are often **cloaked in** mystery before they are released; before the launch of the iPad, even tech reviewers had little idea what the new device would be.

Coalesce – Come together, unite; fuse together.

> While at first, everyone on the team was jockeying for power and recognition, eventually, the group **coalesced** and everyone was happy to share credit for a job well-done.

> East and West Germany **coalesced** into a single country in 1990.

Coercion – Force; use of pressure, threats, etc. to force someone to do something.

Coexistence – Existing at the same time or in the same place. *Coexistence* is often used to mean *peaceful coexistence,* as in *The goal of the Camp David Accords was the coexistence of Israel and Egypt.*

Cogent – Very convincing, logical.

> Most GMAT Critical Reasoning arguments are not terribly **cogent**— they depend on unspoken and unjustified assumptions.

Cognitive – Related to thinking. *Cognition* is the mental process of knowing (awareness, judgment, reasoning, etc.).

Collude – Conspire; cooperate for illegal or fraudulent purposes.

> After two competing software companies doubled their prices on the same day, leaving consumers no lower-priced alternative, the federal government investigated the companies for **collusion**.

Compliant – Obeying, submissive; following the requirements.

> Those who are not **compliant** with the regulations will be put on probation and possibly expelled.

Compound – Add interest to the principal and accrued interest; increase. When talking about substances, *compound* can also mean *mix, combine,* as in *to compound two chemicals.*

> The town was greatly damaged by the hurricane—damage that was only **compounded** by the subsequent looting and even arson that took place in the chaos that followed.

> Your success in studying for the GMAT can only be **compounded** by healthy sleep habits; in fact, the brain requires sleep in order to form new memories and thus solidify your knowledge.

Compromise – Reduce the quality or value of something. Of course, to *compromise* can be good in personal relationships, but often *compromise* means to give up something in a bad way, as in *to compromise one's morals.* So, if you say that the hull of your boat has been *compromised,* you mean that you are going to sink!

> It is unacceptable that safety is being **compromised** in the name of profits.

Concede – Give in, admit, yield; acknowledge reluctantly; grant or give up (such as giving up land after losing a war).

> The negotiations were pointless, with each side's representatives instructed by their home countries to make no **concessions** whatsoever.

> Quebec was a French **concession** to Britain in the Treaty of Paris in 1763.

> I suppose I will have to **concede** the argument now that you've looked up evidence on Wikipedia.

Condone – Overlook, tolerate, regard as harmless.

> While underage drinking is illegal, at many universities, it is tacitly **condoned** by administrations that neglect to enforce anti-drinking policies.

Confer – Consult, compare views; bestow or give.

> A Ph.D. **confers** upon a person the right to be addressed as "Doctor" as well as eligibility to pursue tenure-track professorship.

> Excuse me for a moment to make a call—I can't buy this car until I **confer** with my spouse.

15

Consequently – As a result, therefore. (Don't confuse with *subsequently*, which means *afterwards*.)

> The new medicine is not only a failure, but a dangerous one; **consequently**, drug trials were halted immediately.

Considerable – Large, significant.

Considerations – Factors to be considered in making a decision. Used in the singular, *consideration* can mean care for other people's feelings; high esteem or admiration; or a treatment or account, as in *The book began with a thorough consideration of the history of the debate.*

Consolidate – Unite, combine, solidify, make coherent.

> She **consolidated** her student loans so she would only have to make one payment per month.

> As group leader, Muriel will **consolidate** all of our research into a single report.

Contemplative – Contemplating, thoughtful, meditative.

Contend – Assert, make an argument in favor of; strive, compete, struggle. A *contention* is simply a claim, often a thesis or statement that will then be backed up with reasons. *Contentious* means controversial or argumentative, as in *The death penalty is a contentious issue.*

Contextualize – Place in context, such as by giving the background or circumstances.

> Virginia Woolf's feminism is hard to truly understand unless **contextualized** within the mores of the highly restrained, upper-class English society of her time.

Contract – Shrink, pull together, and thus become smaller (used in this way, *contract* is the opposite of *expand*). You can also *contract* a disease or a debt, in which case *contract* just means *get* or *acquire*. To *contract* can also simply mean to make a contract (to *contract* an agreement).

Conventional – Traditional, customary. This could be related to morals and culture (*Her family was surprised that she had eschewed the conventional wedding ceremony in favor of a bohemian ceremony on the beach*) or to technology, business methods, etc. — a *conventional* oven is simply a regular oven (without certain modern enhancements).

Converge – Move towards one another or towards a point; unite.

> I know we're driving in to the wedding from different states, but our routes ought to **converge** when each of us hits I-95—maybe we could **converge** at a Cracker Barrel for lunch!

Conversely – In an opposite way; on the other hand.

> I am not here to argue that lack of education causes poverty. **Conversely**, I am here to argue that poverty causes lack of education.

Convoluted – Twisted; very complicated.

> Your argument is so **convoluted** that I'm not even able to understand it enough to start critiquing it.

> To get from the hotel room to the pool requires following a **convoluted** path up two staircases and down two others—to get to someplace on the same floor we started on!

Copious –Plentiful, bountiful.

> Although she took **copious** notes in class, she found that she was missing a big picture that would have tied all the information together.

Corresponding – Accompanying; having the same or almost the same relationship.

> Our profit-sharing plan means that increases in profit will be matched by **corresponding** increases in employee compensation.

Corroborate – Support, add evidence to.

> You're telling me you were thirty miles away riding a roller coaster when the school was vandalized? I have a hard time believing that—is there anyone who can **corroborate** your story?

Countenance – Approve or tolerate. *Countenance* can also literally mean "face" (*Her countenance was familiar—did we know each other?*). The metaphorical meaning makes sense when you think about a similar expression: "I cannot *look you in the face* after what you did." (You would usually say "I cannot face you" when the *speaker* is the guilty party.)

> I saw you cheating off my paper, and I can't **countenance** cheating—either you turn yourself in or I'll report you.

Counterintuitive – Against what a person would intuitively expect.

> Although it seems **counterintuitive**, for some extreme dieters, eating more can actually help them to lose weight, since the body is reassured that it is not facing a period of prolonged starvation.

Counterpoint – Contrasting item, opposite; a complement; the use of contrast or interplay in a work of art.

> The play's lighthearted, witty narrator provides a welcome **counterpoint** to the seriousness and grief expressed by the other characters.

> The hot peppers work in **counterpoint** to an otherwise sweet dish.

15

Counterproductive – Defeating the purpose; preventing the intended goal.

The candidate's attempt to win swing votes in Ohio was actually **counterproductive**—following his speech in Toledo, his poll numbers actually went *down* 5%.

Credibility – Believability, trustworthiness.

Many famous "experts" with "Dr." before their names are not medical doctors at all. Any television "doctor" who turns out to have a Ph.D. in botany, for instance, ought to suffer a serious drop in **credibility**.

Culminate – Reach the highest point or final stage.

A Ph.D. program generally **culminates** in a written dissertation and its defense to a committee.

Currency – Money; the act of being passed from person-to-person (*These old coins are no longer in currency*); general acceptance or a period of time during which something is accepted. *Cultural currency* refers to cultural knowledge that allows a person to feel "in the know."

The call center in Mumbai trained its workers in American slang and pop culture, giving them a **cultural currency** that, it was hoped, would help the workers relate to customers thousands of miles away.

Curtail – Cut short or reduce.

Cynical – Thinking the worst of others' motivations; bitterly pessimistic.

Debase – Degrade; lower in quality, value, rank, etc.; lower in moral quality.

Members of the mainstream church argued that the fringe sect was practicing a **debased** version of the religion, twisting around its precepts and missing the point.

I can tell from the weight that this isn't pure gold, but rather some **debased** mixed metal.

You have **debased** yourself by accepting bribes.

Debilitating – Weakening, disabling.

Debunk – Expose, ridicule, or disprove false or exaggerated claims.

Galileo spent his last years under house arrest for **debunking** the widely held idea that the Sun revolved around the Earth.

The show MythBusters **debunks** pseudoscientific claims.

MANHATTAN
GMAT

Decry – Condemn openly. The "cry" in *decry* has the sense of "cry out against," as in *The activist decried the destruction of the animals' habitat.*

Deem – Judge; consider.

> "You can take the black belt exam when I **deem** you ready, and not a moment before," said the karate instructor.

Deflect – Cause to curve; turn aside, especially from a straight course; avoid.

> The purpose of a shield is to **deflect** arrows or bullets from an enemy.

> Every time he was asked a difficult question, Senator Warrington **deflected** by changing the topic, saying he'd answer later, or even—insincerely, it seemed—calling for a moment of prayer.

Delimit – Fix, mark, or define the boundaries of.

> The role of an executive coach is **delimited** by our code of conduct—we may not counsel people for psychological conditions, for instance.

Denote – Be a name or symbol for. A *denotation* is the literal meaning of a word; a *connotation* is the feeling that accompanies that word.

> There's nothing in the **denotation** of "crotchety" (grumpy, having strong and irrational preferences) that indicates any particular group of people, but because of the expression "crotchety old man," the word connotes, for many people, an image of an especially unpleasant male senior citizen.

Deride – Mock, scoff at, laugh at contemptuously.

> The manager really thought that **deriding** his employees as "stupid" or "lazy" would motivate them to work harder; instead, it motivated them to hide his office supplies as an act of revenge.

Deterrent – Something that restrains or discourages.

> Some argue that the death penalty is a **deterrent** to crime—that is, the point is not just to punish the guilty, but to frighten other prospective criminals.

Dichotomy – Division into two parts or into two contradictory groups.

> There is a **dichotomy** in the sciences between theoretical or "pure" sciences such as physics and chemistry, and the life sciences, which often deal more with classifying than with theorizing.

15

Disclosure – Revealing, exposing the truth; something that has been revealed. *Full disclosure* is an expression meaning telling everything. In journalism, the expression is often used when a writer reveals a personal connection to the story. For instance, a news article might read, "MSNBC may have forced the departure of popular anchor Keith Olbermann (full disclosure: I was employed as a fact-checker for MSNBC in 2004)."

Discount – Ignore, especially to ignore information because it is considered untrustworthy; to underestimate, minimize, regard with doubt. To *discount* an idea is to *not count* it as important.

> After staying up all night to finish the presentation, he was understandably unhappy that his boss **discounted** his contribution, implying that she had done most of the work herself.

Discredit – Injure the reputation of, destroy credibility of or confidence in.

> Congresswoman Huffman's opponent tried to use her friendship with a certain radical extremist to **discredit** her, even though the Congresswoman hadn't seen this so-called "extremist" since sixth–grade summer camp.

Discrepancy – Difference or inconsistency.

> When there is a **discrepancy** between a store's receipts and the amount of money in the register, the cashier's behavior is generally called into question.

Discrete – Separate, distinct, detached, existing as individual parts. This is NOT the same word as *discreet*, which means *subtle, secretive.*

> Be sure to use quotation marks and citations as appropriate in your paper in order to keep your ideas **discrete** from those of the experts you are quoting.

> The advertising agency pitched us not on one campaign, but on three **discrete** ideas.

Discretionary – Subject to someone's *discretion,* or judgment (generally good judgment). *Discretionary funds* can be spent on anything (for instance, a budget might contain a small amount for "extras"). *Begin at your discretion* means *Begin whenever you think is best.*

Discriminating – Judicious, discerning, having good judgment or insight. Many people automatically think of *discriminating* as bad, because they are thinking of racial discrimination. However, *discriminating* is simply telling things apart and can be an important skill—it is important to *discriminate* legitimate colleges from fraudulent diploma mills, for instance.

> He is a man of **discriminating** tastes—all his suits are handmade in Italy, and I once saw him send back an entree when he complained that black truffle oil had been substituted for white. The chef was astounded that he could tell.

> You can tell a real Prada bag by the **discriminating** mark on the inside.

Disinterested – Unbiased, impartial; not interested. Don't confuse with *uninterested,* which means not interested, bored, apathetic.

> Let's settle this argument once and for all! We'll get a **disinterested** observer to judge who can sing the highest note!

Disparate – Distinct, different.

> He chose the college for two **disparate** reasons: the strength of the computer science program, and the excellence of the hip-hop dance squad.

Dispatch – Speed, promptness (noun); send off or deal with in a speedy way (verb).

> So, you want to be a bike messenger? I need messengers who approach every delivery with alacrity, care, and **dispatch**—if the customers wanted their packages to arrive slowly, they'd use the post office.

> Acting with all possible **dispatch**, emergency services **dispatched** a rescue squad to the scene.

Disperse – Scatter, spread widely, cause to vanish. *Dispersal* is the noun form.

> Because the demonstrators didn't have a permit, the police showed up with megaphones, demanding loudly that the crowd **disperse**. The eventual **dispersal** of the crowd resulted in smaller protests at various points throughout the city.

Dismiss – Put aside or reject, especially after only a brief consideration; allow to disperse or leave; fire from a job. To *dismiss biases* (*biases* is the plural of *bias*) in science is to rule out possible prejudices that could have influenced results.

> "Before I **dismiss** class," said the teacher, "I want to remind you of the importance of **dismissing** biases in your research by ruling out or adjusting for factors other than the variable you are testing that may have led to your results."

Disseminate – Scatter, spread about, broadcast.

> In the 1760s, revolutionary ideas were **disseminated** via pamphlets such as Thomas Paine's "Common Sense."

Divest – Deprive or strip of a rank, title, etc., or of clothing or gear; to sell off holdings (opposite of *invest*).

> When she found out that the most profitable stock in her portfolio was that of a company that tested products on animals, she immediately **divested** by telling her broker to sell the stock.

> Once his deception was exposed, he was **divested** of his position on the Board.

Dovetail – Join or fit together.

> When the neuroscientist married an exercise physiologist, neither thought they'd end up working together, but when Dr. Marion Ansel received a grant to study how exercise improves brain function and Dr. Jim Ansel was assigned to her team, the two found that their careers **dovetailed** nicely.

Dubious – Doubtful, questionable, suspect.

> This applicant's résumé is filled with **dubious** qualifications—this is a marketing position, and this résumé is mostly about whitewater rafting.

Echelon – A level, rank, or grade; the people at that level. A *stratum* is the same idea (*strata* is the plural, as in *rising through the upper strata/echelons of the firm*).

> Obtaining a job on Wall Street doesn't guarantee access to the upper **echelon** of executives, where multi-million dollar bonuses are the norm.

> I'm not sure I'm cut out to analyze poetry; I find it hard to dig beyond the most accessible **echelon** of meaning.

Eclectic – Selecting the best of everything or from many diverse sources.

> **Eclectic** taste is helpful in being a DJ—crowds love to hear the latest hip-hop mixed with '80s classics and other unexpected genres of music.

Eclipse – 1) One thing covering up another, such as the sun hiding the moon or a person losing attention to a more famous or talented person; 2) To cover up, darken, or make less important.

> Billy Ray Cyrus, who had a hit song, "Achy Breaky Heart," in the '90s, has long since found his fame **eclipsed** by that of his daughter, Miley.

Effectively – Of course, *effectively* can just mean *in a successful manner*, as in *He did the job effectively*. But it can also mean *in effect, but not officially*. For instance, when Woodrow Wilson was president of the United States, he was incapacitated by a stroke, and some people believe that Wilson's wife, Edith, *effectively* served as president. That doesn't mean she was any good at it (she wasn't). Rather, it means that she was doing the job of the president without officially being the president.

> He went on a two-week vacation without asking for time off or even telling anyone he was leaving, thus **effectively** resigning from his position.

Efficacy – The quality of being able to produce the intended effect. Don't confuse **efficacy** with *efficiency*. Something **efficacious** gets the job done; something *efficient* gets the job done without wasting time or effort. **Efficacy** is frequently used in reference to medicines.

> Extensive trials will be necessary to determine whether the drug's **efficacy** outweighs the side effects.

Egalitarian – Related to belief in the equality of all people.

> It is very rare that someone turns down an offer to be knighted by the Queen of England; however, he was **egalitarian** enough to feel uncomfortable with the entire idea of titles and royalty.

Egregious – Extraordinarily or conspicuously bad; glaring.

> Your conduct is an **egregious** violation of our Honor Code—not only did you steal your roommate's paper off his computer and turn it in as your own, you also sold his work to a plagiarism website so other cheaters could purchase it!

Emancipate – Free from slavery or oppression. Lincoln's *Emancipation Proclamation* legally ended slavery in the U.S. In law, to *emancipate* a minor is to declare the child (generally a teenager) no longer under the control of his or her parents.

Eminent – Prominent, distinguished, of high rank.

Emphasize – Give special force or attention to. This word often occurs in GMAT Reading Comprehension answer choices. Hint: While the purpose of a particular sentence could be to *emphasize* a point that came before, the main idea of an entire passage is never just to *emphasize* something.

Empirical – Coming from, based on, or able to be verified by experience or experimentation; not purely based on theory.

> The Ancient Greeks philosophized about the nature of matter (concluding, for instance, that everything was made of earth, water, air, and fire) without any **empirical** evidence—that is, the very idea of conducting experiments hadn't been invented yet.

> People always knew **empirically** that when you drop something, it falls to the ground; the theory of gravity later explained why.

Emulate – Copy in an attempt to equal or be better than.

> The ardent *Star Trek* fan **emulated** Captain Kirk in every way possible—his brash and confident leadership might have gotten him somewhere, but the women he tried to impress weren't so impressed.

15

Enigma – Puzzle, mystery, riddle; mysterious or contradictory person.

> The enormous rock sculptures in Stonehenge, Scotland, are truly an **enigma**—were they created as part of a religious observance, in deference to a great ruler, or for some other reason?

Enjoy – Of course, enjoy means "receive pleasure from," but it also means "benefit from." Thus, it is not true that only people and animals can *enjoy*. For instance:

> The college has long **enjoyed** the support of wealthy alumni.

Ensure vs. **Insure** – If you buy insurance for something, you have *insured* it. If you guarantee something, you have *ensured* it.

> If you go past this security checkpoint, I cannot **ensure** your safety.

Enumerate – Count or list; specify one-by-one.

> The Bill of Rights **enumerates** the basic rights held by every citizen of the United States.

Equitable – Fair, equal, just.

> As the university president was a heavily biased towards the sciences, faculty in the liberal arts felt they had to fight to get an **equitable** share of funding for their departments.

Equivalence – The state of being equal or essentially equal.

Equivocal or **Equivocate** – Use unclear language to deceive or avoid committing to a position.

> Not wanting to lose supporters, the politician **equivocated** on the issue, tossing out buzzwords related to each side while also claiming more study was needed.

Erratic – Inconsistent, wandering, having no fixed course.

> When someone engages in **erratic** behavior, family members often suspect drugs or mental illness. However, sometimes the person is just building a top-secret invention in the garage!

Erroneous – Mistaken, in error.

> Hilda was completely unable to assemble her new desk chair after the instructions **erroneously** instructed her to screw the left armrest onto a small lever on the bottom of the seat.

Erstwhile – Former, previous.

> A novelist and **erstwhile** insurance salesman, he told us his story of the long road to literary success, before he was able to quit his day job.

Escape velocity – The minimum velocity that an object must attain in order to completely escape a gravitational field.

Estimable – 1) Worthy of esteem, admirable; 2) Able to be estimated.

> As the first Black president of the Harvard Law Review, Barack Obama presented an **estimable** résumé when he ran for president in 2008.

> Riding a roller coaster is safer than driving on the highway, but there is still an **estimable** risk.

Ethos – The character, personality, or moral values specific to a person, group, time period, etc.

> At the prep school, the young man happily settled into an **ethos** of hard work and rigorous athletic competition.

Exacerbate – Make worse (more violent, severe, etc.), inflame.

> Allowing your band to practice in our garage has greatly **exacerbated** my headache.

Exacting – Very severe in making demands; requiring precise attention.

> The boxing coach was **exacting**, analyzing Joey's footwork down to the millimeter and forcing him to repeat movements hundreds of times until they were correct.

Execute – Put into effect, do, perform (to *execute* a process). *Execute* can also mean *enforce, make legal, carry out the terms of a legal agreement*. To *execute* a will is to sign it in the presence of witnesses. To *execute* the terms of a contract is to fulfill an obligation written in the contract.

Exhaustive – Comprehensive, thorough, exhausting a topic or subject, accounting for all possibilities; draining, tending to exhaust.

> The consultant's report was an **exhaustive** treatment of all possible options and their likely consequences. In fact, it was so **exhaustive** that the manager joked that he would need to hire another consultant to read the first consultant's report.

Exotic – Foreign, intriguingly unusual or strange.

Expansionist – Wanting to expand, such as by conquering other countries.

Expedient – Suitable, proper; effective (sometimes while sacrificing ethics).

> "I need this report by 2pm, and I don't care what you have to do to make that happen," said the boss. "I expect you to deal with it **expediently**."

> When invited to a wedding you cannot attend, it is **expedient** to send a gift.

15

Explicit – Direct, clear, fully revealed. *Explicit* in the context of movies, music, etc., means depicting or describing sex or nudity, but *explicit* can be used for anything (*explicit instructions* is a common phrase). The antonym of **explicit** is *implicit* or *tacit,* meaning "hinted at, implied."

> The goal of my motivational talk is to make **explicit** the connection between staying in school and avoiding a life of crime.

Extraneous – Irrelevant; foreign, coming from without, not belonging.

> This essay would be stronger if you removed **extraneous** information; this paragraph about the author's life doesn't happen to be relevant to your thesis.

> Maize, which originated in the New World, is **extraneous** to Europe.

Extrapolate – Conjecture about an unknown by projecting information about something known; predict by projecting past experience. In math and science, to *extrapolate* is to infer values in an unobserved interval from values in an observed interval. For instance, from the points (1, 4) and (3, 8), you could *extrapolate* the point (5, 12), since it would be on the same line.

> No, I've never been to Bryn Mawr, but I've visited several small, private women's colleges in the Northeast, so I think I can **extrapolate**.

Facilitate – Make easier, help the progress of.

> A good meeting **facilitator** lets everyone be heard while still keeping the meeting focused.

> As a midwife, my goal is simply to **facilitate** a natural process.

Faction – A group (especially an exclusive group with strong beliefs, self-interest, bias, etc.) within a larger organization. This word is usually meant in a negative way (once people have joined *factions,* they are no longer willing to hear the issues and debate or compromise).

> The opposition movement was once large enough to have a chance at succeeding, but it has since broken into numerous, squabbling **factions**, each too small to have much impact.

Faculty – An ability, often a mental ability. Most often used in the plural, as in *A stroke can often deprive a person of important mental faculties.* (Of course, *faculty* can also mean the teachers or professors of an institution of learning.)

Fading – Declining.

> In the face of **fading** public support for national health care, the Senator withdrew his support for the bill.

Fashion – Manner or way.

> The watchmaker works in a meticulous **fashion**, paying incredible attention to detail.

Fathom – Understand deeply.

> I cannot even remotely **fathom** how you interpreted an invitation to sleep on my couch as permission to take my car on a six-hour joyride!

Finding – "The finding" (or "the findings") refers to a discovery, report, result of an experiment, etc.

> When the attorneys received the results of the DNA report, they were shocked by **the finding** that John Doe could not have committed the crime.

Fishy – Suspicious, unlikely, questionable, as in *a fishy story.* This expression probably arose because fish smell very bad when they start to spoil.

Fledgling – New or inexperienced. A fledgling is also a young bird that cannot fly yet.

> The Society of Engineers is available for career day presentations in elementary schools, where we hope to encourage **fledgling** talents in the applied sciences.

Fleeting – Passing quickly, transitory.

> I had assumed our summer romance would be **fleeting**, so I was very surprised when you proposed marriage!

Foreshadow – Indicate or suggest beforehand.

> You didn't know this was a horror movie? I thought it was pretty clear that the children's ghost story around the campfire was meant to **foreshadow** the horrible things that would happen to them years later as teenagers at a motel in the middle of the woods.

Forestall – Delay, hinder, prevent by taking action beforehand.

> Our research has been **forestalled** by a lack of funding; we're all just biding our time while we wait for the university to approve our grant proposal.

Glacial – Slow, cold, icy, unsympathetic. *Glacial* can also just mean "related to glaciers."

> Progress happened, but at a **glacial** pace everyone found frustrating.

> He had wanted to appear on the reality singing competition his whole young life, but he was not encouraged by the judges' **glacial** response to his audition.

15

Grade, Gradation – A *gradation* is a progression or process taking place gradually, in stages; to *grade* is to slant (the road *grades* steeply) or to blend (the dress's fabric *grades* from blue to green).

> The hill's **gradation** was so gradual that even those on crutches were able to enjoy the nature trail.

> The marshland **grades** into the water so gradually that it is difficult to tell the land from the bay.

Graft – Join together plant parts or skin so that two living things grow together (for instance, a *skin graft* for a burn victim); or the act of acquiring money or other benefits through illegal means, especially by abusing one's power.

> The part of the book describing the financial crisis is good, but the "What You Can Do" section seems **grafted** on, almost as though written by a different author.

> It's not cool for your boss to pressure you into buying Girl Scout cookies from his daughter. If she were selling something larger, we'd call that **graft**.

Grandstand – Perform showily in an attempt to impress onlookers.

> I was really passionate about the candidate when he spoke at our school, but now that I think about it, he was just **grandstanding**. I mean, who could disagree that young people are the future? And doing a cheer for the environment doesn't actually signify a commitment to changing any public policies about it.

Guesswork – A set of guesses or estimates; work based on guesses or estimates.

Guile – Clever deceit, cunning, craftiness.

> The game of poker is all about **guile**, manipulating your own body language and patter to lead other players to erroneous conclusions about the cards you're holding.

Hallmark – A mark of indication of quality, purity, genuineness, etc.; any distinguishing characteristic.

Fast-paced rhymes, an angry tenor, and personal attacks on celebrities are **hallmarks** of Eminem's music.

Hallucination – A delusion, a false or mistaken idea; seeing, sensing, or hearing things that aren't there, such as from a mental disorder.

Handpick – To pick by hand, to personally select.

> The retiring CEO **handpicked** his successor.

Hardly – *Hardly* can mean *almost or probably not,* or *not at all.* Of course, *I can hardly see you* means *I can see you only a little bit.* But in the following sentence, *hardly* means *not:*

> The news could **hardly** have come at a worse time. (The meaning is *The news came at the worst possible time.*)

Hardy – Bold, brave, capable of withstanding hardship, fatigue, cold, etc.

> While the entire family enjoyed the trip to South America, only the **hardier** members even attempted to hike to the top of Ecuador's tallest volcano.

Hearken or **Hark** – Listen, pay attention to. The expression *hearken back* or *hark back* means to turn back to something earlier or return to a source.

> The simple lifestyle and anachronistic dress of the Amish **hearken** back to an earlier era.

> The nation's first change of leadership in decades is causing the people to **hearken** closely to what is happening in government.

Hedge – Avoid commitment by leaving provisions for withdrawal or changing one's mind; protect a bet by also betting on the other side.

> When the professor called on him to take a stand on the issue, he **hedged** for fear of offending her: "Well, there are valid points on both sides," he said.

Hegemony –Domination, authority; influence by a one country over others socially, culturally, economically, etc.

> The discovery of oil by a previously poor nation disrupted the larger, richer nation's **hegemony** in the region—suddenly, the **hegemon** had a competitor.

Heterogeneous – Different in type, incongruous; composed of different types of elements. *Homogeneous* (of the same kind) is the opposite of *heterogeneous.*

> Rather than build the wall with plain brick, we used a **heterogeneous** mixture of stones—they are not only different colors, but a variety of sizes as well.

Hierarchy – A ranked series; a classification of people according to rank, ability, etc.; a ruling body.

> The Eco-Action Coalition was led by a strict **hierarchy** — members followed orders from district leaders, district leaders from regional leaders, and regional leaders from the national head.

Holdings – Property, such as land, capital, and stock. *The company liquidated its holdings* means that the company sold off everything. Of course, the word *hold* has many meanings. *In a holding pattern* is an expression that means *staying still, not changing.*

15

Host – A large amount. *A host of problems* means a lot of problems.

Hyperbole – Deliberate exaggeration for effect.

> Oh, come on. Saying "That movie was so bad it made me puke" was surely **hyperbole**. I strongly doubt that you actually vomited during or following *The Back-up Plan*.

Iconoclast – Attacker of cherished beliefs or institutions.

> A lifelong **iconoclast**, Ayn Rand wrote a controversial book entitled *The Virtue of Selfishness*.

Imminent – Ready to occur, impending.

> In the face of **imminent** war, the nation looked to Franklin D. Roosevelt for reassurance.

Immunity – The state of not being susceptible to disease; exemption from a duty or liability; exemption from legal punishment. *Diplomatic immunity* is an example of *immunity* meaning *exemption from legal punishment.* For instance, every year, New York City loses millions of dollars from United Nations diplomats parking illegally and then not paying their parking tickets, since the diplomats are not subject to U.S. laws.

Impair – Make worse, weaken.

> Playing in a rock band without earplugs will almost certainly **impair** your hearing over time.

Impartial – Unbiased, fair. *Disinterested, dispassionate,* and *nonpartisan* are all related to being fair and not having a bias or personal stake.

> Judge Gonzales removed himself from the case because, having a personal connection to the school where the shooting took place, he did not think he could be appropriately **impartial**.

Impasse – Position or road from which there is no escape; deadlock, gridlock.

> If the union won't budge on its demands and the transit authority won't raise salaries, then we are at an **impasse**.

Impede – Hold back, obstruct the progress of.

> I didn't realize business school would be entirely group work—sadly, there's always at least one person in every group who **impedes** the group's progress more than helps it.

Impinge on – Trespass on, violate.

> Civil liberties experts argued that a school system's regulating what its students do on Facebook outside of school is an **impingement** of their right to free speech.

Implode – Burst inward. Metaphorically, to collapse or break down.

> The startup struggled for years before it simply **imploded**—the management team broke into factions, all the clients were scared off, and employees who hadn't been paid in weeks began taking the office computers home with them in retribution.

Imply – Hint at, suggest, "say without saying."

Impute – Credit, attribute; lay blame or responsibility for.

> The ineffectual CEO was nevertheless a master of public relations—he made sure that all successes were **imputed** to him, and all of the failures were **imputed** to others.

Inadvertently – Accidentally, carelessly, as a side effect.

> In attempting to perfect his science project, he **inadvertently** blew a fuse and plunged his family's home into darkness.

Inasmuch – Since, because. Usually *inasmuch as.*

> **Inasmuch as** a whale is not a fish, it will not be covered in this biology course specifically about fish.

Incentive – Something that encourages greater action or effort, such as a reward.

> A controversial program in a failing school system uses cash payments as an **incentive** for students to stay in school.

Incidentally – Not intentionally, accidentally. *Incidentally* can also mean *by the way* and is used to introduce information that is only slightly related. *Incidentals* can refer to expenses that are "on the side" (*The company gives us $100 a day for meals and incidentals*).

> The environmental protection law was **incidentally** injurious to the rubber industry.

> I think we should move forward with the new office. **Incidentally**, there's a great Mexican restaurant opening up right across the street from it!

Incinerate – Burn, reduce to ashes, cremate.

Inconsequential – Insignificant, unimportant. The sense here is that the thing is so small that it doesn't even have *consequences.*

> You wrote a bestselling book and got a stellar review in the *New York Times*—whatever your cousin has to say about it is simply **inconsequential**.

Incorporate – Combine, unite; form a legal corporation; embody, give physical form to.

> When a business **incorporates**, it becomes a separate legal entity—for instance, the business can declare bankruptcy without the owners doing so.

> Local legend has it that ghosts can **incorporate** on one night of the year and walk among the living.

Indeterminate – Not fixed or determined, indefinite; vague.

> The results of the drug trial were **indeterminate**; further trials will be needed to ascertain whether the drug can be released.

> The lottery can have an **indeterminate** number of winners—the prize is simply divided among them.

Indicative – Indicating, suggestive of. Usually used as *indicative of.*

> Your symptoms are **indicative** of the common cold.

Induce – Persuade or influence (a person to do something); bring about, cause to happen (to *induce labor* when a birth is not proceeding quickly enough).

Inert – Inactive; having little or no power to move.

> All of the missiles at the military museum are **inert**—they're not going blow up.

> When she saw her father's **inert** body on the floor, she thought the worst, but fortunately, he was just practicing very slow yoga.

Inevitable – Not able to be avoided or escaped; certain.

> Benjamin Franklin famously said that only two things in life are **inevitable**: "death and taxes."

Inexplicable – Not able to be explained.

Inextricably – In a way such that one cannot untangle or escape something. If you are *inextricably tied* to something (such as your family), then you have so many different obligations and deep relationships that you could never leave, disobey, etc.

Infer – Conclude from evidence or premises. Remember, on the GMAT, *infer* means *draw a DEFINITELY TRUE conclusion.* It does NOT mean "assume"!

Inform – Inspire, animate; give substance, essence, or context to; be the characteristic quality of. Of course, **inform** most commonly means "impart knowledge to"; thus, many students are confused when they see the word used in other ways on the GMAT.

> Her work as an art historian is **informed** by a background in drama; where others see a static tableau, she sees a protagonist, a conflict, a denouement.

Ingenuity – Inventive skill, imagination, cleverness, especially in design.

Ingrained – Deep-rooted, forming part of the very essence; worked into the fiber.

> Religious observance had been **ingrained** in him since birth; he could not remember a time when he didn't pray five times a day.

Inherent – Existing as a permanent, essential quality; intrinsic. (See the similar *intrinsic* in this list.)

> New research seems to support the idea that humans have an **inherent** sense of justice—even babies become upset at puppet shows depicting unfairness.

Initial – First, at the beginning. An *initial deposit* might be the money you put down to open a new bank account.

Inordinate – Excessive, not within proper limits, unrestrained.

> Students taking practice computer-adaptive tests at home often take an **inordinate** number of breaks—remember, on the real thing, you can't stop just because you're tired or hungry.

Instrumental – Serving as a means of doing something. Just as you might call a weapon an *instrument of war*, saying *He was instrumental in the restructuring* has the sense that the person was used as an *instrument* of getting something done.

Insular – Pertaining to an island; detached, standing alone; narrow-minded (like the stereotype of people from small towns or places).

> The young actress couldn't wait to escape the **insularity** of her small town, where life revolved around high school football and Taco Bell was considered exotic international cuisine.

Interplay – Interaction, reciprocal relationship or influence.

> Bilingual readers will enjoy the **interplay** of English and Spanish in many of the poems in this anthology of the work of Mexican-American poets.

15

Intractable – Difficult to control, manage, or manipulate; hard to cure; stubborn.

> That student is positively **intractable**! Last week, we talked about the importance of staying in your seat during the lesson—this week, she not only got up mid-class, but she actually scrambled on top of a bookcase and refused to come down!

> Back injuries often result in **intractable** pain; despite treatment, patients never feel fully cured.

Intrepid – Fearless, brave, enduring in the face of adversity.

> **Intrepid** explorers Lewis and Clark led the first U.S. expedition to the West Coast, facing bitter winters and rough terrain.

Intrinsic – Belonging to the essential nature of a thing. (See the similar *inherent* in this list.)

> Despite all this high-tech safety equipment, skydiving is an **intrinsically** dangerous proposition.

> Communication is **intrinsic to** a healthy relationship.

Inundate – Flood, cover with water, overwhelm.

> As the city was *inundated* with water, the mayor feared that many evacuees would have nowhere to go.

> I can't go out—I am *inundated* with homework!

Invaluable – Priceless; so valuable that the value cannot be measured.

Investiture – Investing; formally giving someone a right or title.

> The former dean had her academic robes dry cleaned in preparation for her *investiture* as university president.

Involved – Complicated, intricate; confused or tangled.

> The story is quite **involved**—are you sure you have time for it?

Invulnerable – Immune to attack; not vulnerable; impossible to damage, injure, etc.

Isotope – Forms of the same chemical element, but with different numbers of neutrons in the nucleus or different atomic weights. There are 275 isotopes of the 81 stable elements, plus 800 radioactive isotopes. Different isotopes of the same element have almost identical properties.

Jettison – Discard, cast off; throw items overboard in order to lighten a ship in an emergency.

> We got so tired while hiking the Appalachian Trail that we **jettisoned** some of our fancy camping supplies just so we could keep going.

> Sadly, when school budgets are slashed, the first thing **jettisoned** is usually an art or music program.

Jumbo – Unusually large, supersized.

Juncture – Critical point in time, such as a crisis or a time when a decision is necessary; a place where two things are joined together.

> We are at a critical **juncture** in the history of this organization: either we can remain a non-profit, or we can register as a political action committee and try to expand our influence.

> The little canoe started to sink when it split at the **juncture** between the old wood and the new material used to repair it.

Juxtapose – Place side-by-side (either physically or in a metaphorical way, such as to make a comparison). If a Reading Comprehension answer choice says something like, "Juxtapose two theories," ask yourself if the main purpose of the entire passage was to *compare* two theories. (Hint: Probably not. Usually if an author introduces two competing ideas, only one of them turns out to be the main point of the passage.)

> Making a decision between two engagement rings from two different stores was difficult, he noted—it would be much easier if he could **juxtapose** them and compare them directly.

Kinetic – Pertaining to motion.

> Marisa told her mother what she had learned in science class: a ball sitting on a table has potential energy, but a ball falling towards the ground has **kinetic** energy.

Lackluster – Not shiny; dull, mediocre; lacking brilliance or vitality.

> Many young people today are so accustomed to being praised by parents and adults that they are shocked when a **lackluster** effort in the workplace receives the indifference or mild disapproval it deserves.

Landmark – Object (such as a building) that stands out and can be used to navigate by; a very important place, event, etc.

> The Civil Rights Act of 1964 was a **landmark** in the battle for equality.

> In Lebanon, many roads are unmarked, and people navigate by **landmarks**—for instance, "third house down from the water tower."

Latent – Potential; existing but not visible or active. A similar word is *dormant*.

Certain experts believe that some people have a genetic propensity for addiction; however, if such a person never comes into contact with drugs, the propensity for addiction can remain **latent** for life.

Lateral – Sideways, related to or located at the side. A *lateral move* in a career is taking a new job at the same level.

Lax – Not strict; careless, loose, slack.

My parents were really **lax** about homework—they never checked to see if I did it or not. Sadly, this legacy of **laxity** is not serving me well while studying for the GMAT.

Laypeople – Regular people, non-specialists.

The doctor's books were so successful because he was able to explain complicated medical concepts in colloquial language for the **layperson**.

Levy – Collect tax from or wage war on; act of collecting tax or amount owed, or the drafting of troops into military service.

When England **levied** yet another tax on the colonists, the colonists were pushed one further step towards **levying** war. Soon, the worried British began to **levy** troops.

Liberal – Favorable to progress or reform; believing in maximum possible individual freedom; tolerant, open-minded; generous. *("Liberal"* in modern American politics isn't quite the same as the dictionary definition. For instance, *liberal* Democrats tend to favor social programs that require a larger government to administer, while some conservatives say that *liberalism* means having the smallest government possible in order to maximize freedom.)

Split pea soup benefits from a **liberal** application of pepper.

Liberal reformers in Egypt pushed for freedom of speech, freedom of the press, and freedom of assembly.

Lift – Remove (such as a restriction); improve or lighten (such as a person's mood).

If the city government **lifts** the water rationing restrictions, we'll be able to hold a car wash.

Likewise – Also, in addition to; similarly, in the same way. In conversation, **likewise** can mean "Me, too." ("Nice to meet you." "Likewise.")

Chip was baffled by all the silverware set before him, so when his host began eating salad with the smallest, leftmost fork, Chip did **likewise**.

Log – Keep a record of, write down; travel for or at a certain distance or speed; a written record.

> Lawyers who bill by the hour have to be sure to **log** all the time they spend on every client's case.

> You cannot get your pilot's license until you have **logged** 40 hours of flight time.

Machination or **machinations** – Crafty schemes or plots.

> It's cute to think that teen idols became famous because their talent was simply so great that the music industry reached out to them, but usually, any teen idol is the product of intense coaching and parental **machinations**.

Magma – Molten material (such as very hot liquid rock) beneath or within the Earth's crust.

Magnate – Very important or influential person, especially in business.

> Many students pursue MBAs in hopes of becoming wealthy and powerful **magnates**; some students never quite make it there, instead spending their careers staring at spreadsheets and taking orders from **magnates**.

Makeshift – Improvised, relating to a temporary substitute. The expressions *thrown together* or *slapped together* express a similar idea of a *making do* with the resources on hand. Similarly, to *jury rig* something is to assemble it quickly with whatever materials you have available.

> Lost in the woods for over 24 hours, the children were eventually found sleeping under a **makeshift** tent made from branches and old plastic bags.

Malleable – Able to be bent, shaped, or adapted. *Tractable, pliable,* and *plastic* can also mean physically bendable, or metaphorically bendable, as in "easily influenced or shaped by others." *Mutable* means changeable.

> The more **malleable** the material, the easier it is to bend into jewelry—and the easier it is to damage that jewelry.

> My mother is a little too **malleable**—she said she liked all the things her first husband liked, and now she says she likes all the things her second husband likes.

Manifest – Obvious, apparent, perceptible to the eye (adj.) or to become obvious, apparent, perceptible to the eye (verb). Also to show, make clear, or prove (verb). As a noun, a *manifest* is a list of people or goods aboard a plane, ship, train, etc. A *manifestation* is often when something "under the surface" breaks out or becomes apparent.

> Lupus is difficult to diagnose, but sometimes **manifests** as muscular weakness or joint pain.

> The protest was a **manifestation** of a long-brewing discontent.

Mantle (of the Earth) – Layer of the Earth between the crust and the core. The mantle is about 1,800 miles thick and makes up about 85% of the total volume of the Earth.

Max out – Take to the limit (in a good or a bad way). To *max out* your credit cards is to incur as much debt as is permitted; to *max out* your productivity is to achieve maximum productivity.

Maxim – A general truth or fundamental principle, especially expressed as a proverb or saying.

> My favorite **maxim** is "Seize the day!" How much would it cost to get that on a tattoo? How much more for "Curiosity killed the cat"?

Mediated by – Brought about by means of; assisted as an intermediary. Of course, to *mediate* a dispute is to bring about a resolution, but *mediated* in science also has the idea of being "in the middle." For instance, a study might show that poverty leads to inattentiveness in school. But how? Research might reveal that poverty leads to inattentiveness, *mediated by* poor nutrition. That is, poverty causes poor nutrition, which causes inattentiveness (because the kids are hungry). *Mediation* can help make sense of what seems like an indirect correlation.

Mercurial – Quickly and unpredictably changing moods; fickle, flighty.

> It's tough being married to someone so **mercurial**. I do pretty much the same thing every day—some days, she thinks I'm great, and other days, the exact same behaviors make her inexplicably angry.

Militarism – Glorification of the military; government in which the military has a lot of power or in which the military is the top priority.

Mired – Stuck, entangled (in something, like a swamp or muddy area), soiled. *Morass* and *quagmire* are also words (often used metaphorically) for soft, swampy ground that a person can sink into. The Vietnam War was famously called a *quagmire*. The expression *muck and mire* means, literally, "animal waste and mud" and can be used metaphorically. To *muck up* is to mess up or get dirty, and to *muck about* or *around* is to waste time.

> **Mired** in her predecessor's mess and mistakes, the new CEO found it difficult to take the company in a new direction.

> The federal prosecutor spent weeks wading through the **muck and mire** of the scandal—every uncovered document showed that the corruption was deeper and worse than previously thought.

Modest – Humble; simple rather than showy; decent (especially "covering up" in terms of dress); small, limited.

> The reporter was surprised that the celebrity lived in such a **modest** house, one that looked just like every other plain, two-story house on the block.

Her first job out of college was a rude awakening—her **modest** salary was barely enough for rent, much less going out and having fun.

Moreover – In addition to what has been said, for instance; besides.

His actions cost us the job; **moreover**, he seriously offended our client.

Mores – Customs, manners, or morals of a particular group. Pronounce this word as two syllables (rhymes with "more ways").

An American in Saudi Arabia should study the culture beforehand so as to avoid violating conservative cultural **mores**.

Municipal – Relating to local self-government. A *municipality* is a city, town, etc.

Narrative – Story, report, narrated account.

Nebula – A cloud of gas and dust in space. Nebulas can form star-forming regions—all the materials clump together to form larger masses, thus attracting further matter and ultimately creating stars. A *nebula* can also be a cloudy spot on a person's eye, and *nebulous* can mean cloudy, unclear.

Net – Remaining after expenses or other factors have been deducted; ultimate; to bring in as profit; to catch, as in a net.

In one day of trading, my portfolio went up $10,000 and down $8,000, for a **net** gain of $2,000.

All those weeks of working weekends and playing golf with the boss ought to **net** her a promotion.

Nevertheless or **nonetheless** – However, even so, despite that. Note that both *nevertheless* and *nonetheless* are single words—the GMAT has tested this on Sentence Correction ("none the less" is NOT an expression in English and cannot be substituted for "no less").

While losing the P&G account was a serious blow, we **nevertheless** were able to achieve a new sales goal this month because of the tireless efforts of the sales team in bringing in three new clients.

I really can't stand working with you. **Nonetheless**, we're stuck on this project together and we're going to have to get along.

Nontrivial – Important or big enough to matter.

The chief of staff told the assembled doctors, "We all make mistakes. But this mistake was **nontrivial**, and there is going to be an investigation."

15

Normative – Implying or attempting to establish a norm; expressing value judgments or telling people what to do (rather than merely describing that which is happening).

> The reason we are not understanding each other in this argument about grammar is that you are arguing **normatively**, telling me how people *should* talk, and I am simply reporting how people *actually* talk.

Nostalgia – Longing for the past.

> The retail store Urban Outfitters uses **nostalgia** as a marketing strategy, branding many products with cartoon characters popular 10–20 years ago. Sure enough, many adult women do want to buy Jem or Spongebob t-shirts and lip balm.

Nuances – Subtle differences in tone, meaning, expression, etc.

> People with certain cognitive disabilities cannot understand the **nuances** of non-literal speech. For instance, "You can come if you want to, but it's really going to be mostly family" really means that you shouldn't try to come.

Nucleus – Structure within a cell containing the cell's hereditary material; any central or essential part; core, kernel.

> As a member of the president's cabinet, he found himself in the **nucleus** of power.

Offhand – Casual, informal; done without preparation or forethought; rude in a short way, brusque.

> I was pretty happy with my salary until my coworker Deena mentioned **offhandedly** that she was thinking about buying a house now that she made six figures.

Offset – Counteract, compensate for. *Offset* is usually a verb, but as a noun: My company provided me with *an offset* against moving expenses.

> Property taxes did go up this year, but we didn't really suffer because the hit to our finances was **offset** by a reduction in fees paid to our homeowners association.

Oligarchy – Government by the few, especially by a class or a small group or clique.

Omit – Remove, delete, take out.

Operative – Operating; having influence, force, or effect; effective, key, significant. The expression *operative word* refers to the one most meaningful word within a larger phrase. An *operative* can be a worker, or a detective or spy.

> In the doctor's prescription of daily cardio exercise, the *operative word* is "daily."

Optimal – Best, most desirable or favorable. To *optimize* is to make perfect, such as by "maxing out" or striking just the right balance.

> Many believe that the U.S. Constitution's genius lies in its striking an **optimal** balance between freedom and order.

Oral narratives – Stories told verbally, especially by people who are not literate or whose cultures do not have writing (or didn't at the time). An *oral tradition* is a practice of passing down a culture's history verbally.

Outstrip – Surpass, exceed; be larger or better than; leave behind.

> Our sales figures this quarter have **outstripped** those of any other quarter in the company's history.

Revamp – Renovate, redo, revise (verb); a restructuring, upgrade, etc. (noun). The similar word *overhaul* means repair or investigate for repairs.

> I have my whole room decorated in *Twilight: Eclipse* paraphernalia. When *Breaking Dawn* comes out, I will surely have to **revamp** my decor.

Paradigm – Model or pattern; worldview; set of shared assumptions, values, etc.

> Far from being atypically bawdy, this limerick is a **paradigm** of the form—nearly all of them rely on off-color jokes.

Paradox – Contradiction, or seeming contradiction that is actually true.

> Kayla was always bothering the youth minister with her **paradoxes,** such as "If God is all-powerful, can He make a burrito so big He can't eat it?"

Paragon – Model of excellence, perfect example.

> Unlike his sister, he was a **paragon** of responsibility, taking in her three children when she went to jail, and even switching jobs so he could be there to pick them up from school.

Partial – Biased, prejudiced, favoring one over others; having a special liking for something or someone (usually *partial to*). Partial can also mean "in part," of course.

> Although I grew up in New York, I've always been **partial** to country music.

> His lawyers are appealing on the grounds that the judge was **partial** to the plaintiff, even playing golf with the plaintiff during the trial.

15

Patent – Obvious, apparent, plain to see (adj.); a letter from a government guaranteeing an inventor the rights to his or her invention (noun).

> Her résumé was full of **patent** lies: anyone could check to see that she had never been president of UNICEF.

Peddle – Travel around while selling; sell illegally; give out or disseminate.

> After an unsuccessful year spent **peddling** cutlery door-to-door, he turned to **peddling** drugs, thus landing himself in jail.

> "I don't want these people **peddling** lies to our children," said Mrs. Hoffman, protesting an event in which fringe political candidates were invited to speak to kids.

Penumbra – Outer part of a shadow from an eclipse; any surrounding region, fringe, periphery; any area where something "sort of" exists.

> The Constitution doesn't specifically mention a right to privacy, but some experts consider this to exist in the **penumbra** of the Constitution, as a guarantee of privacy is needed in order to exercise the rights that are enumerated.

> The rent in Chicago was too high, so they moved to a suburb in the **penumbra** of the city.

Per – The most common use of *per* is "for each," as in, *We will need one sandwich per child*. However, *per* may also mean "by means of" or "according to," as in *I have delivered the package per your instructions*.

Periodic – Happening at regular intervals.

Perpetuate – Make perpetual, cause to continue.

> Failing public schools in already distressed neighborhoods only **perpetuate** the cycle of poverty.

Physiological – Relating to the normal functioning of a living thing. This word is easy to remember: it looks a lot like *physically logical*.

> A rapid heart rate is a **physiological** response to fear.

Piggyback – "Riding" on something bigger or more important. *Piggyback* literally refers to one person riding on the back of another (the way one sometimes carries a larger child). This word can be an adverb, adjective, or noun.

> The jobs bill arrived **piggyback** on the urgent disaster relief bill—a pretty dirty trick, if you ask me.

Maybe we can **piggyback** this smaller design project onto the bigger one and end up saving some money with our web designers.

Pilot program (or project) – Program planned as a test or trial.

Before rolling out the program nationwide, a **pilot program** was launched in just three cities.

Plutocratic – Related to government by the wealthy.

Polarized – Divided into sharply opposed groups.

The school board was used to rationally discussing issues, but when it came to the teaching of evolution in schools, the board was **polarized**, immediately splitting into two camps, with the discussion devolving into a shouting match within minutes.

Polemic – Controversial argument, especially one attacking a specific idea.

Laura Kipnis's 2003 book *Against Love: A **Polemic*** has been called "shocking" and "scathing." Perhaps Kipnis used the word **polemic** in the title to indicate that she's making an extreme argument as a means of starting a debate. After all, who's really *against love?*

Postulate – Claim, assert; assume the truth or reality of in order to form an argument.

Before proceeding further, let us **postulate** that men and women have some fundamental differences. If we can accept that, we can talk about what type of policies should exist to ensure workplace equality.

Pragmatic – Practical; dealing with actual facts and reality.

The congresswomen personally believed in animal rights, but she knew she had to be **pragmatic**—if she proposed animal rights legislation, she probably wouldn't get reelected.

Predatory – Living by preying on other animals; given to plundering, exploiting, or destroying others for one's own benefit.

Many "check-cashing" outlets are actually **predatory** lenders who charge interest rates that would be illegal in many nations.

Predisposed – having an inclination or tendency beforehand; susceptible. A *predisposition* is an inclination or tendency.

His defense attorney argued that his abusive childhood **predisposed** him to a life of crime.

Predominant – Having the greatest importance or influence; most common, main. A design might have a *predominant color*; a country might have a *predominant religion*. Sentence Correction problems have tested the fact that you need to use *predominant, NOT predominating,* in these situations.

15

Preempt – Prevent; take the place of, supplant; take before someone else can.

The speaker attempted to **preempt** an excessively long Q&A session by handing out a "Frequently Asked Questions" packet at the beginning of the seminar.

Premise – Proposition on which an argument is based. The functional parts of an argument other than the conclusion. Less commonly, *premise* is a verb, as in *The report is premised on (based on) this study.* For somewhat obscure reasons, "the premises" can also refer to a building and its surrounding land.

Prey – An animal that is hunted and eaten. *Predators* are animals that hunt and eat *prey.*

Priceless – Extremely valuable, so valuable that the worth cannot even be estimated.

Pristine – In an original, pure state; uncorrupted. A *pristine* forest has not been touched by humans. Sometimes *pristine* is just used to mean *very clean.*

Progeny – Offspring, descendants.

The study showed that selective breeding could cause the **progeny** of wolves to become more like dogs in a small number of generations.

Prominent – Projecting outward, sticking out; very noticeable. A *prominent* nose might not be a desirable characteristic, according to some people, but a *prominent* citizen is generally a well-known and important person.

Pronounced – Distinct, strong, clearly indicated.

Aunt Shirley claimed we would never know that her "secret recipe" for brownies involved lots of healthy vegetables, but the brownies had a **pronounced** asparagus flavor.

Propagated – Breed, cause to multiply.

Some plants can be **propagated** from cuttings—my mother gave me a piece of her houseplant, and it grew roots after just a few days in water.

Prospective – Potential, aspiring. *Prospective students* have not yet been admitted; *prospective entrepreneurs* are people considering becoming entrepreneurs. This word is related to *prospect,* which can be both a noun (a good possibility) or a verb (to look for something good, such as to *prospect for gold*).

A committee was formed to evaluate the new plan's **prospects**. As part of their analysis, members of the committee looked at the past performance of the **prospective** leader of the new division. One member remarked that the **prospect** of opening up a completely new division was exciting, but might stretch the company too thin.

Proximity – Closeness, the state of being near.

Psyche – The spirit or soul; the mind (as discussed in psychology). Pronounce this word "SY-key."

Qualified – Modified, limited, conditional on something else. *Unqualified* can mean not limited or not restrained. If your boss gives *unqualified* approval for your plan, you can do whatever you want. Of course, everyone knows *qualified* in the sense of *qualified for the job*. Use context to determine which meaning is intended. A *qualified* person is suitable or well-prepared for the job; a *qualified* statement or feeling is held back or limited.

> The scientist gave her **qualified** endorsement to the book, pointing out that, while it posed a credible theory, more research was still needed before the theory could be applied.

Radiometric, radioactive, carbon, or radiocarbon dating – Methods for determining the approximate age of an ancient object by measuring the amount of radioactivity it contains.

Recalcitrant – Not obedient, resisting authority, hard to manage.

> The aspiring kindergarten teacher was not prepared for a roomful of twenty **recalcitrant** children who wouldn't even sit down, much less learn the words to "Holding Hands Around the World."

Recapitulate – Summarize, repeat in a concise way.

> I'm sorry I had to leave your presentation to take a call—I only have a minute, but can you **recapitulate** what you're proposing?

Receptive – Capable of or ready and willing to receive, as in *receptive to a new idea*.

Reconvene – Gather, come together again (or call together again), such as for a meeting, as in *Let's break for lunch and reconvene at 1pm.*

Redress – Setting something right after a misdeed, compensation or relief for injury or wrongdoing (noun); correct, set right, remedy (verb).

> My client was an innocent victim of medical malpractice. As would anyone who had the wrong leg amputated in surgery, he is seeking financial **redress**.

Refute – Prove to be false.

> She's not a very valuable member of the debate team, actually—she loves making speeches, but she's not very good at **refuting** opponents' arguments.

Rehash – Discuss or bring up (an idea or topic) again without adding anything new.

> We're not going to agree, so why **rehash** the issue?

15

Remedial – Providing a remedy, curative; correcting a deficient skill.

> After harassment occurs in the workplace, it is important that the company takes **remedial** action right away, warning or firing the offender as appropriate, and making sure the complainant's concerns are addressed.

> For those who need **remedial** reading help, we offer a summer school program that aims to help students read at grade level.

Reminiscent – Looking back at the past, reminding of the past. A *reminiscent* person is remembering; an old-fashioned object could be *reminiscent of* an earlier time.

Render – Give, submit, surrender; translate; declare formally; cause to become. To *render harmless* is simply to *make harmless.*

> When you **render** your past due payments, we will turn your phone back on.

> Only in her second year of Japanese, she was unable to **render** the classic poem into English.

> The judge **rendered** a verdict that **rendered** us speechless.

Repercussions – Consequences.

> One of the worries about the financial industry is that irresponsible executives rarely suffer lasting **repercussions.**

Respectively – In the order given. This is a very useful word! The sentence "Smith and Jones wrote the books *7 Success Tips* and *Productivity Rocks*" is ambiguous—did they work together on both or did they each write one of the books? "Smith and Jones wrote the books *7 Success Tips* and *Productivity Rocks*, respectively" answers the question—Smith wrote *7 Success Tips* and Jones wrote *Productivity Rocks.* The word is typically used to match up two things to two other things, in the same order.

> His poems "An Ode to the Blossoms of Sheffield" and "An Entreaty to Ladies All Too Prim" were written in 1756 and 1758, **respectively**.

Reticent – Not talking much; private (of a person), restrained, reserved.

> She figured that, to rise to the top, it was best to be **reticent** about her personal life; thus, even her closest colleagues were left speculating at the water cooler about whether her growing belly actually indicated a pregnancy she simply declined to mention to anyone.

Returns – Profits.

Revamp – Renovate, redo, revise (verb); a restructuring, upgrade, etc. (noun). Similarly, *overhaul* means to repair or investigate for repairs.

MANHATTAN
GMAT

I have my whole room decorated in *Twilight: Eclipse* paraphernalia. When *Breaking Dawn* comes out, I will surely have to **revamp** my decor.

Rife – Happening frequently, abundant, currently being reported.

Reports of financial corruption are **rife**.

Rudimentary – Elementary, relating to the basics; undeveloped, primitive.

My knowledge of Chinese is quite **rudimentary**—I get the idea of characters and I can order food, but I really can't read this document you've just given me.

Sanction – Permission or approval, or to give permission or approval OR a legal action by one or more countries against another country to get it to comply (or the act of placing those sanctions on another country). Whoa! Yes, that's right—*sanction* can mean two different things that are basically opposites. Use context to figure it out—if it's plural *(sanctions)*, it's definitely the bad meaning.

Professional boxers may only fight in **sanctioned** matches—fighting outside the ring is prohibited.

America's **sanctions** on Cuba mean that it is illegal for Americans to do business with Cuban companies.

Satire – Literary device in which foolishness or badness is attacked through humor, irony, or making fun of.

Save – But or except. As a verb, of course, *save* means *keep safe, store up, set aside*. But as a preposition or conjunction, *save* can be used as follows:

All of the divisions of the company are profitable **save** the movie-rental division. (This means that the movie-rental division was not profitable.)

He would have been elected president, **save** for the scandal that derailed his campaign at the last minute. (Here, *save* means *except.*)

Scant – not enough or barely enough. *Scanty* is used in the same way (both are adjectives).

The new intern was **scant** help at the conference—he disappeared all day to smoke and didn't seem to realize that he was there to assist his coworkers.

The soldiers were always on the verge of hunger, complaining about their **scanty** rations.

Scarcely – Hardly, barely, by a small margin. Sometimes the adjective *scarce* is used where it sounds like the adverb *scarcely* is needed. This is an idiomatic usage:

She lived a lavish lifestyle she could **scarce** afford.

15

15

Scrutiny – Close, careful observation.

Seemingly – Apparently, outwardly appearing to be a certain way. If an author says that something is *seemingly X,* the author is probably about to say that it is *actually Y.* The word *seemingly* means that something *seems* a certain way (but maybe isn't really).

> He's a **seemingly** honest man—I'll need to get to know him better to say for sure.

Semantic – Relating to the different meanings of words or other symbols.

> Bob said plastic surgery should be covered under the health care plan and Marion said it shouldn't, but it turns out that their disagreement was purely **semantic**—what Bob meant was *reconstructive* surgery and what Marion meant was *cosmetic* surgery.

Settled – Fixed, established, concluded. Sediment can *settle* in water, people who marry can *settle down,* and a *settled judgment* is one that has been firmly decided.

Siphon – Tube for sucking liquid out of something (some people steal gasoline from other people's cars by *siphoning* it). To *siphon funds* is to steal money, perhaps in a continuous stream.

Skeptical – Doubting, especially in a scientific way (needing sufficient evidence before believing).

> Don't confuse **skeptical** and *cynical* (thinking the worst of others' motivations; bitterly pessimistic). In a GMAT Reading Comprehension passage, an author might be **skeptical** (a very appropriate attitude for a scientist, for instance), but would never be *cynical.*

Sketchy – Like a sketch: incomplete, imperfect, superficial.

Skirt – Border, lie along the edge of, go around; evade.

> Melissa spent all of Thanksgiving **skirting** the issue of who she was dating and when she might get married.

> The creek **skirts** our property on the west, so it's easy to tell where our farm ends.

Slew – A large number or quantity. Of course, *slew* is also the past tense of *slay* (kill), so you could actually say *She slew him with a slew of bullets.*

> As soon as we switched software packages, we encountered a whole **slew** of problems.

Slight – Small, not very important, slender or delicate; treat as though not very important; snub, ignore; a discourtesy.

> She was very sensitive, always feeling **slighted** and holding a grudge against her coworkers for a variety of **slights**, both real and imagined.

Natalie Portman has always been **slight**, but she became even thinner to portray a ballerina in *Black Swan*.

Smelt – Fuse or melt ore in order to separate out metal.

Sparing – Holding back or being wise in the use of resources; deficient. Be *sparing* with the ketchup in order to make it last longer, but don't be *sparing* in praising your employees for a job well done.

Spate – Sudden outpouring or rush; flood.

After a brief **spate** of post-exam partying, Lola is ready for classes to begin again.

Spearhead – Be the leader of. A *spearhead* can, of course, be the sharp head of a spear. It can also be a person at the front of a military attack, or a leader of anything.

Lisa agreed to **spearhead** the "healthy office" initiative, and was instrumental in installing two treadmills and getting healthy food stocked in the vending machines.

Staggered – Starting and ending at different times, especially also occurring in overlapping intervals. (Of course, you can also *stagger* around drunk, weaving from side to side.)

Employees who work on **staggered** schedules may only see each other for part of the day.

Static – Fixed, not moving or changing, lacking vitality. *Stasis* is the quality of being *static*.

The anthropologist studied a society in the Amazon that had been deliberately **static** for hundreds of years—the fiercely proud people disdained change, and viewed all new ideas as inferior to the way of life they had always practiced.

Stratum – One of many layers (such as in a rock formation or in the classes of a society). The plural is *strata*.

From overhearing his rich and powerful passengers' conversations, the chauffeur grew to despise the upper **stratum** of society.

I love this dish—it's like a lasagna, but with **strata** made of bread, eggs, and pancetta! Oh, look at the menu—it's actually called a **strata**! That makes perfect sense.

Subjective – Existing in the mind or relating to one's own thoughts, opinions, emotions, etc.; personal, individual, based on feelings

We can give names to colors, but we can never quite convey the **subjective** experience of them—what if my "red" is different from your "red"?

Subjugation – Conquering, domination, enslavement.

Subordinate – Having a lower order or rank, inferior, secondary.

15

Subset – A set that is contained within a larger set.

Subvert – Overthrow, corrupt, cause the downfall of.

Succeeding – Coming after or following. *The succeeding sentence* is simply the sentence that comes after.

> After the sale of the company, you will receive 5% of the profits from the current year, and 1% in all **succeeding** years.

> In 1797, George Washington was **succeeded** by John Adams.

Suffrage – The right to vote. *Women's suffrage* was ensured in the U.S. via the 19th Amendment.

Suppress – Prohibit, curtail, force the end of. A repressive government might *suppress* dissent against its policies.

Surge – Sudden, transient increase (*power surge*), heavy swelling motion like that of waves. A *surge* of troops is sending a lot of soldiers at once. A *surge* in interest is sudden.

Surpass – Transcend, exceed, go beyond, as in *It's only August, and we've already surpassed last year's sales.*

Synchronized – Happening at the same time, simultaneous, in unison.

Syntax – The rules governing grammar and how words join to make sentences (or how words and symbols join in writing computer code), the study of these rules, or any system or orderly arrangement.

> Now that my linguistics class is studying **syntax**, it makes a little more sense when my computer flashes "SYNTAX ERROR" at me.

> Anyone learning a language is bound to make **syntactical** mistakes—even if he or she knows the appropriate vocabulary, it is still difficult to assemble the words perfectly.

Synthesis – Combining of complex things to create a unified whole.

Table – In American English, *to table* something means to postpone discussion of it until later. (In British English, to *table* a bill is the opposite—to submit it for consideration.)

> I see we're not going to agree on whether to scrap our entire curriculum and develop a new one, so let's **table** that discussion and move on to voting on the budget.

Tardy – Late, not on time.

Taxonomy – Science or technique of classification. The *taxonomic* system in biology classifies organisms by Phylum, Class, Order, Species, etc.

Temperament – Natural personality, as in *an angry temperament* or *a pleasant temperament.*

Temperance – Moderation, self-control, especially regarding alcohol or other desires or pleasures; total abstinence from alcohol. Relatedly, *temperate* means *moderate,* as in *a temperate climate.*

> After the end of the Civil War, economic change led to an increase in alcohol problems and the birth of the **Temperance** Movement, which ultimately led to Prohibition.

> Grandma is a model of **temperance**—she drinks red wine every night, but only the one-third of a glass that she read was the minimum amount needed to help prevent heart attacks.

15

Terrestrial – Relating to the Earth or to land; worldly.

> Mr. and Mrs. Daruza were certain they had seen a UFO, plus aliens running around in the night. What they really saw was an especially dense flock of birds in the air, and some mundane, **terrestrial** animals on the ground.

Thenceforth – From that time forward.

> In 1956, Grace Kelly married Rainier III, Prince of Monaco, and was **thenceforth** known as Princess Grace.

Theoretically – In theory (but not necessarily in reality). People sometimes just say *theoretically* when talking about theories, but they also often say it when they mean that something will not work in real life.

> Theoretically, the new process will result in reduced particle emission. (This could mean, "So we will need to try it in order to find out," or it could mean "But I doubt that it will really work." You need the next sentence to know which meaning is intended.)

Thesis – Proposition supported by an argument.

Thorny –Controversial, full of difficulties. Literally, having thorns, prickly (as a rose bush).

Tides – Periodic rise and fall of the ocean about every 12 hours, caused by the attraction of the Sun and moon. Metaphorically, you can say *the tides of refugees,* for instance—implying the refugees are arriving periodically, in large groups.

Token – Sign, symbol, mark, badge; souvenir, memento; sample, or person, thing, idea taken to represent an entire group. Of course, a token can also be a coin-like disk used as currency for subways, arcade games, etc. As an adjective, it means "not very important."

> I am starting to realize that this law firm hired me to be its **token** woman. There I am, smiling in all the ads—but I never actually get to work on important cases.

Hollywood movies are often guilty of **tokenism**—many have exactly one black character (the "token minority"), often present to give advice to the (usually white) main characters.

I am giving you this "Best Friends Forever" necklace as a **token** of our friendship.

Trajectory – The curved path of an object in flight, as in *the missile's trajectory.*

Transient – Moving around, not settled; temporary, not lasting.

In the last decade, podcasting was thought to be the "next big thing," but it turned out to be a largely **transient** phenomenon.

Transmute – Transform, change from one form to another.

Transplantation – Moving from one place to another. Certainly you have heard of a *heart transplant,* for instance. It can also be used metaphorically: a person who has just moved to a new state might refer to herself as a *transplant from Texas.*

Truce or **Armistice** – Suspension of fighting for a specified period because of mutual agreement; cease-fire.

After the earthquake, the two warring nations agreed to a **truce** and sent their soldiers to help the quake's victims.

Undergird – Strengthen, support. To *undergird* an argument is to make it stronger—the opposite of *undermine!*

Undermine – Weaken, cause to collapse by digging away at the foundation (of a building or an argument); injure or attack in a secretive or underhanded way.

Rather than searching impartially for the truth, these pharmaceutical company "scientists" willfully ignored any evidence that **undermined** the conclusion they were being paid to produce.

You are nice to my face, but you are **undermining** me behind my back, suggesting to others in the office that I am making mistakes in my work and that you have been fixing them!

Underpin – Strengthen, corroborate, support from below.

Her argument was **underpinned** with the results of several recent studies.

Underscore – Emphasize (or, literally, to underline text).

"You're not going to mess with Joey anymore," said Joey. His new bodyguards stepped forward threatening, as though to **underscore** Joey's point.

Undifferentiated – Not distinguished from one another, the same.

Unfettered – Free, liberated.

Unforeseeable – Not able to be predicted.

> Our company had disaster insurance and a succession plan in case something happened to the president, but we had no plans for the **unforeseeable** circumstance that our office would be completely overtaken by rats.

Unprecedented – Never before known or seen, without having happened previously.

> When Nixon resigned, American bravado was at an all-time low—the resignation of a sitting president was disgraceful and **unprecedented**.

Untempered – Not toned down; not moderated, controlled, or counterbalanced. Often *untempered by*.

> I wouldn't call it "tough love"—his harshness is **untempered by** any kind of affection.

> The report was an **untempered** condemnation of the company's practices—the investigators didn't have a single good thing to say.

Untenable – Not defendable (as an argument), not able to be lived in (as a house).

> GMAT Critical Reasoning is full of **untenable** arguments that rest upon unproven assumptions.

Unwarranted – Not justified or authorized.

Utopian – Related to ideals of perfection; unrealistically idealistic.

> Reducing homelessness to zero is a **utopian** goal, but our agency views reducing the street population by 25% and getting children off the streets as more practical aims.

Via – Through, by means of, by way of (by a route that goes through or touches). *Per* can also be used in this way.

> We will be flying to Russia **via** Frankfurt.

> Many of the students at our college got here **via** special programs that assist low-income students in preparing for college.

Wanting – Lacking, insufficient, or not good enough (as in, *I read the book and found it wanting*). This makes sense when you think about the fact that people generally *want* good things, of course—so if a person is *left wanting*, he did not get those good things. Conversely, a person who *wants for nothing* is someone who already has everything.

Warranted – Justified, authorized (*warrant* can mean to justify or a justification, but it can also mean to vouch for or guarantee).

> The pundit's comments don't even **warrant** a response from our organization—they were mere name-calling, not suitable for public discourse.

> Your criticism of Anne is **unwarranted**—as your assistant, she has done everything you've asked her to do.

> He doesn't have his documents with him, but I'll **warrant** that he is indeed a certified forklift operator.

Whereas – While on the contrary, considering that.

> Mr. Katsoulas had always assumed his son would take over the family buiness, **whereas** his son had always assumed he would go away to college and never come back.

> **Whereas** squash and peppers are vegetables, a tomato is technically a fruit.

Whet – Stimulate, make keen or eager (especially of an appetite).

> Dinner will take another twenty minutes, but maybe this cheese plate can **whet** your appetite?

Wholesale – Sale of goods in quantity to resellers (opposite of *retail)*. The word can also mean *extensive, in a large way.*

> Neckties have an enormous markup—a tie that sells for $50 often has a **wholesale** cost of less than $5.

> Pol Pot's war crimes included the **wholesale** slaughter of his people.

Winnow – Sift, analyze critically, separate the useful part from the worthless part.

> We got 120 résumés for one job—it's going to take me awhile just to **winnow** this down to a reasonable stack of people we want to interview.

Yoke – A frame for attaching animals (such as oxen) to each other and to a plow or other equipment to be pulled, or a bar across a person's shoulders to help carry buckets of water, etc. Metaphorically, a *yoke* is a burden or something that oppresses. To *yoke* is to unite together or to burden. To *throw off the yoke of oppression* is to free oneself from oppression.

> The speaker argued that humanity had traded the **yoke** of servitude to kings and tyrants for the **yoke** of consumerism, which enslaves us just as much in the end.

Vocab Drill 15.1

Match each word on the left with one of the definitions on the right.

1. Whereas   (A) Also, in addition to, similarly

2. Save   (B) In addition to what has been said, for instance; besides

3. Nonetheless   (C) However, even so, despite that

4. Moreover   (D) On the contrary, considering that

5. Likewise   (E) But or except

Vocab Drill 15.2

For each question, circle the two words that are synonyms (or near-synonyms).

1. Checked	Debilitated	Tempered	Impinged	Warranted
2. Underpin	Undergird	Underscore	Undermine	Unfetter
3. Penumbra	Nebula	Stratum	Enigma	Echelon
4. Patently	Kinetically	Laterally	Baldly	Paradigmatically
5. Enumerate	Delimit	Extrapolate	Infer	Polarize

Vocab Drill 15.3

For each word, circle the nearest SYNONYM below.

1. Partial
(A)   biased
(B)   pleased
(C)   rude
(D)   invaluable

2. Mores
(A)   rights
(B)   language parts
(C)   customs
(D)   decisions

3. Dubious
(A) troubled
(B) immoral
(C) pessimistic
(D) doubtful

4. Eclipse
(A) cover
(B) hide
(C) expose
(D) end

5. Discrete
(A) secretive
(B) equal
(C) special
(D) distinct

Vocab Drill 15.4

Select the most appropriate word for each blank.

1. This report about the changes in the American family structure and the decline of marriage is purely descriptive rather than _____.

    (A) delimited   (B) normative   (C) debased

2. While the rich get richer, the ranks of the poor are greatly expanding and the middle _____ is disappearing completely.

    (A) hierarchy   (B) stratum   (C) gradation

3. Some believe that a propensity for addiction is genetic, but it lies _____ until "activated" through use of drugs or alcohol.

    (A) wanting   (B) lateral   (C) latent

4. While the analysts have collected a great deal of data, there are still many unknowns, and thus our results are _____.

    (A) exhaustive   (B) indeterminate   (C) discretionary

5. This new device has a faster processor and twice as much memory, and is thus easily able to _____ the performance of the previous version.

    (A) outstrip   (B) revamp   (C) offset

Vocab Drill 15.5

For each question, circle the two words that are SYNONYMS.

1.	paradigm	impasse	gridlock	magma	maxim
2.	dichotomy	host	paradox	slew	paragon
3.	impartial	disinterested	eclectic	inert	fledgling
4.	debunk	aggravate	eclipse	fathom	exacerbate
5.	explicitly	baldly	dubiously	cynically	fadingly

Answers to Vocab Drill 15.1

1. Whereas	(D) On the contrary, considering that
2. Save	(E) But or except
3. Nonetheless	(C) However, even so, despite that
4. Moreover	(B) In addition to what has been said, for instance; besides
5. Likewise	(A) Also, in addition to, similarly

Answers to Vocab Drill 15.2

1. *Checked* and *Tempered* both mean limited, held back.
2. *Underpin* and *Undergird* both mean strengthen or support (an argument).
3. *Stratum* and *Echelon* both mean a layer of something.
4. *Patently* and *Baldly* both mean explicitly, openly.
5. *Extrapolate* and *Infer* both mean to draw a conclusion from available data.

Answers to Vocab Drill 15.3

1. (A)
2. (C)
3. (D)
4. (A)
5. (D)

Answers to Vocab Drill 15.4

1. (B)
2. (B)
3. (C)
4. (B)
5. (A)

Answers to Vocab Drill 15.5

1. *Impasse* and *gridlock* both mean a standstill.
2. *Host* and *slew* both mean a large number.
3. *Impartial* and *disinterested* both mean unbiased.
4. *Aggravate* and *exacerbate* both mean make worse.
5. *Explicitly* and *baldly* both mean bluntly, in a straightforward or obvious way.

15 RC Idioms for the GMAT

The following are expressions that are appropriate for use in the type of writing excerpted on the GMAT, and that often appear in writing about business, science, and history. To increase retention of this material, try to use these expressions in your own sentences. Soon, you will be talking like a dignified old professor!

The idioms are followed by a 20-question drill allowing you to test your understanding of these expressions when used in complex sentences.

"..." – Quote marks can indicate 1) that the word or phrase is not to be taken literally, or 2) the introduction of a new, made-up word or phrase. So, some context is needed to understand the meaning.

> The factory employs several people who add defects and rough edges to its popular line of **"antique"** furniture. (The furniture is not really antique.)

> The company has sent its top people to ethics training and courses on Aristotle in an attempt to build a **"philosophically correct"** business. (The idea of a "philosophically correct" business is really weird, perhaps something that the company itself came up with.)

Accorded to – Given or granted to. (Sometimes *accorded* is used without *to*, as in *I was surprised by the adulation accorded the elderly author at the high school assembly.*)

Account for – 1) Take into consideration or make adjustments based on; 2) Cause. This is not the same as *give an account of*, which just means *explain.*

> I **accounted for** the fact that Joe is always late by telling him to meet us at 1:30 when the event is really at 2. (Here, *accounted for* means *made adjustments to compensate for.*)

> I did get us the meeting, but Ellen's hard work **accounted for** the rest of our success. (Here, *accounted for* means *caused.*)

"A given" – The use of *a given* as a noun is different from the use of *given* alone. For instance, a person's *given name* is the one *given* by his or her parents (a "first name" in the U.S.), and you might also say, "The truth differs from the *given* explanation." Here, *given explanation* just means *the explanation that someone gave.* Simple. However, *a given* means something taken for granted, something assumed or that does not require proof.

> When I was planning my wedding, it was **a given** that my parents would invite anyone they wanted, since they were paying for everything.

> It's **a given** that everyone here is against human trafficking—what we disagree about is the best way to fight it.

Albatross or **albatross around the neck of (a person or group)** – A constant burden or worry; an obstacle. Literally, an albatross is a bird. The expression *an albatross around one's neck* creates the silly image of a person wearing a (dead?) bird—but that certainly sounds like a constant burden or worry! (This expression comes from *The Rime of the Ancient Mariner,* in which an old man had to wear an albatross around his neck as punishment for his sins.)

> The city has done an admirable job rebuilding its infrastructure and marketing itself, but the crime rate continues to be an **albatross** around the city's neck in trying to attract tourists.

All but – Almost definitely. *The bill's passage is all but assured* means that the bill will almost certainly pass.

> Your objections have arrived too late; the matter is **all but** decided.

And yet – A stronger way of saying *yet.* The expression *and yet* seems ungrammatical (two conjunctions right next to each other is very strange—you don't say *and but*), but it is an idiom used for emphasis. It indicates a surprising twist, an ironic realization, etc. It is often used at the beginning of a sentence for emphasis, and can even be used on its own, although this usage is casual.

> The company was lauded for its commitment to the environment. **And yet** its employees regularly fly in private jets, creating carbon footprints that would embarrass any true environmentalist.

> He was surprised to see her standing on his doorstep in the rain. "I said I was leaving you and never wanted to see your face again!" she said. "**And yet,**" he replied.

Arms race – Competition between two countries to build up the best and largest supply of weapons. This term is often associated with the Cold War between the U.S. and the Soviet Union. Metaphorically, an arms race is a competition that implies a sort of "more, more, more!" mentality and may not be entirely rational.

> Analysts carefully watched stock prices as the two Internet giants competed in an **arms race**, expanding rapidly by buying up smaller companies with little due diligence.

Aside from – In addition to, not even counting.

> **Aside from** the obvious financial benefits of investing in a socially responsible fund, you can

rest assured that your money is used to maximize social good.

(Adjective) as it is,... – This pattern is used to contrast the part after the comma with the part before. For instance, *Charming as she is, I just don't want to be friends with her anymore.*

> **As pleased as we are** to see more minorities on the board than ever before, discrimination in hiring and promotion is still a serious problem.

As well as – Sometimes, *as well as* just means *and,* as in *I had ramen for lunch, as well as a hot dog.* But *as well as* can also be used to mention one thing as a way to contrast with or emphasize another.

> You know what I discovered? My French teacher speaks Chinese, **as well as** French! (Here, the point of the sentence is that it is amazing that the French teacher also speaks Chinese. Of course, everyone already knows that the French teacher speaks French—that part is only mentioned to highlight how amazing it is that the teacher knows *another,* unrelated language.)

> Therefore, vitamins may protect against emotional instability, **as well as** physical deficiencies. (If this were the conclusion to a Critical Reasoning argument, it would be good to realize that the *physical deficiency* part is not relevant. Everyone knows that vitamins protect against physical deficiency, so that part is only included to contrast with or emphasize the *amazing* fact that maybe vitamins also counteract emotional instability.)

At best – At the most, interpreted in the most favorable way. *The seminar drew 20 people at best* means that 20 or fewer people attended.

> My college algebra teacher can barely factor a polynomial! He is qualified to teach elementary school math, **at best.**

At fault – Guilty.

> The insurance company is investigating who is **at fault** for the collision.

At loggerheads – In conflict, at a standstill.

> The strike is not likely to end soon—the transit authority and the union representatives have been **at loggerheads** for weeks.

At odds – In conflict.

> The teachers' union and the state government are always **at odds.**

At once – 1) Immediately; 2) At the same time.

> Once the hurricane veered near the coast, the governor ordered that we evacuate **at once.** (Here, *at once* means *now.*)

We've received three proposals that are all excellent, but we can do them at **at once**. (Here, *at once* means *at the same time*.)

The better part – The largest or longest part. *The better part* does NOT have to be good! The word *better* is a bit confusing here.

> For **the better part** of human history, slavery has been a reality. (The speaker is NOT saying that slavery is good. The speaker is saying that, for most of human history, slavery has existed.)

> When the oil magnate died, he left **the better part** of his fortune to his third wife, and only a small sliver to his children.

Beside the point – Irrelevant, off-topic.

Bite the hand the feeds you – This expression means exactly what it sounds like (think of a mean and not very smart dog). Although informal sounding, this expression has appeared in business writing.

> The music industry **bites the hand that feeds it** when it penalizes consumers who share (and therefore publicize) their favorite songs with friends.

(Adjective) but (adjective) – This pattern is used for two adjectives that provide a contrast. They can be opposites, or one good and one bad, etc. For instance, *a boring but lucrative job.*

> The food available in such neighborhoods is inexpensive but insalubrious. (Here, you could use the structure to infer that, since *inexpensive* is good, *insalubrious* must be bad. What might be bad about inexpensive food? As it turns out, *insalubrious* means *unhealthy.*)

By no means – Not at all. The use of *means* here is similar to its use in "The ends justify the means," a controversial expression meaning that, as long as the goals (the "ends") are good, it's acceptable to do anything (the "means") in order to achieve the goals. So, *means* can have the meaning of *ways of getting something done.* You can also say, *This scheduling software is the means by which we intend to manage the project.* So, the expression *by no means* indicates that there is no way, or *means,* to interpret something in the manner you are about to say.

> This is **by no means** a new idea. (The idea is certainly not new.)

(Verb) by so (verb)ing – The second verb is equivalent to or causes the first verb. He *defaults by so refusing* means *when he refuses, he is defaulting* (that is, neglecting to fulfill the duties of a contract). *By so agreeing* also occurs on its own, meaning *by agreeing to do the thing that was just mentioned.*

> He agreed to run as the Green Party candidate though he already holds a Democratic party chairmanship, which he effectively **abandoned by so agreeing**.

By the same token – This expression means that the speaker will then say something else based on the same evidence he or she just used to make a different point.

MANHATTAN
GMAT

15

As a libertarian, he wants to abolish the IRS. **By the same token**, he wants drugs legalized.

The case at issue – The matter at hand, the thing that is being discussed.

> Usually, raising prices results in a drop in demand, but in **the case at issue**, the price jump convinced consumers that the product was a luxury good, thus spurring demand from aspirational consumers.

Caught red-handed – Caught in the act of doing something wrong, so that the person cannot deny guilt. The expression refers to having blood on one's hands.

> The scientists on the company payroll could no longer claim that the fish in the river were all dying from natural causes once the company was **caught red-handed** dumping waste at the river's mouth.

Colored by – Influenced or prejudiced by.

> Her opinion about the prison system was **colored by** having grown up effectively an orphan while both her parents served sentences in separate prisons.

Couldn't have come at a better time – The same as *could hardly have come at a better time*, this expression means that something happened at the best possible time, such as at a very convenient moment or just in time to prevent disaster.

Curry favor – To try to gain favor (such as preferential treatment from a boss) through flattery or servile behavior. The expression is derived from French and is not related to *curry*, the food.

Cut bait – Give up, abandon an activity. Often part of the expression *fish or cut bait*, to *cut bait* is to stop fishing.

> As much as he wanted to be an entrepreneur, after a year of struggling, he **cut bait** and asked his former boss for his old job back.

Due diligence – Research or analysis done before taking action (such as investing); care that a reasonable person would take to prevent harm to others

En masse – All together, in a group. This expression is from French and is related to the word *mass*. Like many foreign expressions, *en masse* is often written in italics.

> The protesters marched ***en masse*** to the palace.

Entrée into – Admittance, permission to enter. Most people in the U.S. think of an entrée as the main dish of a meal, but it originally was an appetizer—a dish that leads into the main course (the word is related to "enter"). A person who wants to rise in society might seek an *entrée* into a certain social group. (You can also say "seek *entrée*"—sometimes in that expression, the word *an* is omitted.)

For disadvantaged young people, good public schools can provide an **entrée** into the middle class.

For all X, Y – This sentence pattern means, "Despite X, actually Y"—that is, X and Y will be opposites, or one will be good and one will be bad. The word "actually" (or a similar word) often appears in this pattern, but doesn't have to.

> **For** all of its well-publicized "green" innovations, the company is one of the worst polluters in the state.

> **For** all of the criticism she has received for her actions during the merger, she's actually a really nice person if you get to know her.

Former and latter – When two things are mentioned, the first one is the *former* and the second one is the *latter*.

> Your grades are slipping and you've been very secretive about your behavior—it's **the latter** of these things that worries your father and me the most.

> I intend to choose a business school based on reputation and cost, the **former** more so than the **latter**.

For show – For appearances only.

> The company was voted the best in the country for working mothers, but the actual women employees report that it's all **for show**; for instance, the much-publicized free on-site daycare is tiny and has a three-year waiting list.

For years to come – Until much later. *The consequences won't affect us for years to come* means that they WILL affect us, but not for the next several years.

> My parents are only in their sixties and are healthy and active, so I am hopeful that my children will get to enjoy their grandparents **for years to come**.

Full throttle – With much speed and energy. On a related note, sometimes *juice* is used to mean *energy*.

> The plan was a good idea with little **juice** behind it; because it was never implemented with much gusto, it's hard to say whether it could have succeeded. We'll have to wait until another company goes **full throttle** with a similar idea to observe the outcome.

Garden-variety – Ordinary, common.

Gloss over, paper over, whitewash – These are all expressions for covering up a problem, insult, etc., rather than addressing it or fixing it. Think of a dirty floor that you just put a pretty rug on top of instead of cleaning. Because *gloss* is slippery (think of lip gloss), *gloss over* often has the sense of trying to smoothly and quickly move on to something else.

> He made a snide remark about short people and then tried to **gloss over it** when he realized his 5'2" boss had overheard.

> The journalist accused the government of trying to **whitewash** the scandal, implying that the officials covered up the incident out of concern for national security rather than to protect themselves.

Go down the tubes – Become much worse, fail. One theory is that this expression is about the plumbing attached to toilets.

Go sour – Think of milk going bad—that's the idea behind the expression *go sour*. A relationship *goes sour* before the couple breaks up. An economy *gone sour* can't be good. This is not the same as the expression *sour grapes,* which refers to pretending something you can't have wasn't any good anyway, as in, *Her hatred of the rich is just sour grapes—if she could afford luxury, she'd take all she could get.*

Hand-wringing – An excessive expression of concern, guilt, or distress.

> There has been much **hand-wringing** (or **wringing of hands**) over falling test scores, with so-called "experts" acting as if the world will end if students do 1% worse in math and science.

Hardly – *Hardly* can mean *almost or probably not,* or *not at all.* Of course, *I can hardly see you* means *I can see you only a little bit.* In the sentence *The news could hardly have come at a worse time,* hardly means *not*—thus, the overall meaning is *The news came at the worst possible time.*

Hold the line vs. **toe the line** – *Hold the line* means *keep something the same.* It is a reference to (American) football, in which you don't want the opponent to get the ball past the line of scrimmage in the middle of the field. To *toe the line* is to conform to a policy or way of thinking, or follow the rules. One theory about the origin of the expression is that, on ships, barefoot sailors were made to line up for inspection—that is, to put their toes on an actual line on the deck of the ship.

> My boss doesn't want to hear original ideas at all—he just wants me to **toe the line.**

> If colleges cannot **hold the line** on rising tuition costs, students will have to take on even more crippling loan burdens.

However much, as much as – Even though, no matter how much.

> **However much** people may agree that saving money is a virtue, the majority of Americans don't have sufficient funds for any kind of emergency.

As much as I'd like to attend your wedding, I just can't afford a trip to Taiwan.

In contrast to – This phrase is important in inference questions on Reading Comp. If a writer says *In contrast to X, Y is A*, you can draw the conclusion that *X is not A*.

> *In contrast to our competitor's product, our product is made with organic materials.* (This means that the competitor's product is NOT made with organic materials, which very well could be the answer to a question about what you can infer from the passage.)

Just cause – *Just* as an adjective means *justified, legal, fair. Just cause* means a legally sufficient reason. In some legal codes, an employer must show *just cause* for firing an employee.

Legions or **is legion** – *Legions* are large military units, generally consisting of a few thousand soldiers. Saying that a group is *legion* is saying that it is large.

> Surely, the developers could have foreseen that **legions** of Mac users would protest when news emerged that the new version of the software would not be Mac compatible.

> The former governor has been called a demagogue by many commentators who nevertheless must grudgingly admit that her supporters **are legion**, populating rallies in every state.

"No X OR Y" vs. "no X AND Y" – When you are talking about having two things, saying "salt AND pepper" is very different from saying "salt OR pepper." However, when you are talking about a lack of two things, *and* and *or* can often be used to express the same idea. The following two sentences have the same meaning:

> Pioneer towns were characterized by little access to the outside world **and** few public institutions.

> Pioneer towns had almost no access to the outside world **or** public institutions.

Not (adjective) – Of course, putting *not* before an adjective indicates the opposite. However, sometimes it indicates a softer or more polite way to say something. If someone asks if you like the meal he cooked or the outfit he is wearing, and you know him well enough to be honest, you might say *It's not my favorite*. Or, sometimes you say something like *not irrelevant* instead of simply *relevant* in order to indicate that you are correcting someone else's misconception:

> Concern about foreign debt is **not misplaced**. (Here, this mean that you should be concerned! The phrase also may be implying that others incorrectly think you should *not* be concerned.)

Not only X but also Y – This is a two-part expression, introducing the first part before adding on the second, more extreme or surprising part.

> The executive was **not only** fired, **but also** indicted for fraud.

He **not only** bought his girlfriend an iPhone for her birthday, **but also** took her entire family on a vacation to the Catskills.

Not X, let alone Y – The meaning is *Not X and definitely not this even more extreme thing, Y.*

Our remaining funds are **not** enough to get us through the week, **let alone** pay next month's payroll. (Here, getting through the week is less expensive than next month's payroll, so if you can't afford the cheaper thing, you *definitely* can't afford the more expensive thing.)

No worse than – Equal to or better than.

Although exotic, this illness is really **no worse than** the common flu.

On face – At first appearance, superficially. If someone says *on face,* you can expect that later on, the person will give the "real story." In a Reading Comprehension passage, seeing *on face* is a good clue that the author's main idea will probably be the opposite of what *seems* true at first glance.

On its face, the donation seems like a selfless act of philanthropy. However, the wealthy donor mainly made the donation for the tax benefits.

On face, the theory seems sound. However, new research has uncovered serious flaws.

Only looks (adjective) – Appears (some certain way) but isn't really.

She **only looks** homeless—she is actually a famous and wealthy artist who lives eccentrically.

On par with – Sometimes *on a par with,* this expression comes from golf and means *about equal to* or *equivalent to.*

Opening salvo – A *salvo* is a simultaneous firing of guns or release of bombs. Metaphorically, an *opening salvo* is something that starts a fight.

The introduction of Bill H.R. 2, given the inflammatory name "Repealing the Job-Killing Health Care Law Act," was seen by some as an **opening salvo** by the Republicans.

Outside of the home – Working *outside of the home* means having a regular job, such as in an office. However, working *out of your home* is actually working at home. If that's hard to understand, think of the expression *living out of your car,* which actually means living *in* your car—the idea is that you leave the car to go "out" but return back to the car as your base, just as someone who works *out of their home* leaves the home to go to meetings, for example, but uses the home as a central point.

The study compared incomes of women who had worked **outside of the home** to incomes of women who worked **out of their homes** as freelancers or owners of small businesses.

Per se – In itself, by itself, intrinsically. From Latin, often written in italics. *Per se* is often used to indicate that while something isn't *naturally* or *the same as* something else, it still has the same effect.

The policy isn't sexist, *per se*, but it has had a disproportionate impact on women that deserves further study.

Press for – Argue in favor of. Think of *pushing people* towards what you want them to do.

The advocates **pressed for** greater regulation of child-care providers.

Rabid – Rabies is a disease that some animals (dogs, raccoons, etc.) contract and that causes the animal to become insane and violent. Thus, the word *rabid* (having rabies) is used metaphorically to mean *zealous* or *excessively or angrily passionate*. One symptom of rabies is *foaming at the mouth*, which is also an expression for being extremely (and violently or irrationally) angry.

15

One debater called himself a "peace activist" and his opponent a "**rabid** right-wing gun nut." His opponent called himself a "champion of the American way" and his opponent a "**rabid** anti-American zealot."

Ranks of – The people in a group other than the leaders. Many people know the word *rank* as "a level or grade," as in *A general has a higher rank than a sergeant*. The other use of *ranks* is also originally related to the military: the *ranks* or sometimes the *rank and file* means all the regular soldiers (not the officers). *Ranks* also refers to soldiers standing in a particular formation, so the expression *to break rank* means to rebel, disobey, disagree, or disrupt a situation in which everyone is doing the same thing.

Among the **ranks** of our alumni are two senators and many famous authors.

The author **broke rank** with her colleagues in the field of personal development by suggesting that "positive thinking" may be doing more damage than good.

Reap and **sow** – These are metaphors related to farming, and specifically the idea that the seeds that you plant (or *reap*) determine what you will later harvest (or *sow*). *Sow* is pronounced the same as *so*, and the past tense is *sown*, as in *Having sown the love of knowledge in the minds of children, the teacher's influence extended well past her own lifetime*. A common expression is *You reap what you sow*.

He worked night and day in the strange new country, never stopping to rest, for he knew he would **reap** his reward when his family greeted him as a hero for all the money he had sent back home.

Red flag – Warning sign or something alarming.

Bernie Madoff's sustained, ultrahigh returns should have been a **red flag** for the banks with which he did business.

Red herring – Something irrelevant that distracts from the real issue. A herring is a fish, of course. One theory for the origin of the expression is that criminals trying to escape the police would sometimes rub a smelly fish across their trail as they ran away, in order to mislead the dogs used to track them down.

15

Johnson's new Maserati turned out to be a **red herring** in investigating where the stolen funds had gone—it turns out, Johnson's wife bought the car with her inheritance, and the real culprit behind the theft was the mild-mannered junior accountant no one had suspected.

Reign vs. **reins** – These two words are pronounced the same as *rain* and *rains,* but the meanings are different. *Reign* means rule, as in *Conditions have improved under the king's reign.* Using this word metaphorically, such as for a CEO, implies that the leader is a bit like a king. *Reins* are leather straps used by a rider to control a horse. Metaphorically, you might say *Since the new CEO took the reins of this organization....*

In an era of near-total transparency, some would say that the media now **hold the reins** in our society in a manner formerly reserved for the government.

(Adjective)-ridden – Dominated, burdened, or afflicted by (adjective). In the phrase *disease-ridden slum,* it's pretty obvious that the meaning is bad, but actually, adding *-ridden* to anything makes the meaning bad. If someone said *an equality-ridden society,* that person is actually against equality! *Ridden* can also be used alone, as in *The neighborhood was ridden with crime.*

Save – But or except. As a verb, of course, *save* means *keep safe, store up, set aside.* But as a preposition or conjunction, *save* can be used as follows:

All of the divisions of the company are profitable save the movie-rental division. (This means that the movie-rental division was not profitable.)

He would have been elected president, save for the scandal that derailed his campaign at the last minute. (Here, *save* means *except.*)

Scarcely or **Scarce** – Sometimes *scarce* is used where it sounds like the adverb *scarcely* is needed. This is an idiomatic usage.

She lived a lavish lifestyle she could **scarce** afford. (She could not afford the lifestyle.)

School of thought – A group of people with similar beliefs or perspective on things, or the beliefs themselves. If a GMAT writer says *One school of thought argues X,* it is probably the case that the author is about to say the opposite (calling something a *school of thought* can emphasize that it's not the only way to think about the issue).

One **school of thought** says that companies don't need to "give back" to communities, since the companies make profits from voluntarily trading with others; **a competing school of thought** says that companies benefit from a nation's infrastructure, the school systems that educate their employees, etc., and thus have responsibilities similar to those of citizens.

Sight vs. **Site** vs. **Cite** – To **sight** is to see, or discover by looking. A **site** is a location. To **cite** is to reference or give credit to.

The sailors had nearly given up hope when the finally **sighted** land. When they reached the shore, they planted a flag on the **site** of their landing.

A good research report **cites** relevant studies.

So much as – This phrase is used an adverb to intensify. In *My teacher is so awful, she won't so much as answer a question,* the meaning is that, whatever the teacher will do, it is not "as much as" answering a question—it is something less than that.

> After her husband decided to take up day trading and lost $100,000 in one day, she wouldn't **so much as** look at him.

Sound the depths – Explore, investigate, or look into something really deeply. This expression is a metaphor based on the idea of a "sounding line," which is a rope with a weight on the bottom that you drop to the ocean floor to see how deep the ocean is.

> Other books have dealt with the topic in a superficial way, but this is the first book to really **sound the depths** of the response of the British lower class to the American Revolution.

Steeped in – Immersed in, saturated with. A teabag **steeps** in hot water. A person **steeped in** classic literature probably thinks about almost everything in terms of old, famous books.

> The Met's new campaign seeks to answer affirmatively the question of whether music lovers **steeped in** hip-hop and pop can learn to love opera.

Stem from – Grow out of, be caused by. This is related to the idea of a plant's *stem.*

> The psychologist believed that his neurosis **stemmed from** events in his childhood.

Sway or **hold sway over** – Persuade, influence.

> The lawyer attempted to **sway** the jury with an emotional account of the defendant's tough childhood.

> Repressive governments are suspicious of those who **hold sway** over the people, and often imprison or execute such people.

Take umbrage – Become offended.

> With fifteen years of experience on all kinds of campaigns, she **took umbrage** to her sexist coworker's suggestion that she was only qualified to develop advertising for "women's products."

Tracks with – Is consistent with, makes sense in relation to. Think of *train tracks* running parallel to each other—if two ideas *track,* that means they are going in the same direction. You can say that information *tracks with* something you already know when you want to say that what you are hearing sounds like it *could be* true (although you don't know for sure).

Trappings – Accessories, the characteristic items, products, etc., that come with or are associated with something. Think of the side dishes or condiments that come with a meal. The *trappings* of fame include invites to fancy parties and free items from companies.

> Mr. and Mrs. Seguro moved to the U.S. because they wanted a better education for their children. The children, however, were soon decked out in the *trappings* of American teenage life—cell phones, iPods, and fashionable clothes—with little care for studying.

Vanguard and **avant-garde** – The *avant-garde* (French for *in front of the guard*) were the leading soldiers at the front of an army. *Vanguard* is derived from *avant-garde* and means the same thing. Metaphorically, the *avant-garde* (noun or adjective) or vanguard (noun) are innovators, those at the forefront of any movement or those "ahead of their time." Sometimes, the *avant-garde* seems a little crazy or scary at first.

> While Google has won the search engine wars, in 1994, Yahoo was on the **vanguard** of search technology.

> She arrived at the mixer in a dress that was a little ***avant-garde*** for the otherwise conservative Yale Club—she would have looked more appropriate at an art gallery or Lady Gaga concert.

The very idea (or *the very notion*, etc.) – This expression is used to express a strong contrast.

> The author conjures up a drifting yet haunting word picture that challenges **one's very notion** of what constitutes a story. (This means that the author's strange "word picture" story goes against the most basic things that you think must be true about stories.)

With a grain of salt – To take something (a statement, claim, etc.) *with a grain of salt* is to maintain a small amount of skepticism. The origin of this expression is related to an old belief that a small amount of salt could help protect against poison.

> Take the consultant's advice **with a grain of salt**—the software he's recommending is produced by a company that is also a client of his.

With respect to, in some respects – These expressions are not really about giving respect. *With respect to* (or *in respect to*) just means *about*. The expression *in some respects* just means *in some ways*.

> **With respect to** your request for a raise, I'm afraid no one is getting one this year. This year is, **in some respects**, the worst year we've ever had.

Wreak havoc – Cause destruction. The past tense of *wreak* is *wrought*.

> Unsurprisingly, a combination of heroin abuse and living on the streets can really **wreak havoc** on a person's health.

Drill 15.6 — Decoding Idioms

Each sentence below is written in American English that is idiomatic, but still appropriate for business writing. Pick the multiple choice answer that best expresses the meaning of the original sentence.

Complete this quiz "open book"—feel free to go back and look up anything you want in this book, and to use any online dictionary (such as dictionary.com). You will gain much more from the process of looking things up and decoding the statements than you would by merely testing yourself in the usual manner.

15

1. In contrast to the Swedish social welfare system, Ireland's does not provide paid paternity leave.

    (A) Ireland's social welfare system does not provide paid paternity leave and Sweden's does.
    (B) The Swedish and Irish social welfare systems are different in many ways, and Ireland's does not provide paid paternity leave.
    (C) Both the Swedish and Irish social welfare systems provide paid paternity leave.

2. He can hardly be called a liberal, for his voting record belies the beliefs he professes to hold.

    (A) He is not really a liberal because he votes in a way that goes against liberalism.
    (B) He is a very strong liberal and always supports liberal beliefs with his vote.
    (C) He is slightly liberal, and his voting record goes along with his beliefs.

3. However much the committee may be deadlocked now, the progress made to this point has been non-trivial.

    (A) The committee is now committed to one course of action and is making progress.
    (B) The committee members are fighting with one another, but have made progress on one point they were discussing.
    (C) Although it is true that the committee is stuck and not moving forward, it has already made significant progress.

4.   Although the book has addressed the issue of educational equity head on, it has sidestepped the thorny question of school vouchers.

    (A)   The book talked about owning stock in education, but it has talked in an indirect way about the painful issue of school vouchers.

    (B)   The book talked directly about equality in education, but it avoided talking about the controversial issue of school vouchers.

    (C)   The book talked in a smart way about fairness in education, but it only gave an overview of the controversial issue of school vouchers.

5.   Her appointment to the office is all but assured.

    (A)   She has a meeting at the office, but the time is not set.

    (B)   She will almost certainly be given a new job or leadership role.

    (C)   She may be promoted, but it is not likely.

6.   You discount the consultant's prescription at your peril.

    (A)   You put yourself in danger by dismissing the consultant's recommendations.

    (B)   Paying less for the consultant's advice is not a wise idea.

    (C)   You have gotten a good deal on a dangerous medicine.

7.   Davis seemingly spearheaded the project and has taken credit for its success. Nonetheless, those in the know are aware of his patent appropriation of the ideas of others.

    (A)   Davis seems to have led the project, and he took credit for it. However, those who know the real situation know that he openly stole other people's ideas.

    (B)   Davis was the leader of the project and got the credit, and those who know about what happened know that he used the intellectual property of other people in an appropriate way.

    (C)   Davis seems to have damaged the project, but took credit for its success. However, those who know the real situation know that he used other people's ideas.

8.   The experiment only looks like a success.

    (A)   It is not possible to see the experiment as anything but a success.

    (B)   The experiment seems successful, but we don't know for sure.

    (C)   The experiment has the appearance of a success, but really is a failure.

9.   On its face, the dispute is about the study's integrity. But in actuality, the lead scientist will brook no opposition to his own theories.

      (A)   The dispute is directly about the honesty of the study. But really, the lead scientist will not "go with the flow" of opposition to his own theories.
      (B)   The dispute at first seems to be about the study's honesty. But really, the lead scientist will not tolerate opposition to his own theories.
      (C)   The dispute is directly about the honesty of the study. But really, the lead scientist will not encourage opposition to his own theories.

10.   We will not likely reconcile the apparent discrepancy for years to come.

      (A)   It will probably take us many years to show that what looks like a contradiction really isn't.
      (B)   We do not want to work out a difference of opinion in the coming years.
      (C)   Over the next several years, we will probably not attempt to work out what seems like an error.

11.   The dictator had long sown discontent, and as dissident thinkers began to hold sway over the populace, no one could be surprised when the regime was subverted.

      (A)   The dictator was dissatisfied, and as rebellious thinkers began to have policial power over the people, it was not surprising when the government became corrupt.
      (B)   The dictator had been planting seeds of unhappiness that were destined to grow, and as thinkers who disagreed with the government began to influence regular people, it was not surprising when the dictator was overthrown.
      (C)   The dictator had been more and more dissatisfied over time, and as thinkers whose ideas went against the government began to influence the people, it was not surprising when the dictator lost his power.

12.   A variable-rate mortgage is no worse in this respect than a fixed-rate one.

      (A)   There is something bad about a fixed-rate mortgage, and that same quality is better or equally bad in a variable-rate mortgage.
      (B)   A variable-rate mortgage does not indicate less respect than a fixed-rate mortgage.
      (C)   If you look at it a certain way, a variable-rate mortgage is the same or better than a fixed-rate one.

13. As to whether Dr. Stuttgart is a token academic on a board of otherwise mercenary executives, you need look only at the board's response to the latest crisis, when Dr. Stuttgart was at once turned to for counsel and granted discretionary power over the board's funds.

(A) If there is a question about whether the main reason Dr. Stuttgart is on the board is so the executives who only care about money can look good, then the only way to answer that question is to look at the board's response to the latest crisis, when Dr. Stuttgart was put in charge and given power over the board's money.

(B) If you want to know whether Dr. Stuttgart is really an academic even though he is on a board of executives who will do anything to win, then the best place to look for an answer is at the board's response to the latest crisis, when Dr. Stuttgart was asked for his advice and allowed to secretly control the board's money.

(C) If you are questioning whether the main reason Dr. Stuttgart is on the board is so the executives who only care about money can look good, then you can easily answer that question by looking at the board's response to the latest crisis, when the board asked for Dr. Stuttgart's advice while at the same time giving him power to spend the board's money on whatever he thought was best.

14. The author is seemingly a garden-variety Marxist.

(A) The author seems to be a Marxist who has a lot of diversity in his or her opinions.

(B) The author is a Marxist who is concerned with many different Marxist issues.

(C) It seems as though the author is a typical Marxist, but that may not really be true.

15. The windfall could hardly have come at a better time: by agreeing to a company restructuring he didn't really understand, he had just inadvertently reduced his holdings in the family business.

(A) The disaster happened at a very bad time, because he had also just agreed to a company reorganization that he didn't understand and that improperly reduced his control over the family business.

(B) He suddenly received some money at a very convenient time, because he had just agreed to a company reorganization that he didn't understand and thus had accidentally reduced how much of the family business he owned.

(C) The good fortune could have happened at a better time, because he had also just agreed to a company reorganization that he didn't understand and that reduced his portion of the family business.

16.   Which of the following, if true, best reconciles the apparent discrepancy?

   (A)   Which of the following is true and shows that a contradiction does not really exist?

   (B)   Which of the following, if it happened to be true, would show that what looks like a contradiction really isn't?

   (C)   Which of the following, if it happened to be true, would help us accept a contradiction?

17.   The evidence has been taken as supporting Fujimura's conclusion.

   (A)   Other people have interpreted the evidence in a way that makes it seem to support Fujimura's conclusion.

   (B)   The evidence definitely supports Fujimura's conclusion.

   (C)   The evidence has been deeply understood by others in a way that allows them to effectively support Fujimura's conclusion.

18.   Hardly a debased example, this shifty, hedging, practically unreadable document is paradigmatic of corporate memos.

   (A)   This memo switches positions often, holds back information, and is very hard to read. It is a very poor example of corporate memos.

   (B)   Although this memo refuses to take a stand, tries to reduce the writer's risk, and is very hard to read, it is a poor example of corporate memos and should not be judged to be representative.

   (C)   This memo is evasive or tricky, avoids taking a stand so as not to risk being wrong or offending anyone, and is almost unreadable. However, this is not an especially bad example of a corporate memo — they are all this bad.

19.   Which of the following best underscores the argument that a failure to enforce the regulation is on par with publicly condoning illegal dumping?

   (A)   Which of the following most weakens the argument that a failure to enforce the regulation is just as bad as publicly tolerating illegal dumping?

   (B)   Which of the following most strengthens the argument that a failure to enforce the regulation is just as bad as publicly tolerating illegal dumping?

   (C)   Which of the following most emphasizes the argument that a failure to enforce the regulation is worse than publicly tolerating illegal dumping?

20. The central idea is juxtaposed with the results of a study that seemingly corroborates a long-derided school of thought.

    (A)   The central idea is placed next to and contrasted with evidence that seems to support the ideas of a group of people whose ideas have been looked down on or made fun of for a long time.

    (B)   The central idea is judged to be better than evidence that seems to support the ideas of a group of people whose ideas have been looked down on or made fun of for a long time.

    (C)   The central idea is placed next to and contrasted with evidence that supports the ideas of a group of people whose ideas used to be looked down on or made fun of.

15

MANHATTAN
GMAT

Answers to Drill 15.6 — Decoding Idioms

1. **(A)**
2. **(B)**
3. **(C)**
4. **(B)**
5. **(B)**
6. **(A)**
7. **(A)**
8. **(C)**
9. **(B)**
10. **(A)**
11. **(B)**
12. **(A)**
13. **(C)**
14. **(C)**
15. **(B)**
16. **(B)**
17. **(A)**
18. **(C)**
19. **(B)**
20. **(A)**

15

Appendix *of* A

Foundations of GMAT Verbal

Helpful Hints for Indian Speakers of English

In This Chapter...

Helpful Hints for Indian Speakers of English

Wrap-Up

Helpful Hints for Indian Speakers of English

Many, many Indian and Indian-American students have come through the doors of Manhattan GMAT.

As such, we've heard our Indian students say all kinds of things that are different from the equivalent expressions in American English. For instance, Americans do not *prepone* meetings, although we have to agree that the idea makes perfect sense (we usually say "move a meeting up," based on the idea that earlier times are higher up on a printed schedule). In the U.S., a store has "hours," not "timings," and a handsome movie star might be called a "leading man," but not a "hero."

All of this is very interesting, but not particularly relevant to the GMAT.

However, there are a few differences between Indian and American English that are indeed relevant to the exam, and we will discuss those here.

We want to be clear that our purpose is not to say that Indian English—or any other dialect of English—is wrong. Americans can hardly claim that their form of the language is the "right" one when, of course, the English were speaking their own language long before America was even a country. In some ways, Indian English is closer to the "original" (British English) than American English is. So our purpose here is simply to help speakers of other dialects master a few nuances of American English, on which the GMAT is based.

In 2010, I traveled to India, noting language used in local newspapers, in advertisements, and by people I spoke to. I was a bit amused when a Citibank ATM said, "Your transaction is getting done." (An American version would probably say, "Your transaction is being processed.") I was even more amused to learn that a "non-veg" joke is a dirty one. But more importantly, I collected much of the information appearing in this appendix.

We are fully aware that there are many regional differences in how English is spoken in India, and that some usages below are only prevalent among Hindi speakers, for instance, or are casual and wouldn't be used in business writing even in India. This shouldn't matter for our purposes—the important thing, of course, is learning the American version for the GMAT.

The Progressive Tense

Some speakers of Hindi have a tendency to overuse the progressive tense in English. For instance, "I am knowing how to do it" (incorrect) instead of "I know how to do it."

A less obvious example is perhaps "I am living on Broad Street." Most Americans would say this if they mean to refer to a time period—for instance, "I am living on Broad Street *these days.*" However, if you simply mean to tell someone where you live, just say, "I live on Broad Street."

INCORRECT: He *is wanting* to apply to Stanford.

CORRECT: He *wants* to apply to Stanford.

Here are some situations in which you *should* use the progressive:

CORRECT: She *is writing* a letter and does not want to be disturbed.

CORRECT: He *is going* to the store.

CORRECT: The professor *is talking* about derivatives.

What is different about these last three examples? Or, in other words, how can you tell when you can use the "is (verb)ing" construction? One guideline is: only use the progressive for things you can physically see people doing:

CORRECT: He is waiting.

INCORRECT: He is needing the report.

This guideline won't work every time, though. "He is thinking" is fine, but "He is desiring" is not. One other guideline might also help you: don't use a complicated verb tense when a simple one will do.

The Subjunctive

Sentences in the Command Subjunctive take this pattern:

CORRECT: The CEO demanded that we be on time.

CORRECT: I suggest that you run faster.

Some Indian speakers tend to say things like:

INCORRECT: I request you to do it.

This does not match the pattern above. You need the word *that,* and the word *to* is incorrect:

CORRECT: I request *that* you do it.

For more guidance, see the section on the Subjunctive Mood on page 122.

"Could" and "Would"

INCORRECT: I *could be able* to attend the meeting.

CORRECT: I *am able* to attend the meeting.

CORRECT: I *could* attend the meeting *if you gave me a ride.*

Could is used for things that are not certain to happen—in the last case, the speaker is only able to attend the meeting IF a condition is met. *Could* is also the past tense of *can* (*Back in 1985, I could speak German*). *Could have* is used for actions a person had the ability to do but did not (*I could have married a very rich man, but instead I married for love*).

In real life, people often say things like, "Sure, I *could* get that done by Tuesday." By itself, this is not entirely grammatical—rather, it is a way to avoid responsibility. It is implied that there is some unspoken "if"—as in, *If I feel like doing it and everything goes perfectly, sure, it's possible that it could be done by Tuesday.*

A stronger statement would be, "I can get that done by Tuesday." A person who was really committing to do the job would say, "I'll get that done by Tuesday."

Now that we've discussed *could,* let's discuss *would:*

> INCORRECT: Six of us *would* be attending the conference.

> CORRECT: Six of us *will* be attending the conference.

> CORRECT: Our company *would* have paid for our lunch *if we had kept the receipt.*

Don't use *would* in place of *will*. If something is definitely happening or has been planned, use *will*. Use *would* for imagined situations (*I would love to be a rock star),* as the past tense of *will* and *won't* (*He said he would do it*), or for conditionals (as in the example above with *if we had kept the receipt*).

The Past Perfect

> INCORRECT: The company had gone bankrupt.

> CORRECT: The company went bankrupt.

Don't use complicated past tenses (the *past perfect*) when the regular past tense will do. As you learned in the chapter on Verbs (specifically pages 45–55), only use a "had" verb when expressing an action in the past of another action also in the past:

> CORRECT: The company had been on the brink of bankruptcy before it was saved by an investor.

Here, *had been* is correct and is in the past of *was saved*.

"As" after "Called," "Named," Etc.

> INCORRECT: Aretha Franklin is called *as* "The Queen of Soul."

> CORRECT: Aretha Franklin is called "The Queen of Soul."

INCORRECT: I consider you *as* a friend.

CORRECT: I consider you a friend.

Do not use *as* after consider, named, called, etc.

"To" After Comparisons

INCORRECT: She is more experienced *to* the other candidates.

CORRECT: She is more experienced *than* the other candidates.

Follow comparatives by *than: taller than, smarter than, more intelligent than....*

"Up To" and "In Spite"

Each of these is two words. *She went up to the roof in spite of the warning.* "Upto" and "inspite" are not words in American English.

Countable vs. Non-countable Nouns

Pay attention to which nouns in your reading and study are pluralized and which are not. For instance, *suggestion* can be pluralized—I could give you three *suggestions,* for instance. However, *advice* cannot be pluralized. I CANNOT give you "*three advices.*" Instead, I would give you "a lot of advice" or "three *pieces* of advice." (Also, *advice* is a noun. The related verb is *advise.*)

Adverbs (or the Lack Thereof)

There is a definite lack of adverbs in some Indian English. For instance, many street signs say "Go Slow." (Since *slow* modifies a verb, it should be *slowly.*) Watch out to make sure you do not modify verbs with adjectives.

And, as was noted in the section on Adverbs (page 55), in India, *timely* is used as an adverb, as in *Please do it timely.* In American English, this is NOT correct. While *timely* ends in "–ly," it is actually an adjective, so *Please do it timely* is incorrect, just as *Please do it quick* and *Please do it cheerful* are wrong. Instead, say *Please do it in a timely manner.*

Usage Issues Related to GMAT Math

There should not be any language differences that affect your taking of the actual GMAT.

However, if you attended school in India and then attend an American GMAT class, or try to read an American test prep book, you may run into a few small differences that we can clear up right now.

MANHATTAN
GMAT

It may help avoid confusion to know that, in American English, "two into ten" equals 5, not 20. (The wording "into" is quite casual and will not appear on the GMAT itself, but it is something that an American GMAT instructor would be very likely to say while teaching.)

Americans use "into" as a short version of "divided into" and "by" as a short version of "multiplied by." Thus:

6 into 12 = 2

5 by 10 = 50

Again, these phrases are informal and often spoken out loud, but not written in textbooks or used on exams such as the GMAT. It would be very common for someone to say that he lived in a "10 by 12 bedroom," meaning a bedroom with dimensions of 10 and 12 feet and an area of 120 square feet. Such a usage is very common in construction, real estate, buying carpeting or other home supplies, etc. The real GMAT tends to avoid this problem entirely by simply saying "length" and "width."

A few other issues: Undoubtedly, you have already familiarized yourself with the different use of separators in the American numbering system—for instance, taking as an example the number twelve million, four hundred thousand, two hundred nine:

Indian:	1,24,00,209
American:	12,400,209

Numbers of this size just don't occur that often on the GMAT, and in cases such as 5,600,000 (or 56,00,000), it is best to simply put the number in scientific notation anyway: 5.6×10^6.

In the U.S., "thrice" is considered a very fancy word. Educated people will understand it, but they might look at you a little funny. This is just a cultural quirk; to Americans, *twice* is a totally normal word, but *thrice* makes you sound like someone who thinks he's British royalty.

Relatedly, Americans tend to say every number in a series even when there are repeats. For instance, the phone number 229–3334 is *two, two, nine, three, three, three, four*. Of course, anyone will understand you when you say *double two, nine, triple three, four*, but it might throw the person off enough that he or she has trouble writing down the number and needs to ask you to repeat it.

Finally—and I'm not sure what language or cultural difference is causing this confusion—I have seen many students incorrectly interpret this:

What is the average of $a + b + c + d$ and 7?

Many students write $(a + b + c + d + 7) / 5$. This is incorrect! Our best guess as to the confusion is that you might be mixing up the summation (represented by the plus sign, +) with the *and* that is used to list the two numbers to take the average of. If you routinely think of $5 + 2$ as "five and two," you might make this mistake. In American English, $5 + 2$ would typically be read as "five *plus* two."

If the GMAT intended the variables as individual items, it would have separated *a*, *b*, *c*, and *d* with commas. As is, "*a* + *b* + *c* + *d*" is all one item. Use the commas to count items! For instance, "the average of *a* + *b*, 2, and *c* + *d*" means that there are three items being averaged (2 commas separating 3 items). To recap:

The average of *a* + *b* + *c* + *d* and 7 is written as $(a + b + c + d + 7) / 2$.

The average of *a*, *b*, *c*, *d* and 7 is written as $(a + b + c + d + 7) / 5$.

Wrap-Up

All of that said, I would like to share with you an email from the first of my GMAT students to ever match my own GMAT score at the time:

> Hi Jen,
>
> Good news—I gave my GMAT this morning and got a 780.
>
> Thank you very much for all your help. I will let you know once I start hearing back from the schools.
>
> Regards,
> Anirudh

In American English, we would say, "took my GMAT." (Isn't it interesting that "gave" and "took" are opposites?) But who cares? My student got a 780!

So, don't think that being a non-native speaker of American English has to hold you back. It doesn't.